Defying the Odds

By
John R. Harris

Aspect Books
Brushton, New York

Testimonial For *Defying the Odds*

Defying the Odds is on of those rare books that has the power to command the attention of the reader immediately and to retain that attention and interest from start to finish. It is written in a superbly brilliant yet easy-to-read style that paints vivid word pictures chronicling the life of a dedicated Christian man who defied the odds to become a civic, religious, and educational leader worthy of the utmost respect and admiration.

Defying the Odds takes one on a beautiful journey, during which the author is revealed to be a dutiful son, a loving brother, a devoted husband, a caring father, a highly skilled educator, a faithful religious leader, and a worthwhile citizen of society—with all of the emotional ups and downs, triumphs and tragedies, inherent in everyday life.

This book should be on the "Must Read" list of everyone who has ever felt that he or she is surrounded by insurmountable odds and obstacles. Hopefully, all who read it will find it to be a blessing and a rich source of enjoyment and inspiration.

Dr. Thelma D. Anderson
Retired Professor, Albany State College

CONTENTS

ACKNOWLEDGMENTS

There are a number of individuals who contributed to this book including the following:

Mrs. Chesley Wiger, who went beyond the call of duty in typing the manuscript, for which I am most appreciative.

Mr. Les Wiger, who made many constructive suggestions including proofing and editing.

My niece, Rhonda Elaine Robinson, even though not in the best of health, edited several chapters of the manuscript.

Dr. Thelma Anderson deserves the major portion of the credit for editing and proofing the manuscript.

Finally, Mrs. Kate P. Slaton provided information that she thought was appropriate for inclusion in this book.

I am also appreciative to the many others who encouraged me to complete the task.

INTRODUCTION

"It was the best of times. It was the worst of times." In my opinion this quote from Charles Dickens' *A Tale of Two Cities*, could have been written about my life.

The year was 1927. It is interesting that this was the year Charles Lindbergh successfully completed the first nonstop solo flight over the ocean; the United States president was Calvin Coolidge and serving with him as vice president was Charles G. Dawes; and talking movies were introduced.

In the November 17, 1927, edition of the local newspaper, The Early County News, sixteen pounds of sugar sold for $1.00 and a can of Wesson oil for $.25. Men's overalls were $1.49, Florsheim shoes $6.00, and men's work shoes were $2.25. A Chevy touring car was $525.00, and the four-door sedan sold for $695.00. Even though prices were low in comparison to today, money was scarce, therefore making many items a luxury.

My place was in the small unincorporated town of Cedar Springs, Georgia. Cedar Springs is in Early County, which is in the extreme southwestern corner of the state near the point where Alabama, Florida, and Georgia converge. The Chattahoochee River, flows within five miles of Cedar Springs on its way to the Gulf of Mexico and serves as the boundary line between Alabama and Georgia from the city of LaGrange to the Georgia border with Florida. At that time, the town of Cedar Springs consisted of a U.S. Post Office and three or four country stores that supplied groceries, work clothes, and basic items.

The origin of Cedar Springs goes back to the early 1800's. The name is said to refer to a cluster of small springs just east of the community where there were numerous surrounding cedar trees. The spot reportedly was popular even with the Creek Indians; and although water still boils up at one point, it is now almost lost in the underbrush.

Cedar Springs was put on the map, so to speak, in the early nineteen sixties when the Great Northern Paper Company located a large paper and plywood mill on the nearby Chattahoochee River. These industries brought hundreds of new jobs to the area; but most of the employees chose to live in the surrounding cities of Dothan,

Alabama, Donalsonville, Blakely, and Bainbridge as opposed to living in the Cedar Springs area.

According to the 1930 census, the population of Early County was 18,273. There were 8,536 whites and 9,737 blacks. The county seat of Early County was, and still is, Blakely, Georgia. In the 1930 census Blakely had a population of 2,106. Blakely is located about twenty miles northeast of Cedar Springs. It is some ninety miles south of Columbus and approximately the same distance north of Tallahassee, Florida. U.S. 27 and Georgia 39 are the major north/south routes, with U.S. 84 and Georgia 62 being the major east/west routes.

Early County has always been a rural county that is predominantly agricultural but also has, in the past, included important saw-milling and major turpentining operations. The timber industry in the county today is significant consisting primarily of the production of container board.

Four things come not back:
The spoken word;
The sped arrow;
Time past;
The neglected opportunity
—Omar Lbn, Al Halif

CHAPTER 1

IN THE BEGINNING

My mother's father, John Wiley Franklin Webb, was from Terrell County, Georgia, and moved to Early County around 1895. He was married at the time and had one child named Bennie Lee. After he moved, he and his first wife were divorced. He taught school in Early County for many years and was affectionately known to all the people in the community as "Professor Webb." I never knew the level of his professional training, but I am sure he was not a college graduate. Being a college graduate was not a prerequisite. It seems that during his teaching experience it was necessary to pass a teacher examination administered by the county school superintendent. Upon passing the exam, the candidate would be granted a license to teach. This practice was observed for many years and was still in place during my mother's early years as a teacher. From documentation of the years 1909–1910 I discovered that he received a salary of $15.00 per month.

I have been told by many of his former students that he was a very outstanding teacher and that he was an exceptionally good disciplinarian because of his ability to maintain order while teaching seven grades and all age students in one room. Throughout my professional career, I have been frequently reminded of his exemplary record.

While teaching in Early County, he fell in love with Mary Mitchell, one of his students, and they were married. They were blessed with ten children, seven of whom survived, with my mother, Charlotte Mae, being the eldest.

I spent many precious hours with him and was very much attached to him. I called him Papa as did my mother and aunts.

I can remember when I was about seven or eight years of age that my aunts who lived in Florida, decided to give Papa a trip to visit them and they wanted him to bring me along. Their rationale was that he was getting old, and it would be much better not to travel alone. Nevertheless, he refused to take me and seemed to have resented the idea that my aunts did not trust his ability to make the trip alone. He

1

made the trip without me, apparently not realizing the disappointment and heartbreak I suffered. In retrospect, I feel this stemmed not only from my desire to accompany my grandfather, but also the desire to experience riding on the train for the first time. I got over it, but I never forgot it.

My mother's mother, whom we called Ma, was very dear to me and frequently persuaded my parents to allow me to spend the night with her. This was always a special treat, not that she did anything elaborate; but it was just the idea of being at their house, which we affectionately called "over home." It seemed as if there was something about her food that made it more delicious than the food my mother served us at home. The distance between our home and "over home" was approximately one mile on a small winding trail through the woods as opposed to the approximately two-mile walk along the dirt road. It was an ongoing rivalry on the part of my siblings and me to see who the lucky one would be. This rivalry culminated with my sister Nellie, whom we called Doll, running away from home to spend the night "over home" with Ma and Papa. As best as I can recall, we came home one evening from the fields and Doll could not be found. All of us were concerned as to what had happened to her, but I think my dad must have had a hunch that she might have gone "over home." He immediately set out on the trip to confirm his suspicion and put his mind at ease. Upon his arrival, his hunch was correct for he found her safe and sound in the company of Ma and Papa. He discovered that she had packed a few items of clothing in a flour sack and made her get-a-way undetected. I am not sure whether my dad allowed her to spend the night or required her to return home with him. Anyway, she or none of my other siblings ever tried it again.

My mother was a teacher also and was my teacher during my early elementary grades. In retrospect I find it difficult to understand how my mother was able to be a full-time mother, housewife, home-maker, school teacher, and very active in church and all of its responsibilities.

I never knew my paternal grandfather. I am not sure whether it was because my father never felt comfortable discussing this with us or he really didn't know him; but for whatever reason, we never knew anything other than rumors.

My dad's mother, Mary, lived with us for a number of years after she was no longer able to work in the homes of white families in Cedar

Springs. In her latter years she lost her sight. We never knew whether it was cataracts, glaucoma, or what; but she spent the ten or more years of her life in darkness. My grandmother was extremely good about sending basic food items such as sugar, flour, salt fish, and pink salmon by the rolling store to our large and struggling family.

My father, a lifetime farmer, didn't have the benefit of very much education however, he was endowed with a lot of native ability. I specifically recall his skill in installation of radios, not only our own, but also the neighbors in the community. Unlike today's modern radio, the radios of that time required at least three dry cells batteries, an outside antenna, and an outside ground wire. My dad was able to read and understand the diagrams for the installation and became very proficient in bringing radios to life.

I recall that he designed or invented a manure spreader. It was never patented, but he used it on our farm. He was very creative in many aspects of daily living for making tasks easier for him and for the neighbors.

> He who can not forgive others
> breaks the bridge over which
> he must pass himself
> —George Herbert

CHAPTER 2

BIRTH, EARLY CHILDHOOD, AND ELEMENTARY SCHOOL

I was born in 1927, on November 29 in Cedar Springs, Georgia. I was the second of twelve children born to Rufus and Charlie Mae Harris.

The house where my older sister, Dorothy, and I were born has undergone extensive renovations and is still occupied to this day. The land on which it is located is known as the Stone Place. I do not know why it had this name, but perhaps it was formerly owned by someone by that name.

When we moved from the Stone Place, we moved to the house previously owned by my mother's father, and their remaining ten children were born at that location. It may be interesting that I, and all my brothers and sisters were born at home with a midwife attending. My grandfather had built another home; therefore, he sold his old home to my dad.

Upon the death of my sister, Dorothy, when I was three, I became my parents' oldest child. This had its advantages and disadvantages in that the oldest child was expected to set the example for the younger children. This was not always easy; nevertheless, I tried and, as best as I can recall, was reasonably successful. Throughout my entire life, I tried to set a good example for my younger siblings in order to motivate them to become the best that they could in their educational endeavors and preparation for life.

My early educational endeavors were with my mother as my teacher, and I consider myself to this day extremely fortunate to have had this unique experience. The name of the school where she taught was Allen Chapel and was located on the same lot as the African Methodist Episcopal church by the same name. The two weather-beaten frame buildings stood parallel to each other and were 25 to 30 feet apart. The school building was one large room 30 feet by 60 feet and included a stage at the north end. It was originally built for a church but when the new church was constructed, the building was

Rufus and Charlie Mae Harris
(The author's parents)

converted to a school and thereafter was used exclusively for school purposes. The physical condition of the schoolhouse left a lot to be desired as it had numerous cracks in the floor, windows, and ceiling. The homemade seats and desks were well constructed though somewhat uncomfortable, but at the time we were so glad to be away from farm chores that being in school was a welcome relief.

There was also a big live oak tree in the back yard of the school, which provided an abundance of shade in fall and spring months. It also produced an ample supply of acorns. Some of us boys ate them. I do not know if they were considered edible, but I do not recall that any one of us ever became ill as a result of having ingested them.

There was no well on the school grounds, so drinking water was brought from the nearest house. That house which belonged to Mr. Turner Ford was in sight of the schoolhouse. When water was needed, a couple of boys would be excused to fetch water with the school's water bucket. Upon arriving at the well, they would lower the bucket

5

until it reached the water 15 to 20 feet below. Mr Ford's well had a rectangular siding made of wood we called "curbing." This was a sort of protective wall to keep out small animals, usually rodents, and to prevent people from falling in accidentally. There was a separate curbing inside the well beginning just above the surface of the water and extending down to the bottom to prevent the sides of the well from caving in. The well's bucket was attached to a chain which was fed through a device called a "whirl" which resembled a small pulley that hung from a crossbeam which was supported by two upright posts on opposite sides of the curbing. This was considered to be an improvement over the windlass type well which used a crank to wrap a rope around a wooden beam and required much more effort to operate.

Each student was responsible for bringing their own drinking cup to use during the day. The lack of water and indoor plumbing made it necessary for us to use outdoor toilets which were located on the rear of the campus, approximately 150 feet from the school house.

Much of my mother's teaching in those early days was done under rather adverse conditions in a one or two-room school. Resources were very limited, and she had to do a lot of improvising, something most of our teachers today do not have to do. There were no free textbooks or supplementary materials. Like her father before her, she had a multi-grade arrangement, first through seventh, with the students ages ranging from six to twenty. In spite of the lack of so many educational resources, she was able to motivate her students and make school a lot of fun. It was largely her inspiration that influenced me to become a teacher.

The beginning of the school year was always an exciting time, one of the reasons being that most everyone would be showing off their new school clothes. For my peers and me, it was almost like Christmas, since I could usually count on new overalls, flannel shirt, jacket, and brogan boots. These items were usually purchased from the Sears, Roebuck and Co. and were ordered out of their mail order catalog, often referred to as the "Wishbook." I spent many hours looking through the book before my mother placed the order for the items that she and my dad could afford. They reminded me that I was just one of several siblings who were also in need of winter clothing. After the order was placed, the eager anticipation of the receipt of the merchandise would begin. This usually took anywhere from a week to ten days. Finally, the mailman would arrive with the package; and there would be much rejoicing and excitement as my mother or dad opened the package and everyone examined and tried on his or her individual selections. At that stage of my childhood, that was an exhilarating experience. Our clothes were always bought at least one size larger than necessary so that we would have room for extra growth before wearing them out or passing them down to one of our smaller siblings.

A childhood experience that I fondly recall was the packages that my Aunt Bennie Lee, who lived "up north," would consistently send us. These packages would usually be shipped via railroad express and would have to be picked up in Hilton, Georgia, or Columbia, Alabama. This was a distance of twelve to fifteen miles, depending on which of the two places my dad would have to go to claim the package. Most times he would allow me to accompany him on these trips, which were made by buggy or wagon. Even though it took from two to three hours, I always enjoyed it. The trip included at least two frightening experiences; namely, having to go through a covered wooden bridge and crossing the old bridge that spanned the Chattahoochee River if we had to go into Columbia. The problem was that the horse or mule that my dad would be driving was afraid to go through or over these bridges. It would take a lot of coaxing and persuasion on dad's part to get the animal to cooperate. There were times when, to me, these experiences appeared to have been life threatening. Nevertheless, I would be eager to go back as soon as the next opportunity came.

Once we returned home from the railroad express section with Aunt Bennie Lee's "Care Package," the joy and excitement rivaled that displayed when the mailman arrived with the package from Sears, Roebuck and Co. As the case with the Sears' package, my Aunt's package would include something for everyone. Those items were not new, but we appreciated them just as much. She was my mother's half sister; and, as far as I can remember, I never saw her, but she was very special to me during that stage of my life, and I am eternally grateful for her love and concern for my siblings and me.

The recess period and the lunch hour were especially exciting. There were no school lunches available; so we brought a brown bag lunch from home, which often consisted of a cold "tater" with sugar sprinkled on it and a biscuit. It took a very short time to eat as we were anxious to play a variety of games. As I recall "shooting marbles" was a favorite for the boys and "hide and seek" for the girls.

In the winter, it was the responsibility of the parents to provide firewood for the old potbellied stove that heated the classroom. They would take turns dropping off a load of firewood about once a week. However, there were times when it had to be supplemented. My mother solved this problem by sending several of the larger boys into the nearby forest to pick up small pieces of wood and bring them back by the armful to deposit in the woodbox located in the corner of the classroom. The largest boy, usually the one in charge of the chore, would take an ax along and chop or split the bigger pieces into more manageable sizes that were small enough to get into the door of the stove.

The boys were thrilled to start the fire and pack as much wood into the stove as possible. We then watched in eager anticipation as it gradually became red hot and the room returned to a more comfortable temperature. Unfortunately, the wood was usually consumed in short order and the process had to be repeated all over again. Therefore, it was necessary to continually monitor the status of the fire so that the classroom temperature could be maintained at a fairly comfortable level.

Another thing that I remember about the old potbellied stove is that it was situated in a sand box 40 inches by 40 inches by 6 inches and was filled with white sand. It would catch any burning embers that might have fallen out of the stove, and they would slowly burn themselves out. This was a safety precaution that prevented the wooden floor from catching fire.

The stove also had several joints of stove pipes that extended from the top of the stove into the chimney. When we fired the stove up each morning for the first time, the joint above the stove would usually become red hot along with the stove. One problem encountered with the potbellied stove was the pipes. As the winter progressed, the pipes would become clogged with soot with the result being that smoke would fill the classroom instead of going out the chimney. Fortunately, this did not happen but about once per school year; but when it did happen, it took a great deal of effort to get the pipes cleaned and operating normally. Unusual excitement occurred when, for some unexplained reason, the stove pipe would fall sending soot and smoke throughout the classroom.

The school year was very short, five months to seven months. Many of the teenage boys were unable to attend on a regular basis because of having to do farm work. However, my mother permitted those who were interested in individual tutoring to come to our house at night. She was not compensated for this but gladly went the extra mile to help her students obtain at least a basic education. Her primary concern was that they could at least learn survival skills in reading, basic math and writing.

Even though there were so many things that we did not have in that one room school house we still had a lot of fun. Highlights of a school year would include a Christmas concert, where gifts were exchanged, weekly spelling bees, usually on Fridays, school concerts usually involving all students, although some of the individual parts consisted of only a few lines committed to memory, and a special school closing program with dinner being served by the parents.

As I reflect over my childhood experiences, I thank the Lord for having blessed me to have the benefit of loving and concerned parents who were willing to make whatever sacrifice necessary to give me the opportunity to succeed in life. Not only were they willing to do it for me but my siblings as well.

> You can only make others better
> by being good yourself.
> —Hugh R. Hawies

CHAPTER 3

FARM LIFE

At the time of my birth, mechanization of the farm had not reached this area; therefore, manual farm labor was a top priority. For me, this meant being introduced to manual labor at a much earlier age than my city peers. In fact, when I first started to plow a mule, I was only ten years old and slightly taller than the plow handles. You may find it difficult to believe that in the 1930's in most rural areas no one had electricity, indoor plumbing, radio, or T.V. in their community. All of these conveniences were things of the future.

In the winter my father, my brothers and I were responsible for seeing that an ample supply of firewood was maintained to heat the rooms where the open fire places were located. In order to do this, we had to make frequent trips to the woods on the wagon to cut and split loads of lightwood and oakwood so that there would always be an adequate supply on hand. This was hard work because the tools for cutting and splitting were an ax and a crosscut saw. The larger logs would be split into more manageable pieces by using an iron wedge and a wooden maul made of hickory, the most durable wood available from the local area.

Open fireplaces were very inefficient so you could be "burning up in front and freezing behind." This resulted primarily from a lack of insulation in the house as well as the very high ceiling which allowed heat to rise to the top and escape through the cracks. Houses were usually about 2 feet off the ground and the area under the house was not enclosed. No underpinning was used around this open area beneath the house to prevent the cold wind from blowing through the cracks in the floor. This system had the effect of creating a cold draft coming up through the floor and escaping through the ceiling. You can imagine that it took a lot of firewood to maintain a reasonable degree of comfort.

I vividly remember that there were always chores to be done, day or night, rain or shine, hot or cold. Even though I could not appreciate it at that stage of my life when we were working hard to maintain our basic necessities, I am now convinced that it was a positive influence on me as we were reared to believe that an idle mind was the devil's workshop.

There were always more than enough chores to go around, and my parents made sure that we all had an opportunity to participate. One noteworthy example was shelling peanuts around the open fireplace at night after we had eaten our supper. Because the majority of farmers believed that mechanically shelled peanuts would result in damaged seed thereby causing an unsatisfactory number of seeds to germinate at planting time, the practice of hand shelling was prevalent. All of us were given what my parents considered a reasonable amount of peanuts to shell before we could retire to bed. This was a very monotonous chore, but it became less boring after my parents purchased a Silvertone radio from Sears. The radio provided entertainment for us as we listened to country music and shelled our quota of peanuts for the night. This routine would last from four to six weeks each year and we would be delighted when the last pan of seed peanuts had been shelled.

Another chore that stands out in my mind involved harvesting peanuts in late summer or early fall. The picking and threshing was quite an exciting experience for me. The farmers of that day would look at the tops of the peanut vines and could just about tell when they were ready for harvesting. However, to make sure they were ready, the farmer would pull up several vines at intervals in the peanut field and crack the peanuts open; and if the hulls were full and had turned a dark color, they were ready for harvest. It was important that the farmer get his peanuts out of the ground in four or five days of the time they were ripe, or he would lose his crop. The tap roots of the vines were severed by a plow pulled by a mule.

The most difficult part of the harvesting was shaking the dirt out of the peanuts by hand after they had been plowed up and allowed to dry from one to two days on top of the ground. When we had as many as we could carry in or under our arms, we would take them to the stack which was a seven foot pole with two slats nailed to it about twenty-four inches from the ground. This allowed air to flow through and aid in drying. We were required to turn the roots to the inside towards the pole so that the birds would not be able to pick off the peanuts. When a stack was finished, it was capped off with grass to keep the kernels from being exposed to the weather.

At the time of picking and separating the peanuts from the hay, the peanut picker would be located in a strategic place in the peanut field and the tractor aligned with a long drive belt that ran from the main pulley on the peanut picker to the pulley on the tractor. The peanut stacks were pulled from their location in the field to the site of the peanut picker usually on ground slides. The ground slide could take one to five stacks to the peanut picker at a time and required two or three workers.

The ground slide was constructed of two poles spaced about five or six feet apart with boards nailed across them and with a chain attached to the front end for the single tree if using one mule or a double tree if using two mules to pull the ground slide. The primary advantage was that the stacks of peanuts could be rolled on to the ground slide instead of having to lift the stacks when using a wagon.

Once at the site of the peanut picker, the stacks of peanuts would be rolled over to the front end of the picker and the pole and slats pulled out of it. The poles and slats were stacked nearby, usually for use the next season.

The peanuts were "fed" into the mouth of the picker by two or three workers using pitch forks. One worker was assigned to catch the peanuts in burlap bags or in tubs and dump them into a truck or trailer parked nearby.

Two workers forked the hay, the peanut vines after the peanuts had been removed, as it fell to the ground on being expelled from the rear of the picker. Two workers were required to operate the hay baler, one to pack the hay into the mouth of the baler and place a wooden block into the baler to separate the bales as they were being packed. The second worker tied the bales with "hay wire" while they were still in the bales and stacked them in a pile close by. This was very demanding in that the next bale of hay would come out of the baler untied if the worker was not swift enough to tie the bale, stack it and get back to his position at the baler and tie the bale before it had gone too far in the baler. This required the two workers operating the baler to work very closely as a team. For example, if the worker feeding the hay into the machine saw that the next bale was going to get out of the baler before it was tied, he would stop packing hay into the baler until his coworker had time to tie it. At first the baler was mule-powered. The wheels of the baler would have to be lowered by digging trenches for them, so that the mule could step over the frame end of the baler as he made the continuous 360 degree rotations. The mule-powered baler was replaced by a small steam engine mounted on the machine and was much more efficient than the mule. The manpower remained the same with this more modern piece of equipment. I don't recall ever feeding the baler but I was fascinated by the process of the power of this "modern" invention, specifically, how the governors on the engine would open during the process of compressing the hay.

There were times when one of the pieces of equipment would break down, and everyone would get a much deserved break. It was during these breaks, usually in mid or late afternoons, that someone would take a pitchfork of the peanuts that were still on the vines and set fire to them. The worker doing this would stir the vines with his pitchfork while they were burning. Once the process was completed, everyone would partake of the roasted peanuts. They were much more delicious than any that could have been roasted in an oven. By the time everyone had eaten his fill, all of our mouths would be blackened with the soot from the burned peanut hulls. Even though our appearance left much to be desired, the feast on the roasted peanuts was all that mattered.

Cotton was the backbone of the South for a long time and played a major role in the slave-trade. My dad planted several acres every year. The prevailing attitude of the majority of farmers was that a farmer was not considered progressive if cotton was not a part of his operation. Therefore, in spite of the boll weevil epidemic that greatly reduced our yield, we always planted cotton.

Our cotton crop required more hand labor for children and adults than the other farm products. In the cotton fields, after the seed was planted for 30 days and had reached a height of 3–4 inches, all the children eight and above were expected in the field to thin the excess plants so that the remaining plants could take on more bolls. This chore was referred to as chopping cotton. The weeds were hoed 3 to 4 weeks later and only had to be done that one time. When the bolls opened at maturity, each child had his cotton sack and actively participated in picking the cotton. It was common practice that the cotton field would be picked at least twice, once when the earlier cotton bolls first matured and again when the bolls that were not ready during the first picking matured.

Cotton picking was indeed a "family affair" in that all of us were involved, my parents, my siblings who were old enough, and myself.

My mother would join us after having prepared our breakfast and cleaned up the kitchen. She would stop an hour or so before noon to prepare our noon meal. If we were working away from home, she would prepare the food at breakfast time; and we would take it with us and have a cold meal. Those were difficult and challenging times, but we survived, by not giving up and claiming the Lord's promises to sustain us.

In my opinion, picking was the most difficult as there was no easy way in which to pick cotton. You had to crawl on your knees or bend your back. The fiber was picked from the boll, one boll at a time. Most people could only pick about 100 pounds of cotton per day but on rare occasions some people that developed the expertise to pick two bolls at a time could pick 200 to 300 pounds. However, no matter how hard I tried or how early I started, I never qualified for the 200 pounds per day club.

Each individual picker had a sack, usually a long burlap bag, for putting the cotton in by the handfuls as soon as it was picked from the boll. The sack had a strap attached to the upper end, and each individual would put the sack under one arm and pull the strap over his head to rest on the opposite shoulder.

When the sack was filled or too heavy to drag, it would be emptied into a basket or on to a cotton spread made of burlap that could be tied up and weighed at the end of the day. It was then dumped into a crib for holding until 1500–1600 pounds of cotton had been picked. It was at this point that the cotton would be loaded on the wagon for the trip to the cotton gin located in Blakely.

The loading process involved practically everyone. Some were in the crib filling the baskets and dumping the cotton into the wagon. Others were on the wagon and had the task of walking over and over the cotton to pack it as tightly as possible so that it would fit into the body of the wagon. The wagon had sides that were temporarily extended in height to forty-eight inches in order to hold that amount of cotton. The light from a lantern was used for those in the filling of the baskets and the moonlight for those who were on the wagon doing the packing.

The most rewarding experience about cotton picking came when I was fortunate enough to accompany my dad to the cotton gin when we had picked enough to make a bale of 1500–1600 pounds. The trip to the gin started well before daybreak when my dad and I would get up, dress, harness and hitch the pair of mules to the wagon to begin the long twelve mile trip to Blakely.

On those rare occasions when I was allowed to go, I slept very little that night, due to the excitement and enthusiasm generated by this coveted experience. However, once on the road, I would bed down into the cotton, cover myself with a quilt and before long, the rocking of the loaded wagon would lull me to sleep.

We would usually arrive at the gin just a little after sunrise and there would always be several loaded wagons ahead of us. My dad would take his place in the line and patiently await his turn.

After the cotton had been ginned, we would drive the mule team back up town to an area reserved for mules and horses, today's equivalent of a parking lot, to be fed and watered. We would unharness the mules, lead them over to a big watering trough, a 100 gallon syrup kettle, where they drank a generous supply. They were then led back to the wagon and given the feed of corn and hay brought along for that purpose. While they were eating and resting, daddy would go around to the cotton warehouse and find out the weight and grade of the ginned bale of cotton. He would also pick up the seed check, which was usually no more than ten to fifteen dollars. Nevertheless, it was enough for him to buy us some cheese, soda crackers, and a soda pop. I very vividly remember that soda pop costing only a nickel. He would also purchase a few goodies to take home for those who had remained behind. After the mules had eaten and rested, they were led back to the watering trough and offered more water before beginning the long return trip home.

We would usually arrive home by midafternoon and after unharnessing the mules and sharing the goodies with my mother and my siblings, we would return to the cotton field and begin the much despised process all over again.

Another annual chore that we had to perform in the fall of the year was digging our crop of sweet potatoes for our personal use throughout the year. The first step involved plowing a furrow between the rows to remove the long vines. Secondly, a deep furrow was plowed down the middle of the row, at which time the potatoes would turn up on the surface in a variety of shapes and sizes. The third step was to gather them into containers, load them on the wagon, and transport them to a nearby area. Then we would arrange them on pine straw in piles of four or five bushels. The piles would be covered with layers of pine straw, boards, and dirt. If these procedures were care-fully followed, the potatoes would be light and water proof, thus preserving them and avoiding the problem of rotting. When potatoes were removed from the pile, it was necessary to make a small opening and reach the hand inside to remove the desired quantity. Having done this, the opening was tightly closed until more potatoes were needed. This process preserved our potatoes all through the winter and into the spring. Any way we prepared them, they were delicious, whether baked, boiled, roasted in the ashes in the fireplace, or in pies and puddings.

Other farm chores that we had to perform included clearing the fence rows of underbrush so that the rail fences would not burn in the event of a uncontrolled fire. We also cleared woodland by hand employing the use of ax and crosscut saw so that it could be converted to tillable land.

With the exception of my youngest brother, William, who was born after we bought our first tractor, all of the boys were required to plow mules. This at times was quite an ordeal, especially when the animal was inclined to be contrary. One notable example was a horse that we owned called Doc. Old Doc was very slow and would stop whenever he desired, and he would move again when he desired! When he chose to stop, we would repeatedly whip him with the reins to get him to decide to move again. He would just stand there until finally he would go a little further before repeating the same thing all over again. His behavior would really try our patience. Consequently, none of us wanted to have the responsibility of plowing with Doc. At that time we had five mules and horses, and none of us would voluntarily choose Old Doc; so my dad would decide whose turn it was to plow with him.

Plowing was hard work that required you to follow the mule from one end of the row to the other for several hours at a time—sun-up to noon and 1:00 p.m. to sunset. There was a special language used to communicate with the mule. It included such words as "Gee," to go to the right; "Haw," to go to the left; "Come up" or "Get up," to move and "Whoa," to stop.

In the winter months, the land preparation was called "breaking" the land. This was done with a plow called a "steel beam" and was available in a one or two-horse model. An area of land would be laid off by plowing a furrow around it and continuing furrow after furrow until the entire area had been plowed or broken.

In the early spring the rows were "laid off," the fertilizer applied, and the seeds planted. This was followed by the cultivation of the plants which lasted on into the summer months culminating around the fourth of July. This period was referred to as the "lay by season." Work during the "lay by season" was less demanding since the crops did not have to be plowed. Nevertheless, there were cotton and peanuts to be hoed and weeds pulled. Although the weeds were hoed in the spring, early summer would find a new crop of weeds to be hoed, especially if it was a rainy period.

The most difficult plowing involved breaking newly cleared land which we called "new ground." Sometimes the plow would get hung under a root, and I could barely get it unhung. This was also very dangerous, because the plow would hit the roots unexpectedly and would almost knock me down. However, I learned to be alert for that possibility and escaped any serious injuries.

It was a happy time when we were finally able to purchase a used tractor to do some of the difficult manual labor. The tractor was a "Farmall 12" with metal wheels made by International Harvester Co. The main disadvantage of that model tractor was that it was not equipped with rubber tires. This meant that any time that you drove on a dirt road, you did major damage to it. It was illegal to drive a tractor with metal wheels on a paved road due to the damage that it would do. After several years use, my dad was finally able to equip it with rubber tires. Although it did not have very much horsepower, it seemed extremely powerful when compared to working with mules. We were able to use it for such jobs as pulling the disc harrow and the peanut picker.

Although all the chores were difficult, the one that stands out in my mind as having been the most difficult of all was picking velvet beans.

Velvet beans were usually picked during the months of November and December. The sale of the beans would bring in a little extra money for Christmas which helped to motivate us to endure this painful experience. The difficulty stemmed from the stinging that would develop as we picked them and the sand spurs that got all over our pants legs. Between these two culprits, the velvet bean picking chore rated as the most excruciating and undesirable of farm chores.

My parents were poor and were unable to provide many of the material things that we wanted. Nevertheless, they kept food on the table and clothes on our backs. The food was basic and did not include dessert unless it was a special occasion because sugar was too expensive . We usually had biscuits on Sunday morning. We always had a garden, and my mother canned an abundance of fruits and vegetables to get us through the winter months. Consequently, very little of our food came from the store. We shucked and shelled our corn, after which we took it to a grist mill several miles away where it was ground into meal and grits. The grist mill was water powered by a large wheel that turned the stone as the water poured over it. The miller took a portion of the corn before it was ground for his services. Therefore, no cash was exchanged.

We always had milk cows which provided plenty of milk and butter. There was always a large number of chickens on hand that kept us supplied with eggs and chicken. My dad would hunt wild game in the fall and winter months to supplement our food supply. This usually included doves, quails, squirrels, rabbits, possums, turtles, and ducks. My parents were resourceful; and even though they had twelve children, they were always able, with the Lord's help, to provide for our basic needs.

My dad was one of the best syrup makers in the community and was in much demand to make the neighbors' syrup. They paid him in toll, which meant that for his work, he received every fourth gallon.

The syrup making process was very interesting and fascinating to me. It started with stripping the fodder from the cane stalks, cutting it down, stacking it in piles, hauling it to the cane mill site, and grinding it by feeding several stalks into the cane mill without allowing the stalks to run out or pass through the rollers before they were replaced with other stalks. We called this process "feeding the mill."

Our cane mill consisted of three large steel rollers, estimated weight of 500 pounds each, mounted on three large posts. The three rollers were connected with gears or cogs at the top. The shaft extended through the top to which a tongue was attached. An implement used for hitching the mule's trace chains, a "single-tree," was fastened to the small end of the tongue. A mule or horse was hitched to this attachment, which had a strip nailed to it several feet up the tongue and the mule or horse's bridle would be fastened to it for the purpose of guiding him around the circle. Each time the rollers made a complete revolution the animal made a 360 degree circle. As the rollers turned, it was a full-time job to keep the stalks of cane "fed" into the rollers. The juice was squeezed from the cane stalks and drained into a barrel, from which it was taken to the evaporator that was approximately 25 or 30 feet away. The mule pulling the rollers was usually changed every four or five hours to get a much deserved rest.

The next step in the syrup making process was the cooking and boiling of the cane juice in a long vat called an evaporator. It was about 16 feet long, 6 feet wide and 6 inches deep and mounted on a brick furnace. This container had compartments similar to a maze and was on a slight incline. Instead of the juice being poured directly into the evaporator, it was poured into a small barrel, sometimes a tub, that was equipped with a faucet. The faucet would be turned on and off as needed to keep the desired amount of juice in the evaporator. The juice was poured into the rear end and would make its way through the maze of compartments as more and more of the water would be evaporated. By the time the juice reached the extreme front of the evaporator, it had become syrup. At the peak of this process, juice would be entering the rear end of the evaporator; and syrup would be draining from the front end.

My dad would use what was called a skimmer to remove the foam or residue that would form during the cooking process. This substance was deposited in a keg, or barrel, depending upon the quality, and allowed to ferment. Once it developed into the fermented stage, it was considered beer, and at this point shelled corn was added to it. It was commonly called "buck" by dad and his friends and was in great demand. The distilling process changed the beer from buck to "moonshine" whiskey. I do not know whether this was considered a still and my dad sold the "moonshine" or just got a percentage of what his friends made from the skimmings. The "moonshine" business was illegal; therefore, much care had to be taken to conceal the operation; but as far as I am able to recall, none of them were ever caught. It seemed somewhat ironic, but some of dad's friends were more interested in the "moonshine" derived from the skimmings than they were in the syrup.

It was a very special treat to get some of the freshly ground cane juice and drink it right there at the mill site. Even more enjoyable than drinking the fresh cane juice directly from the mill was to sop some of the hot syrup with some of my mother's homemade biscuits along with some country butter. At the time, it seemed like manna from heaven.

My dad would have to work late into the night cooking down the evaporator and draining all the syrup from it.Water had to be substituted for the juice when the operation was shut down at the end of the day so that the syrup would not stick to the evaporator. My dad used a rag or a towel to keep the juice separated from the water. In a good day's operation, he could make seventy-five or more gallons of the best syrup in the community; in fact, it was "finger licking good."

The older folks in our community showed a special interest in me and would often extend friendly gestures to me. There is one person in particular who stands out in my mind; and this involved Mr. Bob Ford, affectionately called "Uncle Bob," who was also a syrup maker. However, in all fairness, he could not compete with my dad. One reason for that was that he used the old fashioned 100 gallon capacity syrup kettle as opposed to the evaporator used by my dad. Generally, the syrup cooked in an evaporator was of a higher quality than that cooked in a kettle. Nevertheless, at cane grinding and syrup making season each year he would always give me a bottle of his syrup. I could count on that bottle of syrup from Uncle Bob without fail, and this memory has stayed with me for more than fifty years. While this may not have appeared to have been anything important, it made a life-long impression on me.

Uncle Bob's brother, Turner, was our next door neighbor throughout my childhood. I remember him very vividly as an expert basketmaker.

He would select the white oak that he used for the construction of his baskets from the nearby creek swamps. He was very selective about his choice of white oak, since it had to be free of knots so that the thin strips would not break when they were being pealed off of the larger pieces. He would cut it into pieces six feet in length. After he got the wood pieces to his work site, he would split them into smaller pieces, usually quarters. The next step was to split off small strips $\frac{1}{8}$ inch thick and $\frac{1}{2}$ inch wide. The tools that he used were a draw knife and a pocket knife.

It required quite a few strips to make a basket, which was usually large enough to hold approximately two bushels of corn or a hundred pounds of cotton. I would often stand nearby and watch him weave the many strips into an attractive and sturdy basket. It was a fascinating and interesting experience for me as I watched the finished product come from his skilled hands. He was a very creative man which was reflected in the variety of shapes and sizes of his baskets.

Daddy was one of his regular customers and usually bought one or two new baskets from him at the beginning of the harvest season. He and daddy were rivals in watermelon production. I remember one year in particular that daddy's prize melon weighed in at 45 pounds. He was very proud of it and shared the news with Mr. Turner. Later he inquired of him whether or not he had weighed his largest melon. Mr. Turner would always express an excuse for not having weighed it. This went on for the better part of a week before he finally told daddy that he never weighed it but he was satisfied that it weighed 45 or 50 pounds. We laughed about that for years because daddy believed that he did weigh it and that it weighed less than his but he was not willing to admit it.

Even though Mr. Turner lived much closer to us than Uncle Bob, I always felt closer to Uncle Bob. Somehow I believe that the bottle of syrup that he always gave me at the beginning of the cane grinding season each year might have made the difference.

My dad raised hogs to supplement our food supply. The hog-killing day was usually one of the coldest days of the winter so that the meat would cure before it could spoil. The day's activities included killing several hogs early in the morning, usually around sunrise, submerging the carcasses in scalding hot water, then scraping the hair from the carcasses before hanging them on a "gallows" for gutting , quartering and thickly coating with salt to preserve the meat. The quartered meat was hung in the "smoke house" where it was smoked by the slow burning of hickory wood. Hickory was one of the hardest and strongest woods available in our area. The curing process lasted for several days, even weeks, depending on my dad's judgment as to when the meat was adequately cured to preserve it as there was no refrigeration. In the meantime, there were homemade sausages, cracklings, liver, and fresh meat to feast upon.

However, when I was about eight years old, my parents learned that the Bible forbade the eating of pork. The Biblical counsel on which they based their decision to abstain from the eating of pork is as follows: "And the swine, because it divideth the hoof, yet cheweth not the cud, it is unclean unto you: ye shall not eat of their flesh, nor touch their dead carcass." (Deuteronomy 14:8) Hence, from that time, pork was no longer a part of our diet. Subsequently, my dad discontinued raising swine altogether. My parents were sharply criticized by our neighbors and even certain family members for this change in their life style. Nevertheless, they stood by their decision. My dad wavered a little in that there were times when he would eat some pork, but my mother never did.

Fishing occupied a prominent place in my childhood and was a welcome relief from the ever present farm chores. My dad was one of the best fishermen I have known and would catch fish when no one else would. Our fishing experiences were not limited to the "hook and line" but also muddying ponds and striking.

Muddying ponds was a practice that usually took place in the summer when the ponds dried from the heavy spring rains. We would go in with our hoes and stir up the mud in the bottom of the pond until the water became extremely muddy, at which time the fish would come to the surface to get air. As soon as one would surface, one of us would give it a quick and forceful push with our hoe. If our timing was right, and it usually was, the fish would land on the nearby bank and one of us would quickly pick it up and deposit it in a tub or sack. It was not uncommon to get twenty-five or thirty pounds of fish of all shapes and sizes during one of these "muddyings," which usually took place while on our noon-hour lunch break.

Striking was somewhat the opposite of muddying in that it occurred during the wet season, usually in the spring, after the ponds and creeks overflowed their banks and the water would cover long stretches of the road. My dad, my brothers, and I would participate in this sport, which took place at night.

We would cut long strips or splinters of lightwood and light them to furnish the necessary light. Once our lights were in order, we would wade into the water covered road, holding our lights eighteen to twenty-four inches above the surface. When we came near a fish, the light would cause it to swim to the surface at which time we would deliver a fatal blow with one of our "strike irons." This required split second timing or the fish would escape. We usually harvested fewer fish through striking than muddying, but it was just as much fun and even more exciting.

Trapping fish was another favorite activity for men and boys when the heavy rains would come. Many nice fish could be caught this way. The fish trap was made out of wire cloth that was used to make brooders and chicken coops. They were either of mesh-wire or net-wire construction. The latter allowed the small fish to escape. A funnel-shaped mouth was built in one end of the trap. This end was always turned in the same direction as the water was flowing. Keep in mind that fish swim in the opposite direction of the current of the water. A dam was constructed of limbs, wire, rocks, etc. to cause the fish to have to come through the trap to continue navigating the stream.

The farmers would normally check their traps early in the morning and it was common for them to return with a sack containing several kinds of fish. The trap would keep the fish alive for a long time. However, the person checking the trap had to be on the lookout for water moccasins, turtles, terrapins, and the dreaded lamprey-eel that was much feared by local people.

Trapping fish could be done in a stream only a few feet wide to a stream as large as 25 or 30 feet wide. However, the stream had to be fairly shallow so that the dam could be constructed to guide the fish into the trap.

Growing up on the farm had its share of adventure. In my opinion, the summer months were the most thrilling and fascinating in that there was always an abundance of fresh fruits and vegetables. Some of my favorites were watermelons, peaches, pears, figs, black-berries, fresh corn, tomatoes, plums, and cantaloupes. My dad always had a watermelon patch, and it was a delightful experience for me to arise around sunrise to go to the watermelon patch, choose a melon, burst it open, and eat the "heart" of it and throw the remainder away. After the night's dew had fallen on the melons, they were far more delicious than when placed in a refrigerator.

Going to the peach trees during the ripening period was always a thrilling experience. The luscious fruit would almost cause me to over indulge. My only concern was how much of the "mouth-watering" fruit I could eat at one time.

The joy of picking and eating fresh figs right off the tree was a close rival to the peaches. We usually had at least one tree, and most of the neighbors had trees, thereby assuring me of an abundance of this delicious fruit. Fortunately, I was not a picky eater.

My parents believed in home remedies for our minor illnesses and if we went to the doctor, the situation was considered life threatening. This was also the case at the birth of my siblings and me as my mother was attended by a lady in the community called a midwife. The Lord took care of us, and we all survived without any evidence of malpractice on the part of the midwife. My mother gave birth to twelve children with none being born in a hospital.

In the spring of the year, my parents would accompany us into the nearby forest and dig a variety of herbs, including sassafras, fever grass, gopher grass, mullein, alum root, etc. These were kept on hand and used whenever one of us was threatened with an illness. My parents believed it was necessary to have an annual internal cleansing, and one of the chosen herbs would be boiled and allowed to simmer for approximately an hour before we would drink the tea just as warm as we could bear it. The response was usually satisfactory as it served as a laxative. This was a very undesirable experience for us, but the alternative was even worse. The alternative was either a dose of castor oil or calomel, neither of which would kill me but would almost make me wish I were dead. I felt so strongly about this until I promised myself that if I lived to become a man, I would never take castor oil or calomel. Praise the Lord! He has enabled me to keep this promise.

In addition to the small family-size farms, thirty to sixty acres, that were so prevalent in Early County when I was growing up, there was also a significant timber industry. The products produced were lumber, turpentine, and rosin. I recall vividly Uncle Melva and Uncle Hank, my father's brothers-in-law, telling of their work in the sawmills and turpentine industry.

The sawmills were powered by steam engines, and the logs were hauled out of the forest on ox carts or drays. The carts had two wheels and were pulled by a team of oxen. The drays had four wheels and were pulled by a team of mules. The logs that were hauled on the ox cart would have the butt ends supported by heavy chains attached to the front of the cart so that the logs could not plow into the ground, thereby making the load lighter and less difficult for the oxen to pull; however, the opposite ends were allowed to drag. The logs that were hauled on the dray were loaded without any portion being allowed to drag on the ground.

The logs were hauled by ox cart or dray to the ramp that was situated by the railroad that was designed exclusively for transporting logs to the sawmill. This special railroad led only from the forest to the sawmill and was called a tram road. From the ramp, the logs were loaded on the train, which was called a dummy to differentiate between a log train and the passenger or freight train. The ramp was elevated above the railroad cars so that the logs could be rolled down it as soon as a small block was removed from under the front log. When the desired number of logs had been loaded, the small block would be replaced under the front log and it would hold the remaining logs in place until it was time to load another railroad car. After the logs were loaded on the dummy, they were transported to the mill site near Jakin or Blakely, where they were sawed into lumber.

In addition to logging and sawmilling, there was a rather significant turpentine operation in existence in the county. Turpentining goes back in this area to at least 1834 when there was a great demand for pitch, tar, and raw gum to be used in the naval and merchant fleets of the world.

The turpentining process was started by cutting the pine tree in an inverted "v." This was called streaking and was done with a tool called a chipper or a hack iron. A strip of tin was tacked just below the ends of the inverted "v" and served as an apron for the tar to run into the cup placed underneath and held in place by a large nail. The trees were streaked once per week with the new streak being immediately above the previous streak. When the trees had been streaked to approximately shoulder height, a long handled tool called a puller was used to enable the worker to reach higher on the tree. The cups were emptied monthly, and this process was called dipping. Each cup would be removed from the tree and the tar poured into the dip bucket, which was the equivalent of a five-gallon can. When the can was filled with the tar, it would be emptied into a barrel located nearby.

The streaking and the dipping were both done by the same man. Later on, the barrels would be loaded onto a wagon by another man using two skids to form an incline. He would seal the barrel so that it could be turned on its side without emptying the contents. He would then place it on the incline and proceed to manually push and roll the barrel that probably weighed 700 or 800 pounds onto the cart. There would be five to six barrels on the cart to be taken to the still.

The closest still to us was Miller Still located near Lucille, approximately six miles from our house. Throughout the year, a significant amount of tar would accumulate on the face of the tree in the area that had been streaked. Therefore, at the end of the season each year, the worker would scrape all of the tar from that area and collect it in a container called a scrape box. The scrape box would be positioned against the tree under the area to be scraped so that the tar would fall into it when it dislodged from the tree with the scrape iron. The scrape box had legs on it and had to be dragged from one tree to another. When it became full, it was emptied into a 55-gallon barrel and picked up later by a worker.

My Uncle Hank was responsible for about 6,000 trees and received $2.50 per thousand for chipping them each week and $1.00 per barrel for dipping the tar monthly. This was a demanding job and required both skill and strength, but he was one of the best. The most demanding part was having to carry the 5-gallon bucket full of tar, which weighed approximately 75 pounds, from the trees to the large barrel. However, he had worked out a system whereby he would be rather close to the barrel when the bucket became full, thereby minimizing the distance that it had to be carried.

My Uncle Melva worked at Miller Still and was one of a two-man crew that operated it. He was called a cooper and was responsible for assembling the barrels that were used for the shipment of the turpentine and resin. He also would sometimes help out with the straining of the turpentine so that all of the foreign matter would be removed from it. The other worker was called a distiller and was responsible for cooking the tar and getting the by-products of turpentine and rosin into the barrels and ready for shipment.

The raw tar would be dumped into a large vat, which held approximately 8 barrels, and cooked for several hours to distill the turpentine. A full vat of tar would usually yield approximately two 55-gallon barrels of turpentine and was the average daily production. The residue from it was called rosin and was shipped to Savannah, Georgia, to be used in the making of glass

Although the lumber and turpentining industries were prosperous during my childhood, presently there is no longer a turpentining industry and very little lumber. Pulp wood for container board is the major industry in Early County today.

"The poorest of all men is not the man without a cent; it is the man without a dream."

—Anonymous

CHAPTER 4

EDUCATIONAL EXPERIENCES DURING HIGH SCHOOL GRADES 8–11

During my final year in elementary school, 1940–41, the following Black schools and their enrollment were in existence in Early County:

NAME OF SCHOOL	ENROLLMENT
Allen Chapel	54
Bandcraft	44
Bright Star	56
Carver High	158
Cross Road	44
Old Damascus	48
Early County Training	145
Ebenezer	50
Friendship	42
Good Hope	25
Hartley Giff	71
Hayes Grove	60
Jerusalem	73
Kestler	120
Kiokee	62
Macedonia	54
Mt. Meigh	59
Mt. Zion	69
Oak Grove	55
Platsville	69
Piney Grove	47
Pleasant Grove	65
Pleasant Hill	75
Prospect	83
Salem	59
Sardi's	49
Shiloh	29

NAME OF SCHOOL	ENROLLMENT *(cont.)*
St. John	77
St. Maryland	67
Timmons	70
Truevine	40
Union Hill	80
Washington	367
Zion Hill	50
Zion Hope	63
Zion Watch	75

In this year, there was a total of 36 Black schools in Early County with an enrollment of 2,654 students.

Upon the completion of my elementary training, grades one through seven at age 14, I was confronted with a major problem; namely, how to get to and from the high school campus in Blakely each day. The problem stemmed from the lack of public transportation for Black students. Even though it was a real challenge, I made a decision to ride my bike each day, a distance of 12 miles one way that took about 45 minutes. My bike was put together with spare parts, as opposed to being a store-bought model such as many of my friends owned. Nevertheless, it served me well and I was able to make the transition to high school.

As I recall, the most difficult part of the ride was in the morning when the ground would be frozen solid and I had to face a strong north wind. Oftentimes when I arrived at school, my hands and feet would be aching while the remainder of my body would be perspiring. As soon as I arrived on campus, I would go directly to Mrs. Kate Slaton's room to get warmed up before my classes began. I could always count on her room being nice and comfortable, which was a welcome relief from the cold that I had experienced on my long bike ride. There were times when I became discouraged, but I did not give up because by this time my mother had instilled within me an insatiable desire to learn.

Upon my return home from school in the afternoon, and if the weather permitted, I would have to harness one of my dad's mules and plow until dark. If I did not have to plow, there were other chores to do, such as raking and cleaning fence rows. Consequently, my studying had to be done at night by kerosene lamplight and the light from the open fireplace.

My clothing was limited; and many times after getting home from school I would handwash my khaki trousers, dry them in front of the open fireplace, and iron them with the smoothing iron so that I could wear them back to school the following day. The smoothing iron had to be heated in front of the open fireplace and if I did not watch it very carefully, the iron would collect soot and soil the clothes in the process of ironing them. Those were difficult days, but through it all the Lord sustained me; and I successfully completed my first year of high school.

The adjustment from the one-room school, Allen Chapel, with an enrollment of 54 to the Washington Elementary and High School with an enrollment of 367 was not especially difficult. Having to work in a room with 54 students on different grade levels was much more demanding than working in smaller classes all on the same level and subject. I was only there for classes since it was necessary for me to return home or to my job promptly at dismissal. I did not attend the social activities or extra curricula events that were held after school, primarily due to the distance that my family lived from Blakely.

The only noteworthy adjustment experience that I encountered was in the form of teasing by my peers, who seemed to have enjoyed calling me "country boy" or "plow boy." I didn't make a big deal about it, and it soon passed away.

In retrospect, one of the most noteworthy events during my first year was the bombing of Pearl Harbor on December 7, 1941, by the Japanese and the United States becoming involved in World War II. This event had a very significant impact on my life because of the far-reaching changes that occurred, including the rationing of gasoline, sugar, and automobile tires, just to name a few. At school our resources were already at the bare minimum, and the war made the situation even more difficult. My eighth grade social studies teacher, Mr. Joe Matt Brittian, was drafted into the Army along with some of my older schoolmates who had become eligible for the draft. I did not have to serve even though I had gone for my preinduction physical and was cleared for induction when the war finally ended in 1945.

As I recall, our family adjusted to the sugar rationing without too much inconvenience. However, the gasoline and automobile tires were a different matter. My dad had just managed to get his first truck, a 1936 Chevy pickup. At least two of the tires were worn out, but replacements were not available due to the war effort. My dad, in desperation, wrapped them with rubber or leather strips after inserting boots in them; but this arrangement proved very ineffective because the wrapping wore off after a very few miles of driving, and the boots caused the tires to bump each time the wheel made a revolution. Consequently, the truck had to be parked most of the time. When tires did become available, they were made from synthetic rubber and did not last very long. Therefore, the lack of dependable tires and rationed gasoline caused us to limit the driving of the truck. However, we were not alone and considered it our patriotic duty to do our part for the war effort. Nevertheless, it was indeed a happy time when the war finally ended and life returned to somewhat normal conditions.

Our family was blessed in that we did not have any immediate family members killed in the war. I knew many families who were less fortunate; and each time it happened to someone we knew, the trauma was almost as severe as if it been a member of my own family.

My second year of high school was somewhat different in that my oldest sister was a freshman and my parents made arrangements for the two of us to board in town during the school week. This eliminated the need for me to ride my bike as I had done during my freshman year. It also provided me an opportunity to get some part-time work. The most noteworthy was working at a small dairy. This required me to get up around 5:00 a.m. and walk from the northwest side of town to the southeast part, a distance of approximately three miles. Once there it was my responsibility to milk several cows, strain and bottle the milk, load it onto a buggy, and accompany the owner as he drove the horse and buggy around the milk route. When he came to the house of a customer, I would dismount the buggy, deliver the bottle(s) of fresh milk, and pick up the empty bottles so that they could be washed and refilled with milk the following morning. This job was even more demanding than the ever-present farm chores that I had at home. Nevertheless, it was better than nothing and I was thankful to have it.

My next job was at a garage and was after school during daylight hours, which was more favorable than my job at the dairy. For the most part, it was indoors and reasonably comfortable. I was responsible for cleaning the work areas and organizing the tools. The pay was minimal, but it was a good experience and gave me something to do. One of the fringe benefits was that I could use the company's tools for any of my little personal repairs. However, I had not acquired enough mechanical skill to do very much as evidenced by the following experience.

My father allowed me to drive his old 1936 pickup truck on Monday morning so that my sister and I could drive ourselves home when school was out on Friday afternoon. One day I drove it to work and for some reason decided that the gas line needed blowing out; so, I disconnected it from the fuel pump and proceeded to blow it with the compressed air. It was not long before I heard a loud noise that came from the rear of the truck. My investigation revealed that the gas tank had exploded as a result of the pressure that had built up from the compressed air that I had blown into it. The accident stemmed from my failure to remove the gas cap from the spout of the gas tank. Obviously, I was frightened, embarrassed, and disappointed because the success I had hoped for turned out to be a major defeat. In order to repair the damaged tank, it had to be removed, the remaining gas drained from it, welded, and reattached before the truck could be started again. In addition to the aforementioned damage, all of the gas in the tank at the time of the explosion was wasted. Aside from this traumatic experience, I enjoyed this job and appreciated the little cash that it afforded me. I think the most important lesson that it taught me was if you did not know how to do something, ask someone that did.

By the time I entered my junior year of high school, dad allowed me to drive his pickup truck, which permitted my sister Nellie and me to commute to and from school each day. It proved to be a good arrangement since it enabled me to get home earlier and have more time for farm chores.

It was during my junior year in high school that I encountered my first experience as a pallbearer. The circumstances involved one of my female schoolmates who became pregnant and died in childbirth. Her funeral was held at the Wesley Chapel African Methodist Episcopal church in Blakely. The pallbearers were from Washington High School. I do not recall whether or not we volunteered, but it was indeed a very sad and solemn experience. As I remember, teenage pregnancy was not that prevalent in Washington High School during my years as a student. However, I feel reasonably sure that this was not an isolated case, but insofar as I remember, this was the only one that had such a tragic ending. It really got my attention!

It was during this period of my training that I was tremendously inspired by Miss Bessie Scott, who was serving as curriculum director

31

for the Black schools in the Early County school system. She seemed to have taken a special interest in me and encouraged me to stay in school and do my best. I heeded her counsel and have never regretted it. She had come to Early County from Mobile, Alabama, in 1935 and made significant progress in upgrading the quality of education in the Black schools.

Another teacher who inspired me as a teacher and role model was Mrs. Kate P. Slaton. She was my teacher during all of my high-school years and was my principal at the time of my graduation. Even though our high school was unaccredited and possessed only the bare necessities, she improvised and challenged her students to do their best with what they had. I was especially impressed by her promptness in beginning her classes and keeping her students on task. From the time we entered her classroom until dismissal, she was teaching. She informed us right up front as to what her expectations were. She held us to a high standard of work and would not accept anything less than our best.

I remember very vividly how inadequate the materials and equipment were during my high school years. For example, we had no science lab. In fact, I saw my first test tube when I entered college. Textbooks were very scarce and consisted primarily of "hand me down" copies that had been used by the White schools. Also, there were almost no library or reference materials.

The building was substandard, to say the least, with each classroom being equipped with a coal burning heater. The fire would have to be started each morning, which meant that on very cold mornings, the classroom temperature was almost as cold as the outside. Starting and maintaining the fire was the teacher's responsibility, which was usually delegated to a dependable student.

Another memorable event which characterized my high school years was the administrative turnover in our Black schools. Believe it or not, I had a different principal each of my four years in high school. Even today I do not have an official explanation for it. However, I suspect some of them used the position as stepping stones to something better.

In spite of the paucity of equipment, resource materials and other limitations, I consider my high school years to have been productive and rewarding. My teachers, for the most part, were dedicated and committed to doing a creditable job. With very few exceptions, they did not hold college degrees but were capable of doing quality work.

However, my high school years left much to be desired. Specifically, we did not have a hot lunch program most of the time. Farm work made it necessary for many of the students, including myself, to miss many days from school. Lack of transportation was a major inhibitor, in that many of the students were not sufficiently well motivated to walk the long distances from home to school.

I encountered many learning inhibitors during my elementary and high school grades, as previously stated. In my opinion, my most serious obstacle was having to stay out of school so much to assist my dad with the farm work. Even though the school year consisted of only five months during my elementary grades, I still had to miss an excessive number of days. My mother tried as best she could to offset what I missed by giving me private tutoring at home. However, this arrangement helped but left a lot to be desired due to the distractions created by my younger siblings. As a result of my chronic absenteeism, I had to repeat the six or seventh grade. This was a big disappointment for me, but it was in my best interest even though I could not understand it at that time.

After getting into high school, my mother arranged for me to get some additional private tutoring during the summer months by one of her colleagues. Her name was Mrs. Julia Harris, no relation to our family, and she taught at the Union Hill School which was located about two miles from our house. She was an excellent tutor and helped me immensely, especially with my algebraic concepts. Not only was she an excellent tutor, she also took a special interest in me and encouraged me to strive to develop to my full potential, in spite of the difficulties that I had experienced and was continuing to experience to a more or less degree. Her inspiration and encouragement were just what I needed most at that point in my life. This was a critical stage of my development because most of my peers dropped out of school around that level and became full-time farm workers. The fathers, with very few exceptions, considered farm work to be a higher priority than school. In their opinion, their first obligation was to keep food on the table and provide clothes for their children. To accomplish that goal, they felt that they had no choice but to require their sons to join them in that endeavor as soon as they were physically able to do so.

33

To the best of my recollection, I never had a confrontation with my dad about having to stay out of school and work. Even though it was a heart-breaking experience, I always tried to be an obedient son and fulfilled that obligation to the best of my ability. Somehow I felt that it might have been part of the responsibility that went along with being the oldest son.

It is interesting to note that by this juncture of my life I had already lived through the country's worst depression, World War II, and the death of Franklin Delano Roosevelt, who was our president during these turbulent years. He led us so courageously to victory. I still remember his immortal words that he so eloquently spoke to the nation that "We have nothing to fear except fear itself."

Our country has been blessed with other great presidents during my lifetime. Nevertheless, in my opinion, there was something special about him that inspired me. Specifically, I was impressed with the way he led and governed the nation from his wheelchair. Being a polio victim, he could have given in to personal defeat, but instead, went on with living his life to the fullest. In my visits to the Little White House in Warm Springs, Georgia, I was able to capture some of the things that made him great. It was indeed a sad day when I heard over the radio that our beloved president had passed away.

Fortunately, President Harry S. Truman was able to take over the reins of our government and lead us on to victory. I am grateful to him for his leadership in bringing the War to an end with his extremely difficult decision to drop the atomic bomb on Hiroshima and Nagasaki. One of the most far reaching and courageous things that he did that touched my life in particular was his executive order outlawing segregation in the Armed Forces. I do not believe that any other one thing could have boosted the morale of Black servicemen and women as much as this bold act on the part of President Truman. It is interesting how much history I had experienced by my eighteenth birthday.

Out of a graduating class of nine, I was the only boy and the only one to immediately continue on to finish college four years later. Several of my classmates deserve commendation for continuing their education at a later date. To my knowledge, only one of my high school classmates is deceased 47 years after our high school graduation.

At the time of my high school graduation, the school system did not have a suitable facility for the graduation exercises so we were allowed to use a nearby church, Wesley Chapel African Methodist Episcopal church, for the event. Graduation was very special for me because of the struggle that I had experienced along the way. At that time, graduation included a class night, baccalaureate sermon and the commencement address as opposed to the one service currently used.

The summer following my high school graduation was one of decision. I wanted to go to college, but money was scarce. My parents were willing, but I was not their only responsibility. Nevertheless, my mother encouraged me to pursue the possibility; so, I secured college catalogs and familiarized myself with the entrance requirements. At that time, school counselors had not become available in our area on the high school level; consequently, I was on my own. With the help of Mrs. Slaton, Miss Scott, and my mother, I was able to get all of my application materials into the admissions office on time. Meanwhile, my financial situation had not improved. Nevertheless, I continued to work hard—picking cotton, shaking peanuts, assisting with the peanut picking, and any other farm work that needed to be done. I continued to hope and pray all the time that it would all work out. I suppose you might say that I was walking by faith and not by sight.

In spite of the unaccredited status of my high school, I was admitted to Albany State College in Albany, Georgia, 67 miles away. This gave me the motivation, encouragement, and inspiration to go on regardless of the academic and financial hurdles that I would have to overcome.

Even at this point there was an element of reservation on my part as to whether or not I could really succeed on the college level. This stemmed primarily from the fact that no one in my family had ever graduated from college. If I succeeded, I would be the first in my immediate family to accomplish this goal. I considered this a real challenge and in the final days of the summer of 1945, I accepted the challenge. The inspiration that I gained from studying the lives of Booker T. Washington, George W. Carver, Mary McCloud Bethune, and other famous Black leaders did much in helping me to decide that with the Lord's help, I could also succeed. I was firmly convinced that even though it would be a struggle, it was nothing compared to the hardships overcome by these great leaders who were no more than one generation from slavery.

Even though I knew that it would be difficult, I still felt that I could do it—I could accomplish this goal and become a role model for my younger brothers and sisters.

"Let me be a little kinder,
Let me be a little blinder,
To the faults of those about me,
Let me praise a little more;
Let me be when I am weary
Just a little bit more cheery—
Let me serve a little better
Those that I am striving for.

"Let me be a little braver
When temptation bids me waver,
Let me strive a little harder
To be all that I should be;
Let me be a little meeker
With the brother who is weaker
Let me think more of my neighbor,
And a little less of me."

—Anonymous

CHAPTER 5

COLLEGE YEARS

The day I left for college was very much like any other work day for me with the exception of stopping work in time for my Dad to get me to the train station for my 7 P.M. departure. However, I had packed my few belongings well in advance of this date. I still remember how I was able to pack all of my clothing, including bedding, in one footlocker. I purchased my ticket and boarded the train for the long trip to Albany State College, Albany, Georgia, about sixty miles away. I do not recall whether my mother or any of my siblings accompanied me to the train station. This was my second train trip and my first alone. Nevertheless, I made it successfully.

I arrived in Albany around 10:00 p.m. at the end of my train trip from Blakely. After claiming my baggage I hired a taxi to take me to the campus. I do not remember the amount of the cab fare, however, I am sure that I did not have very much money left over after paying it. As I can recall I was just barely able to pay my tuition, room and board and buy my books for the first quarter. I did not have the luxury of having money for sodas and other refreshments available at the student center. Therefore, my social life was somewhat limited but I did not worry about it because with my work schedule and my studies there was not very much free time. From the very beginning I was determined to try to keep my priorities in order.

Upon arrival at campus and to the dorm to which I was assigned I unpacked and made a start on organizing my room. This was my first experience of being away from home and I had a lot of adjustments to make. Being a farm boy, I did not understand much of the life style of many of my peers who were from the city and affluent families. I experienced my share of loneliness and home sickness. This was before telephones were available in rural areas. Therefore, the only thing that I could do was write letters which I did on a very consistent and regular basis during my transition period. My mother could always be counted on to write to me, whether in response to letters that I had written or just letters of encouragement. It was her letters, prayers and sacrifices that enabled me to get to that milestone in my life and I am eternally grateful to her.

Albany State College was founded in 1903 by Dr. Joseph W. Holley. In the beginning it was called Albany Bible and Manual Training Institute and was to provide religious and manual training for Black youths of Southwest Georgia. In this quest, it was helped financially by the Hazard family of Newport, Rhode Island. The first classes were held in the Union Baptist Church in East Albany until fifty acres were purchased on the banks of the Flint River by the donation given so generously by Miss Anna Hazard. The first building, Gibson Hall, was built in 1911, again with the help of the Hazard family followed in 1917 by the administration building named Caroline Hall after its benefactor, Miss Caroline Hazard, president of Wellesley College in Massachusetts.

In 1917 it became known as Georgia Normal and Agricultural College when the state of Georgia was asked to help in the education of its Black citizens. The school now offered work on the junior college level in teacher education, agriculture and home economics. The Hazards continued to play a big role financially in the development of the school.

In 1943 the school came under the able leadership of Dr. Aaron Brown. Under his administration the school became upgraded to four year status and was authorized to grant the bachelor's degree in elementary education and home economics, at which time the name was changed to Albany State College as we know it today. Dr. Brown was eminently qualified for this position. He held a Ph.d from the University of Chicago and was an exceptionally good administrator. The college experienced unprecedented growth under his leadership. After going through freshman orientation and overcoming my loneliness and homesickness, I settled into the routine of college life. As expected, it was somewhat difficult, but by this time my self esteem had developed to the point that I no longer felt insecure and afraid to assert myself.

Because of my limited background in elementary and high school it was necessary for me to study extremely hard to compensate for what I had missed in that phase of my training. My perseverance paid off and I got through my first quarter successfully. Even though I did not make the honor roll, I did not fail any courses. For me this was no small accomplishment and it enabled me to tackle my assignments with a higher degree of confidence. Consequently, my academic performance consistently improved each quarter.

My financial circumstances remained more or less the same throughout my freshman year. Although I needed all of my free time for studying, it was imperative that I work in order to help out with my expenses as much as possible. My work experiences included waiting tables in the dining hall, janitorial work and railroad express station helper.

My janitorial job was on campus and included the policing of the campus, cleaning the restrooms and stoking the boilers during the winter months. I did not find my janitorial duties at Albany State College to be that difficult but it was necessary for me to be outside most of the time. Therefore, when the weather was inclement it was undesirable, but I adjusted to it. I think my farm upbringing might have helped.

My job at the railroad express station was very demanding and required me to handle (load or unload) large quantities of parcels, many of which were rather heavy. While I appreciated the work it did have one major disadvantage, namely being located downtown, a distance of approximately three miles one way that I had to walk each evening that I worked. Walking to work was not a big problem because I would be rested, but walking back to the campus after handling a large quantity of heavy boxes was another matter. Therefore, I was happy when a better job came along which was waiting tables in the dining hall at school.

Waiting tables was one of my better jobs and I became rather proficient at it. Our cafeteria operated on the family service style and it was the waiters responsibility to serve the food for the number of tables assigned them. I think I had five tables. After the students had finished their meals the waiters would clear the tables and set them up for the next meal. I liked this job in the summer because the elementary and high school teachers would be enrolled working towards their degree and they would tip their waiters, usually on Sundays. This provided me with a little spending money which sometimes amounted to several dollars.

The college lacked adequate dormitory accommodations for the men students. Therefore, I was housed in a cottage type building, located on the south end of the campus, a distance of approximately 1/3 of a mile from the dining hall and the administration building. Three other guys shared the cottage with me. I was the only freshman but they were nice to me. The showers and restrooms were housed in another building located about fifty feet southwest of our cottage. I enjoyed living in that arrangement except when there was inclement weather.

World War II had just ended earlier that year (1945) and a large number of veterans was returning to school to study under the G.I. Bill. The college responded to that need by building living quarters out of World War II barracks. That enabled the Veterans to have their families on campus with them. Accommodations were available for both family and individual needs.

By the end of my freshman year I gained the confidence that I needed to achieve academic success. However, my sister Nellie entered college the forthcoming fall quarter and that placed an even greater financial strain on my parents' resources. Therefore, it was necessary for me to drop out for the winter and spring quarters of my sophomore year. By this time, my intellectual appetite had been whetted to the extent that there was no turning back. With my parents' sacrifice and the Lord's help, I was able to resume my studies during the two summer quarters and get back on track.

With the help of Miss Bessie Scott, whom I mentioned earlier, I was able to get some financial aid during my junior and senior years. This along with the work that I did enabled me to remain in school, both during regular school year as well as the summer quarters.

I am also very much indebted to a cousin of mine, John Hunter, Sr., for his financial assistance during my college experience. When all other sources failed, mother could always count on him for a short term loan to tide me over. This is not to suggest that he was wealthy, only a successful farmer who valued education and felt that I was a good risk. My thanks to him take on a special meaning when I consider the fact that he also had a large family and could have very well taken the attitude that he needed all of his resources to educate his own children. Nevertheless, he found a way to help me and I shall always be thankful for the faith and confidence that he had in me.

It was also during this phase of my training that Dr. Aaron Brown, Albany State's second president, took a special interest in me and bestowed on me the honor of being his personal chauffeur. This was a very coveted position and was a fulfilling and rewarding experience for me. Even though it did not pay very much, the experience was invaluable. While serving in that capacity I was privileged to stay in the president's home which I considered a real honor and met many of his friends and colleagues that I would not have otherwise met. This also placed me in an environment that was conducive for studying and learning. I greatly admired and respected Dr. Brown and considered him my mentor in my endeavor to get my college education. I will always remember his favorite quotation by Henry Van Dyke hanging on his office wall:

"Four things a man must learn to do if he would make his record true:

"To think without confusion clearly;
To love his fellowmen sincerely;
To act from honest motives purely;
To trust in God and Heaven securely."

I consider that experience to have been one of the best things to happen to me during my entire college experience.

My extra curricular activities included participating in the dramatics club and singing in the college choir. Mr. A.P. Turner was the sponsor for the dramatics club and cast me in two or three plays presented locally at the college.

Mr. James L. Elkins was the choral director and was one of the best and I was extremely fortunate to have been chosen to sing in his choir. Performances included a local radio program each Sunday morning, presentations at the college, and tours to off-campus institutions. This was somewhat of an elite group, but he tolerated me, even though my musical talent left a lot to be desired. I look back upon the experience with a degree of pride and satisfaction. I was most happy when the group was able to perform in Blakely, my hometown, during the time that I was a member.

My junior and senior years were my best and I consistently made the Dean's List. It was also during my junior and senior years that I became interested in joining a fraternity. I was strongly influenced by the admiration that I had for our president, Dr. Brown, who happened to have been an Alpha man. Also, I do not know whether it was by coincidence or design, but most of the men in key positions at the college during this period were Alpha men. It was in that context that I pledged Alpha Phi Alpha in my junior year in 1948 and was initiated into the Delta Chapter at Albany State College February 26, 1949. I was highly impressed with the principles for which Alpha Phi Alpha stood but rather disappointed with the lifestyle of many of those who were members. Therefore, I became somewhat disenchanted and never transferred to the graduate chapter after completing my college program.

Another rewarding experience that I had while in college was becoming acquainted with Dr. E. S. Portis. At the time he was a medical doctor with a family practice on Pine Avenue. He was also a Seventh-day Adventist. Dr. and Mrs. Portis were "down to earth," common people who were concerned about helping those who were in need. Hence, they took a special interest in me, would invite me home for dinner after Sabbath worship and lend me money when I was between the rock and the hard place. They were devout Christians and made an indelible impression on me at the time when I was still trying to find a sense of direction.

Much sooner than I had realized the time came for me to do my student teaching. I was assigned to teach at the Moultrie Elementary and High School under the supervision of Mrs. Oliver. I was happy with this assignment and considered myself fortunate to have gotten Mrs. Oliver as my supervising teacher because she was a veteran teacher with a proven track record. The Moultrie Elementary and High School was one of the few Black accredited schools in southwest Georgia at that time. Her classes were housed in a World War II army barrack that had been converted to classrooms. Her classes were departmentalized and consisted of six seventh grade math groups. She was very competent, organized and patient. This experience covered a period of twelve weeks and provided me with a wealth of information. However, there was a big gap in what I had been taught and the real world that I faced when I got out on my own. My student teaching was completed at the end of the winter quarter of 1949 at which time I fulfilled all of my requirements for graduation.

Miss Bessie Scott, my friend and mentor from high school, informed me a teacher was going out on maternity leave in Early County and she would like for me to complete the school year for her. I accepted the offer and found myself facing the greatest challenge ever to that point in my life. It involved the Zion Hope school, a one teacher school, housed in a church, located about five miles north of Blakely. The enrollment included grades one through seven and as I recall, there were between twenty-five and thirty students with ages ranging from six to sixteen. It was obvious that I had not received any training in my college courses or my student teaching to prepare me for such a situation. Nevertheless, I tried to be as resourceful as possible and sought help from my mother and others who had experience in teaching multi-grades in a one room setting. One advantage that I had was the exceptionally good behavior of the students. As far as I am able to recall, I do not believe there were any discipline problems at all.

During this time I lived at home with my parents. At that time, my dad was driving his privately owned school bus. This was prior to public transportation being provided for Black students, so my dad was one of the few who pioneered in this area. The parents of the students paid him a small fee to transport their children. As might have been expected, some paid and some did not, however, as far as I can recall the students were permitted to ride the bus whether or not their fees were current. He decided to let me drive the bus and pick up the students on his route and drop them off at the Washington High School campus in Blakely on my way to my school. I then drove the bus to Zion Hope and parked it where it remained until dismissal at the end of the school day. After dismissing my students, I would drive the bus to the Washington High School campus, pick up the students and return them to their homes. This was advantageous to both my father and me as it freed him to continue with his farm work and it provided transportation for me to my school as I was unable to afford a car at this time.

The Zion Hope School only operated for eight months as opposed to nine months for the Washington High School in Blakely. Therefore, at its closing, I continued to drive the bus and transport the students to the Washington High School campus. I was also assigned teaching duties at this school for the ninth month of the school term. I do not recall specifically what these duties were, but there is no doubt in my mind that they were much more satisfactory and in line with my professional preparation.

I returned to Albany State College at the end of the spring quarter for my graduation. This was another milestone in my life that had been reached by consistent perseverance, the prayers and sacrifices of my parents, especially my mother. With the financial assistance of my cousin John, and the blessings of the Lord, I was finally a college graduate, which is no "big deal" presently, but at that time and under the prevailing adverse circumstances was indeed a major accomplishment. I had become the first one in my family to attain this level of professional training. Nevertheless, there was not time for celebration, because this only enabled me to get on first base, so to speak. My long range goal was to become a school administrator.

Therefore, I immediately enrolled in Atlanta University the following summer of 1949 and started my master's program in elementary and secondary school administration. Atlanta University was founded in 1867 and was incorporated for the purpose of providing graduate training for Blacks. In 1929 it became affiliated with Morehouse College and Spellman College at which time it began offering graduate and professional degrees. It was especially appealing to me because it had a quality graduate program in elementary and secondary school administration. Other graduate schools in the state did not admit Blacks; therefore, it was my most logical choice. The courses that summer amounted to nine semester hours and qualified me for provisional certification, P-4, as a principal. I had come that far by faith, by beating the odds, and trusting the Lord.

At the beginning of the school year in the fall of 1949, I found myself, after having graduated from Albany State College in the spring, and the nine semester hours of graduate work at Atlanta University, the principal of Washington High School. I could not help being apprehensive. Nevertheless, Miss Scott, Mrs. Slaton and the local trustees felt that I could do the job. This gave me the necessary courage to try it. Even though my goal was to become a school principal, I never expected it to come so quickly. I faced a rather unique situation in that the majority of the teachers on my faculty had been my teachers while I was a student in high school. While they did not display any overt resentment toward me, they did not exactly feel happy about this "young whippersnapper" coming back as their principal. It was a supersensitive situation and I tried to avoid anything that would have reinforced their feelings of insecurity or rebellion against me. In my opinion, I was reasonably successful and they became very supportive of my efforts.

Another problem that I faced during my first year was that I was twenty-two at the time and not much older than many of my students. I was keenly aware of this and put forth special effort to avoid situations where this could become a problem, especially with female students. I am happy that my efforts in that endeavor were successful.

My first job for an entire school year made it imperative that I have a car. I had no idea how I would be able to manage such a major investment being just out of school and flat broke. After much consideration and prayer, I talked the matter over with my cousin, John, and he agreed to co-sign for me to get my first new car. It was a 1949 Chevy Fleetline. The total cost at that time was $1,800.00. It was a very pretty shade of blue and even though the Lord has blessed me with several cars since then, none of them have been as special as my 1949 Chevy Fleetline.

I continued my program at Atlanta University by attending the following three summer sessions. While there I made many professional contacts and valuable friendships. One of these contacts was Mr. James A. Slaton, who was a native of Early County, but his professional career was in Calhoun County where he served as principal of H. T. Singleton Elementary and High School. He was polished, well read and of impeccable character. Mr. Slaton was an exceptionally good role model and I cherished the friendship that developed between us. My relationship to him was more like father-son than a colleague. I was fortunate to have had him take a special interest in me because at that point, I was professionally proficient but still short on experience. He was one of the best principals that I have ever known and his positive influence over me during this period was one of the better things to happen to me at that juncture of my life. His concern for and interest in my well being did much to get me firmly established as a successful school administrator.

M-Y-S-E-L-F

I have to live with myself and so
I want to live fit for myself to know,
I want to be able as the days go by,
Always, to look myself straight in the eye;
I don't want to stand with the setting sun,
And hate myself for the things I've done.
I don't want to keep on a closet shelf
A lot of secrets about myself
And fool myself as I come and go,
Into thinking that nobody else will know,
The kind of man I really am.
—Edgar A. Guest

CHAPTER 6

SERVICE AT OLD WASHINGTON ELEMENTARY AND HIGH SCHOOL AND CARVER

The 1949–50 school year was my first complete year as principal of a school and in my opinion was reasonably successful. Even though significant gains had been made in upgrading the opportunities for Blacks in Early County since my elementary and high school years, much remained to be done.

The consolidation of the one and two teacher schools was gaining momentum and resulted in a smaller number of schools in operation each year. The consolidation was much needed, but the problem of providing buses to transport the affected students to the larger consolidated schools was a major one. The buses were still privately owned and for each consolidated school the State of Georgia would appropriate $600 as an incentive. Although this helped, it was far from adequate; however, it was a beginning.

The need for buildings in which to house the students after the smaller schools were consolidated was a very serious problem. The local school board of trustees and parent-teacher associations conducted major fund-raisers for building purposes. Despite everyone working together, our efforts yielded only a small fraction of what was needed. The teachers and the students were also actively involved in that endeavor by sponsoring a variety of activities including homeroom contests to see which homeroom group could raise the largest amount of money. We also had fish fries and sold hot dogs and hamburgers both at school and on street corners on weekends.

The lack of adequate textbooks continued to be a major problem and remained so for several more years. The books we received were used and out of date texts given to us when the White schools bought new books. It was not until federal funds, such as Title I and Title III, were made available to all schools—Black and White—was this situation corrected.

Herdisene and the author—Old Carver School, 1953

The two-story Washington High School building was torn down for the purpose of erecting a new building on the campus on Washington Avenue in Blakely in the summer of 1950. The only part of it that was not torn down was the office which was moved to the southwest side of the campus where it continued to serve as a combination office and classroom. Students no longer had a central location when they were bused into Washington Elementary and High School campus. Classrooms were spread between several frame buildings, including a Masonic Lodge Hall that was close to the campus and an army barrack moved from Bainbridge to Blakely and converted to eight classrooms. Not all buildings were on the same campus as several buildings were two or three miles away on property owned by the Holmes family. None of the buildings were up to standard but this was all that could be done under the prevailing circumstances.

The old school was never rebuilt. The school site of approximately five acres was really too small even if it had been possible to build a school building on it. An agriculture building was built from the lumber salvaged from the old Washington High School. This building later became the school bus maintenance shop when the county took over the operation of school buses. It was replaced many years later by today's modern steel and concrete maintenance shop which serves all the public school buses for Early County.

The lack of a building large enough to house the student body in one setting made it impossible to have an assembly program. When it was time for the school day to begin, I would ring a hand held bell and the students would enter the classrooms. We had to depend largely on our individual time pieces and it was not easy to keep them synchronized.

We only had one typewriter and it was given to the school by Col. J. W. Bonner, a local attorney, when he bought a new one. Colonel was an honorary title given to lawyers at that time and had nothing to do with serving in the military. From that small beginning we started a typing class and it produced many good typists. Ruth Brown was one noteworthy example. She went on and earned her degree in business education from Ft. Valley State College and returned to teach typing and shorthand on the high school level. I might add that she was outstanding and her career started from that one typewriter, desk and chair given to the school by Col. Bonner.

At the end of my first year of teaching I was faced with a new experience, namely compiling the principal's annual report. It was a rather detailed statistical report, but I handled it rather well. After getting that behind me, I was off to Atlanta University to continue work on my master's degree in elementary and secondary school administration.

I returned to Washington High School at the end of my summer program and immediately went about the task of planning and organizing for the 1950–51 school year. My homework paid off and the school year got off to a successful beginning. However, it proved to be a very unusual and challenging year for me. The United States had become involved in the Korean conflict and I was drafted into the U. S. Army on November 25, 1950. That was a very unexpected turn of events and I found myself at Ft. Jackson, Columbia, South Carolina, on the afternoon of Thanksgiving Day, 1950.

The trip had been the longest I had ever experienced to that point in my life. It began the day before when I boarded the Trailways bus in Blakely bound to Columbus. Upon my arrival at the bus station, I was met by a couple of soldiers and taken to Ft. Benning. There were two other draftees from Blakely, Red Riley and Glenn Houston, who reported to Ft. Benning with me. However, they shipped out to other military posts leaving me the only one from Blakely to go to Ft. Jackson, South Carolina.

The trip from Columbus, Georgia, to Columbia, South Carolina was by train, which left early that Wednesday night. The other draftees and I shared a Pullman car and we traveled all night. The trip was via Savannah. I have never understood why that route was chosen but I am sure that the military had a good reason for the choice. Thanksgiving dinner was served on the train somewhere between Savannah and Columbia. The other draftees and I arrived in Columbia around midafternoon on Thanksgiving Day 1950. Upon arrival we were met by a couple of soldiers who ordered us to climb into the back of an army personnel carrier for the trip from Columbia to Ft. Jackson.

After getting settled into the routine of army life, I was able to get a pass to attend church in Columbia each Sabbath.

It was during that time that I met my future wife, Herdisene Theresa Robinson. I have concluded that even then the Lord was working things out for my life even though I was not able to see it at that time.

It was not an extended courtship as it lasted from November 1950 to August 1951. While I was still stationed in Columbia, I would have a weekend pass and we would see one another. When I returned home in March, I continued the relationship by writing and calling frequently. I would make the long trip to Columbia by car once a month. The fact that she was an only daughter made her parents overly protective of her; so, our dates consisted primarily of visits within the home, attending church and treats in a nearby ice cream parlor. We never kept late hours for I cannot recall ever being out beyond midnight.

During the period I was stationed at Ft. Jackson, I experienced chronic arthritic problems. Because of this I received my discharge from the U. S. Army on March 5, 1951.

I returned to Washington High School in time to complete the school year. Mr. E. T. Brown had been my stand-in. He had been transferred from Carver to take my place when I was drafted.

At the end of the school year, 1950–51, Miss Bessie Scott, our curriculum director, informed me that she wanted me to transfer to the

Carver Elementary and High School in Jakin, Georgia. Even though her job title was Curriculum Director, in reality she functioned as superintendent for the Black schools. I understood that and went to my new assignment without an abundance of enthusiasm. Mr. E. T. Brown became the principal of Washington High School.

That summer found me back at my studies at Atlanta University for the third of the four summers required for my degree in school administration. I was really enjoying my work there and experienced a very satisfactory degree of success academically.

Between my studies at Atlanta University and before beginning my duties at Carver, I found time to get married on August 19, 1951, and was happier than I had ever been during my entire life.

My transfer to Carver came as somewhat of a disappointment to me after having served two years at Washington High School as I perceived the transfer as a demotion. Carver was a smaller school consisting of grades one through eleven with an enrollment less than 500 and a professional staff of twenty. In addition, there was a comprehensive plan by the Georgia State School Building Authority recommending the building of three new schools for Black students; an elementary and high school in Blakely, an elementary school in Damascus and an elementary school to replace Carver Elementary and High School. All students at Carver in grades eight through eleven would then be bused to Blakely thereby decreasing my total enrollment in the school. I was left with only grades one through seven located in the new Carver school.

The land for the old Carver school site was given by Mr. Albert Rivers, chairman of the local school board of trustees, and was very much appreciated although it was most inconveniently located. When entering or leaving the campus it was necessary to go down a lane and through a set of gates opening and closing the gates as you went through. The gates could not be left open as the livestock which was located on the adjoining farm would wander off.

Another problem was the pond that was located on the school premises. When we had periods of extended rain, the pond would fill rapidly and the flood water would come up to the back steps of the main building.

Even though we did not have the benefit of a gym, we played a number of outside night basketball games on our dirt court. Light was provided by large 200 or 300 watt light bulbs strung up around the

Isabelle Daniels Holston
Former student and Olympic track star

court. Even though it was very cold most of the time, we had a lot of fun and excitement. There were no bleachers for seating but we did have a limited number of chairs that we borrowed from the classroom for the older people. However, the majority of the spectators stood around the edge of the court and cheered our teams as they performed.

As I look back over this experience I find it difficult to understand why we were deprived to such an extent. The status of the Black schools in Early County was not the exception but rather the rule of Black schools in the south under the "separate but equal" doctrine advocated at that time. Nevertheless, we were happy as we now had modern school buildings instead of meeting in churches and lodge halls for our education and tried as best we could to make the most of a very bad situation. We tried to accentuate the positive and not dwell on what we didn't have.

I tried not to let the circumstances discourage me and the Lord blessed my effort. I did not realize at the time, but He was just getting me ready for greater things to come.

Two of the most outstanding students that attended the old Carver Elementary and High School were John Hunter, Jr. and Isabelle Daniels Holston.

Due to the fact that our Black schools were unaccredited, it was difficult for our graduates to get admitted to colleges. One noteworthy example was John Hunter, Jr. who wanted to attend Tuskegee Institute. Very much to our disappointment, Tuskegee refused to accept him. However, we did not give up and his father, John Senior, John

Jr. and I went to Florida Agriculture and Mechanical University in Tallahassee, Florida and presented our case. The Lord blessed us and he was admitted. John made a good record for himself at FAMU, including being commissioned a second Lieutenant in the U. S. Army. After graduation from FAMU he served on active duty for more than twenty years, during which time he became a fixed wing pilot and obtained the rank of major at the time of his retirement. I am proud of his accomplishments and I hope that I might have had a small role in helping him to believe in himself and "give it his best shot," even though the odds were against him. Another important student was Isabelle Daniels. The following article about Isabelle appeared in the booklet, Sports Hall of Fame Annual Awards, February 21, 1987.

"When little grade-schooler Isabelle Daniels started chasing that pig on the family farm over near Jakin, Georgia in Early County, her farmer daddy, Fred, her schoolteacher mother and her four older brothers and as many older sisters never dreamed she would keep going until she had run around the world. But she did.

At the time in those early 1940's, there were not enough youngsters competing in track in rural Georgia schools even to speculate on her chances. Only Isabelle and two others competed in track events on the annual field days. She graduated from elementary school in 1949 after attending the Carver school where her mother, Vera, taught. She also attended Good Hope school in Cedar Springs where her oldest sister, Edith, taught.

Then came Carver High in Jakin, 20 miles from county seat, Blakely, and in 1950, when Isabelle was 13, she won her first event, the 50-yard dash, on high school field day. Winning to her proved contagious. Each of the next three springs she ran in the district track and field meet for Black Georgia schools at Fort Valley State College. The last two years she was a first place winner.

In the spring of 1954, Ed Temple invited her to attend his Tennessee State University Track and Field Clinic for girls which has spawned many Olympians. The rest is history. She participated in her first national competition, The National AAU, in 1954 in Harrisburg, Pa. at 17, finishing second in the 100 and 200 meter runs and her team, which included Mae Faggs, Lucinda Williams and Cynthia Thompson, won the 800-meter medley relay after placing second in the 400 meter relay.

She was off and running across the nation and around the world for the next five years. She had literally followed her oldest brother Edward's urging when he first heard with elation that she had been offered a track scholarship to Tennessee State. "Tweety," he told her, using the nickname he long before had pinned on her, "you go up there, you run like hell."

"Tweety" ran like hell until she had won the 100 meter run in the Olympic Tryouts in Washington, D. C. in 1956 and became a member of the United States Women's Olympic Track and Field Team. She ran until she finished fourth in the 100 meters in 11.8 seconds in the '56 Olympics as Melbourne, Australia, where she and Faggs, Wilma Rudolph and Margaret Matthews won the third place bronze medal in the 400 meter relay.

Competing chiefly in relays and the 50, 100 and 200 meter dashes she ran until in 1957 she established a world and American record of 5.7 in the 50 yard dash, which held up until Wyomia Tyus, another Tennessee State Tigerbelle, broke it in 1966. Sprinting earned her a position on the AAU All-American Track and Field Women's Team every year she was in college—through 1959. She ran until she had competed in more than 25 national and international meets and acquired over 100 awards. She had 18 firsts, 3 seconds in National AAU meets alone.

Fleet "Tweety" ran to victory in the 1952 Pan American Games. She won first places in her specialties around the world—in Mexico City, London, Moscow, Budapest, Warsaw and Athens, Greece.

In Ponca City in the 1955 national AAU, she earned four gold medals, winning the 50 and 100 yard dashes and sharing honors with teammates in 300 and 400 yard relays.

In the 1956 Evening Star Games in Washington, D. C. she had firsts in the 50, 100 and 440 relay. She again was a three-event first placer in the 1957 national AAU at Cleveland. It happened again in the same event in 1958 at Akron, Ohio, in the 50, 220 and 440 relay. It happened one more time, in the 1959 national AAU at Cleveland, this time in the 60 meter, 200 meter and 400 meter relay.

In major meets in the United States she streaked to 22 first places, 14 seconds. In six major events abroad she earned 13 first, nine seconds, three thirds.

Isabelle, who taught physical education in Muscogee County Schools, Columbus, after being graduated from college, has put her

53

expertise to good use as a track coach for the last 18 years in DeKalb County schools, four at Hamilton in Scottdale, the last 14 at Gordon High. Two Coach of the Year Awards from the Atlanta Track Club, three state championships, eight Region titles and three county titles attest to her effectiveness.

Much of Isabelle's success can be attributed to Miss Bessie Scott, who was our curriculum director at that time. She knew the right contacts to make after we had discovered Isabelle's potential.

I believe she is the only Black or White medal winner that the Early County public school system has ever produced. She encountered many odds along the way but with the Lord's help, she beat them all and I am extremely proud of her.

During my three years at old Carver school, I learned to respect and admire Mr. Albert Rivers. Even though his children were through high school and had finished college, he showed a genuine interest for the education of all children. He was a prudent and wise man and much to be respected. He was born in Ft. Gaines in 1872 and attended school through the fourth grade. He was committed to the importance of education and opened the first school for Black students in Jakin in the Methodist Church. Each child was charged fifty cents and Mr. Rivers and a friend, Mr. Ellex Gardner, would contribute to pay the teacher. Mr. Rivers prospered enough to be able to buy 285 acres of land, to educate three daughters, two as teachers and one as a registered nurse who worked many years in the Veterans Hospital in Tuskegee, to build five large houses, and to be the first Black to own a car in that area.

He encountered the wrath of his White neighbors because of his prosperity and was not allowed to live in the first house that he built because it was located on the main road. However, they were willing to permit him to live in his house located away from the main road. Even then they forbade him to paint it white. Consequently, he painted it yellow. He was continually harassed by drive-by shootings and repeated warnings to leave town. One Saturday night some White men came to his house, kidnapped and whipped him and again told him to be out of town in twenty four hours. Being a man of fearless principle, he refused to be intimidated by the threats. He continued to buy land to become as isolated from Whites as possible.

I admired and respected Mr. Rivers for his meek and friendly attitude. In spite of the inhumane treatment that he received from his

White neighbors, there was no overt evidence of any ill will or animosity on his part. In my opinion, this was indicative of a real Christian, who in a real sense, "turned the other cheek" rather than "fight fire with fire." I can only imagine how difficult it must have been for him to labor and toil by the sweat of his brow to build his dream house, so to speak, and not be allowed to live in it. I find it difficult and almost incomprehensible that anyone could be so cruel to another human being. According to the Bible there will be a day of reckoning for those who were responsible for such a despicable act. I was extremely fortunate to have had someone of his caliber to help me get a firm foundation during those formative years of my career.

In addition to the support and counsel of Mr. Rivers, another strong and invaluable supporter was my cousin Mr. John Hunter, Sr. He too did not have the benefit of a lot of formal training, but possessed a rare ability to get along with people. He also was blessed with strong leadership qualities and the vision so much needed at that time to move our educational program forward. I could always count on him when there was a need for lay/parental support for any worthwhile project.

Although he only had the opportunity to obtain little more than a basic education, he valued its importance. As a result, he provided an opportunity for all of his children to receive a college education. When you consider that he had nine children, to provide all of them with the opportunity to obtain a college education was no small accomplishment. His oldest daughter had a hearing disability and remained at home with her parents. One son, Bishop, remained at home and became a successful farmer and businessman. His father took him to Albany State College to pursue his college degree but he chose to come back home and assist his father on the farm. At the present time Bishop is the chairperson for the Early County Board of Education.

Even with the large family Mr. Hunter found a way to keep bread on the table without his wife having to work outside of the home. Consequently, she was able to devote her full time to being a house-wife and mother for the children. Being a farmer on such a large scale, he could have easily felt that he had to keep his children out of school to help with the farm chores, but he was so committed to the value of an education that he kept them in school every day, unless they were ill or there was an emergency. I can really admire him for this sacrificial effort, because at that time most Black farmers felt it necessary to have the assistance of their older children in the chopping of the cotton, hoeing of the peanuts and picking the cotton at harvest time. In my opinion, this really speaks well of him and his children have rewarded him immensely in that they are professional, productive, law abiding citizens.

At that time he was one of the most progressive farmers in the state of Georgia and was featured in July 1972 *Ebony* magazine for his successful farm operation in general and his feed lot cattle operation in particular. Even before mechanical cotton pickers were introduced to this area, he was producing in excess of a 100 bales of cotton annually. This spoke well of his ability to hire and manage dependable laborers.

After three years at the old Carver school with grades one through eleven, the beginning of the 1953–54 school year was moving time from the old frame buildings located inside the gates and on the edge of a pond to the new modern building located on a hill overlooking the nearby rural community between Jakin and Cedar Springs. This new school was to be called Carver Elementary School and it, along with the two other schools in Early County, were the first Black schools to be built under the Georgia State School Building Authority in the second congressional district.

One positive aspect about my move to the newly built Carver school was that it was closer to my home. It had a central heating system, indoor toilet facilities, a modern kitchen and cafetorium.

Personally I think that I was most appreciative for the indoor toilet facilities. We tried to keep the outdoor toilets presentable at the old school, but even doing our best, they left a lot to be desired. After building the school there was no money for furniture so we had to make do with the old homemade furniture from the old school. This posed a major problem but being in a modern, comfortable school building almost made us forget about the disadvantage of lack of furniture. We also had a library, but very few books. Nevertheless, we were happy.

For the first time in my experience, I was provided the service of a part-time janitor who swept the halls, cleaned the restrooms, offices and maintained the grounds but the classroom teachers were still responsible for cleaning their individual classrooms.

The Lord blessed me tremendously during my three years in the new facility and I enjoyed that period of my career. The parents were very supportive and we had a very vibrant P.T. A. One extremely loyal and dedicated P.T.A. worker was Mrs. Ola Williams.

Mrs. Ola Williams was our P.T.A. president during this period of my career. In my opinion she was the most dedicated P. T. A. worker that I had throughout my entire career. This is not to suggest that there were not other diligent workers, but I feel that she was number one. She was very creative and took a very special interest in our P.T.A. scrapbooks. These scrapbooks highlighted P.T.A. activities throughout the school year. Most area schools participated and each year they were judged and received their rating of superior, excellent, good, or fair. The books from our school were very good and several were district winners.

After the high school grades were consolidated with Washington High School, she was elected president for that chapter and served for a number of years with the same zeal and dedication that she had displayed at Carver.

Upon occupying the new Carver school, the students and staff were excited at the prospect of having a hot lunch served to them at noon. In the old school, the students and staff brought their lunches in brown paper bags and by the time they ate them, the food was cold.

While there, with the cooperation of the P.T.A. and local trustee board, we were able to make many improvements including the installment of playground equipment, concrete walks to main entrances, landscaping the front of the campus and erecting a flag pole in front of the building. Also, the library was stocked with a significant number of volumes, even though less than required for accreditation.

It was during this period of my career that I received my master's degree from Atlanta University in elementary and secondary school administration which enabled me to obtain professional certification as a principal.

Another noteworthy event that occurred was the birth of our first child, Mike, on September 2, 1954. It was also during this period of service that the Lord blessed us to build our house. Our second child, Cheryl, was born on January 20, 1956, while I was at Carver.

In retrospect I can see that the Lord was leading although it was not always apparent at the time. All things considered, I feel that my service at Carver was five of the most fulfilling and productive years of my career. The experience in that situation proved invaluable to me as I advanced further in my career. I was never more cordially received than I was in that community. The parents and citizens in general were extremely cooperative and supportive. I can better understand the counsel in Romans 8:28 which states "...that all things work together for good to them that love God, to them who are the called according to his purpose." Little did I realize then that my service at both the old and the new Carver schools was preparing me for the greatest challenges that would confront me in the future.

> Out of the night that covers me,
> Black as the Pit from pole to pole,
> I thank whatever gods may be
> For my unconquerable soul.
>
> In the fell clutch of circumstances
> I have not winced nor cried aloud.
> Under the bludgeonings of chance
> My head is bloody, but unbowed.
>
> Beyond this place of wrath and tears
> Looms but the Horror of the shade,
> And yet the menace of the years
> Finds, and shall find, me unafraid.
>
> It matters not how strait the gate,
> How charged with punishments the scroll,
> I am the master of my fate:
> I am the captain of my soul.
>   —William Ernest Henley

CHAPTER 7

YEARS OF SERVICE AT KESTLER

(1956–57 to 1959–60)

With the advent of the summer of 1956 came my opportunity to move on to a new assignment and a greater challenge; namely, to serve as the principal of the Kestler Elementary and High School in Damascus, Georgia. I went with mixed emotions because I was happy and enjoyed my work at Carver.

It had been only five years since Miss Bessie Scott had informed me that she was transferring me to the Carver Elementary and High School. She now felt that my services were needed at the Kestler School. I readily accepted the position and was very excited about the promotion and opportunity for professional advancement that it represented.

The consolidation of the Black schools was almost complete, the only exception being the high school students at Kestler. It had taken almost twenty years, but the number of schools had finally been reduced from thirty-nine to three and each school was housed in practically new modern buildings.

My predecessor at Kestler was Professor Sam Barkley from Miami, Florida. He was a bachelor and possessed a good deal of charisma. Up until I arrived at Kestler, the turnover in administrative personnel had been abnormally high.

The school consisted of grades one through twelve with an enrollment of more than five hundred and a professional staff of twenty-five, including a professionally trained part time librarian. In my opinion I was able to make a smooth transition and the school prospered. It is worthy to note that I was provided the services of my first full-time janitor who was responsible for sweeping the halls, offices, cleaning restrooms and maintaining the grounds. Classroom teachers were still responsible for cleaning their individual classrooms.

At first there was some concern about my not living in the community. However, I explained that we had just built our house a couple of years earlier and that it was more advantageous for me to commute as opposed to having living expenses in two different places. Nevertheless, I assured everyone concerned that I would not allow my commuting to interfere with my professional obligations and responsibilities. The distance from our house to the Kestler school was approximately twenty-eight miles. This I faithfully did even though there were times when it meant driving the distance twice per day, when there were special events being held. Also, I would frequently visit the churches in the community. It was rather demanding but with the Lord's blessing, I was able to manage.

This was the first time that I had the opportunity to serve as full-time principal. I really appreciated this arrangement because as a teaching principal, there were frequent disruptions when I would have to attend to certain administrative details. As a result, the students were somewhat penalized. This arrangement also relieved me of the responsibility of having to grade papers at night and on weekends.

I did not know the parents in the Kestler community as well as I did those at Carver. However, once I got to know them, I found them to be very supportive and cooperative. I can recall the names of many parents who went beyond the call of duty. However, I shall mention four exceptional parents; namely, Mr. Melton Smith, Mr. J. C. Roberts, Mr. Isaiah Thompson and Mr. Alvin Thompson.

Mr. Smith was a railroad worker and was away from home much of the time but that did not keep him from doing more than his share in supporting the school. This is even more significant when it's taken into consideration that Mr. Smith did not have any children in school. He also served as chairman of our local trustee board and was very active in our P.T.A. Our P.T.A. was strong and vibrant but not as strong as the one that we had at Carver.

Mr. J. C. Roberts was the husband of Mrs. Naomi Roberts who was a very loyal and dedicated member of my faculty. They were the parents of three sons who attended the Kestler school while I was there. Mr. Roberts was a carpenter by trade and was a highly respected citizen in the community because of his involvement in his local school, church and community affairs. He was a member of my local board of trustees.

Mr. Isaiah Thompson, another highly respected citizen in the community, was one of my school bus drivers and a loyal supporter of all my endeavors. His daughter, Lola, served on my faculty and his youngest daughter, Aldenia, was a high school student at Kestler during that time. He seemed to have admired and held me in high esteem as evidenced by his special interests in all I tried to accomplish. I frequently felt more like a son than a friend.

Mr. Alvin Thompson was the younger brother of Isaiah Thompson. Like his brother, he was also one of my school bus drivers. He was very supportive of my efforts and took a very active part in all fund-raising activities in our P.T.A. despite the fact that he did not have children in our school.

Another significant event that happened while I was serving at Kestler was the birth of our third and last child, Wayne Bernard, on June 9, 1957,

The curriculum offerings were still somewhat limited though much more adequate than what we had previously at Washington High School and at Carver. In the vocational area we had industrial arts and home economics but no agriculture.

In January, 1957, Miss Annie Grier became county school superintendent and implemented many changes. One worthy of note was that all principals would report directly to her. Prior to her administration certain administrative details were delegated to the curriculum director, Miss Bayous Scott. For some reason, Miss Grier did not see fit to retain Miss Scott in that position. Consequently, after twenty years of service as curriculum supervisor in the Black schools of Early County, her services were terminated. This was a very personal shock to me. I was only ten years of age when she came to Early County. As far back as my elementary grades, she had shown a very special interest in me. It was she who encouraged me to prepare myself to become a principal. Having prepared myself, it was she who recommended me for my first four positions. Therefore I was saddened when her services were terminated.

The following is a sampling of the contributions made to the upgrading of the status of Negro education in Early County by Miss Bayous Scott during the period of 1937–1957:

- During her tenure in Early County, Black schools were upgraded and consolidated from 39 meager buildings to three modern plants.

- The school term was extended from 100 actual teaching days to 180.
- She was delegated the authority to actually administer the program for the Black schools.
- She was instrumental in Isabelle Daniels Holston's success as she knew the proper channels to pursue in order for Isabelle to develop her athletic potential to the fullest.
- She served as president of Region Nine of the Georgia Teachers and Education Association.
- She fostered literary meets, giving many students the opportunity to develop their talents in public speaking, dramatics, choral readings and also choral singing groups.
- She demanded that teachers improve their certifications.

After leaving Early County at the end of the 1956–57 school year, Miss Scott became the Jeans Curriculum Director for the Appling-Bacon-Pierce county school district. However, she passed away in May of 1958 before the completion of her first school year. It seemed as if she never fully recovered from the trauma of being terminated from Early County.

As a tribute to Miss Scott's untiring service and loyal dedication to education in general in Early County and Black education in particular, the physical education building on the new Washington Elementary and High School campus bears her name. It was erected and dedicated to her memory during the 1966–67 school year and stands as a fitting memorial for her twenty years' service in Early County.

I served another three years at Kestler after Miss Scott's termination. Her successor was Mrs. K. P. Slaton, a former teacher of mine. In fact, she was principal of the old Washington High School when I graduated in 1945. She did a fantastic job of carrying on the excellent work done by Miss Scott. Her primary focus was on curriculum and instruction. As a result, our instructional program was strengthened and expanded.

My tenure at the Kestler school was under the administration of Miss Annie Grier. She was the most meticulous superintendent that I had during my entire career; however, once I understood her expectations, I did not have any real problem in following her directions. It was very difficult to get her to spend funds for what I considered routine supplies. I remember one item in particular, deodorant blocks for the restrooms. She refused to buy them, because in her opinion, if the restrooms were clean there would be no need for deodorant blocks. I could understand her rationale but I still felt that they were justified.

Another thing that bothered me was her refusal to hire Mr. R.K. Sites, her predecessor, in any capacity during her administration. She had run against him for that office and defeated him, which was all a part of the democratic process. However, after the election was over, she steadfastly refused to give him a job.

Finally, I did not agree with her firing Miss Bayous Scott after her twenty years of loyal and dedicated service in the Early County school system. I could have understood her changing her job description but to terminate her, in my opinion, was not justifiable.

I enjoyed my service at Kestler and made some of the same improvements that had been made to Carver, including a paved walk to the main entrance, landscaping the front of the campus and erecting posts and chains around walks and driveway.

At the completion of my fourth year, 1959–60, at Kestler, I knew that the high school grades would be consolidated with the Washington High School in Blakely. However, I did not know, until that following summer that I would also be transferred to that school to serve as principal. In eleven years I had served in all of the three existing Black schools in Early County going from the old Washington Elementary and High School to the old Carver Elementary and High School to the new Carver Elementary to Kestler Elementary and High School and finally to the new Washington Elementary and High School.

My work at Kestler was rewarding and fulfilling and I feel that I was successful as a role model in the community. At that time this was a top priority and the Lord enabled me to fulfill that need.

> One ship drives east and another drives west
> With the selfsame winds that blow.
> 'Tis the set of the sails
> And not the gales
>
> —Which tells us the way to go.
> Like the winds of the sea are the ways of fate,
> As we voyage along through life:
> 'Tis the set of a soul
> That decides its goal,
> And not the calm or the strife.
> —Ella Wheeler Wilcox

CHAPTER 8

YEARS AT WASHINGTON HIGH SCHOOL

My return to Washington High School in 1960 in some respects could have been characterized as being "the best of times and the worst of times" as expressed by Charles Dickens in his *Tale of Two Cities*. I was eleven years into my professional career and had been reasonably successful.

However, for some unexplained reason, which I am not completely certain that I understand even today, that first year was one of extraordinary turbulence. I inherited a faculty that was not completely loyal to me and this disloyalty frequently manifested itself by the sowing of seeds of discord. This attitude could have stemmed in part from the fact that they felt that I was advancing too fast since the principalship at Washington High School was the top and most prestigious position for a Black educator in the school system. However, it should be noted that the position sought me as opposed to my seeking it. Therefore, my conscience was clear, in that I had not done anything underhanded or professionally unethical to get the position.

Mr. Curtis E. Stanley was my predecessor at the new Washington High School. He was from Valdosta, Georgia, and held a master's degree from the University of Pittsburgh. He was recruited by Miss Bessie Scott and served from 1952 to 1960, a total of eight terms. I didn't know then, nor do I know now, the circumstances concerning the nonrenewal of his contract. This could possibly be an explanation why certain faculty members were not supportive of me and my program. After leaving Blakely, he worked at Alabama State College, Montgomery, Alabama, until his death. This situation presented my greatest challenge throughout my entire professional career of forty plus years.

Even under those adverse circumstances, the Lord blessed. When school resumed after the Christmas holidays in January 1961, I was provided my first secretarial help in the person of Miss Bertha Jenkins from Edison, Georgia. She came to this position from Bainbridge, Georgia, where she was employed as secretary for Dr. J. H.

Griffin, a Black physician, who was operating the Griffin Hospital and Clinic at that time. Hiring Miss Jenkins was one of the best things that happened during that first year. Little did I realize that she would remain with me in that capacity for the next twenty-nine years until I retired.

The combined enrollment for the elementary and high school was 1553 and the professional staff numbered 46. At that time the physical plant was one of the largest in the state. Two janitors were employed to sweep the halls, clean the restrooms and maintain the grounds. However, the teachers were still responsible for their individual classroom. This was actually demeaning for the teacher.

Members of my Board of Trustees were: Mr. John Hunter, Sr., Chairman, Mr. John Slaton, Treasurer, Mr. Lucious Brannon, Mr. Will Wiley, Mr. Melton Smith, Mr. J. C. Roberts, and Mr. Isaiah Thompson. The members were very supportive of my efforts and I enjoyed working with them. They were especially helpful in our efforts to get our P. E. building although it didn't become a reality until spring 1967. They served as a direct link between me and the all white Board of Education by meeting periodically with the Board and keeping our need for this facility in focus.

Major accomplishment during the 1960–61 school year included the following:

A. installation of an intercom system,

B. installation of concrete posts and chain around the main driveways to enhance the campus beautification, and

C. installation of paved walks to main entrances.

At the conclusion of that first year, I was faced with a very difficult decision when it came time to recommend professional personnel. I realized that my total program would self destruct if I did not have a loyal and supportive professional staff. Consequently, it was necessary for me to not recommend several teachers for reappointment. I was not happy about it but felt that it was crucial to the survival of my program. Some of those not recommended were excellent teachers but under the circumstances, I did not have any other logical alternative. The need to not recommend a teacher for the upcoming year was always a most distasteful task and one that I detested throughout my years as an administrator. The local trustee board, the Early County Board of Education and the system school superintendent concurred and supported my decision that year.

Dr. Aaron Brown, president emeritus of Albany State College, had this to say about the leadership role of the principal:
"To be successful:

1. He must uphold major objectives and purposes.
2. He must delegate responsibility and give with it corresponding authority.
3. He must consider himself/herself as a symbol of good education.

This is the principal's public relations role:

4. He should recognize the fact that administration is a service to instruction.
5. He/she must be consistent and impartial.
6. When the schools are large enough for an assistant principal, the assistant should be strong in the principal's weak points and not an extension of his/her personality."

He further stated, "in your pursuit of excellence as principals, you must face these issues: you have to let your students know where you stand—there is no 'hiding place'."

The following humorous note is also attributed to Dr. Aaron Brown:

"If he's friendly with the office personnel, he's a politician.
If he keeps to himself, he's a snob.
If he makes quick decisions, he's arbitrary.
If he doesn't have an immediate answer, he can't make up his mind.
If he works on a day to day basis, he lacks foresight.
If he has long range plans, he's a dreamer.
If his name appears in the newspaper, he's a publicity hound.
If no one has heard of him, he's a nonentity.
If he requests a large appropriation, he is against economy.
If he doesn't ask for money, he's a timid soul (or stark mad).
If he tries to eliminate red tape, he has no regard for the system.
If he insists in going through channels, he's a bureaucrat.
If he speaks the language of education, he's a cliche expert.
If he doesn't use the jargon, he's illiterate.
If he writes for the educational journals, he's neglecting his work.
If he has never written an article, he hasn't had a thought of his own for twenty years.
If he is late for work in the morning, he's taking advantage of his position.
If he gets to the office on time, he's an eager beaver.

If the office is running smoothly, he is a dictator.

If the office is a mess, he's a poor administrator.

If he holds weekly staff meetings, he's in desperate need of ideas.

If he doesn't hold weekly staff meetings, he doesn't appreciate the value of teamwork.

If he spends a lot of time with the Board, he's a back slapper.

If he's never with the Board, he's on his way out.

If he goes to conventions, he's on the gravy train.

If he never takes a trip, he's not important.

If he tries to do all the work himself, he doesn't trust anybody.

If he delegates as much as possible, he's lazy.

If he tries to get additional personnel, he's an empire builder.

If he doesn't want more employees, he's a slave driver.

If he takes his briefcase home, he's trying to impress the Board.

If he leaves the office without any homework, he has a sinecure.

If he enjoys reading this description, he's facetious.

If he doesn't think it's clever, he's entitled to his own opinion."

After closing the books on the first year, our total program prospered. My faculty was loyal, dedicated and competent. The morale was high and the climate was conducive for effective teaching and learning.

I deliberately tried to de-emphasize fund-raising so that full emphasis could be focused on the teaching/learning process. However, we did sell apples during the lunch hour which netted a substantial profit, thus making it possible to buy a new Ford Econoline Van for the school. The apples were purchased wholesale by the barrel and supplemented our school lunch provided by our school lunchroom program.

The van proved to be a very valuable asset to our total program in that Early County is a rather large county and many parents were unable or unwilling to pick up their child after school if the child needed to stay over for an after-school tutoring or extra curricular function. With the van we were able to take students home with the result many of them had an opportunity to participate in an array of activities that otherwise would not have been available to them. This was especially true with out-of-town sports events; namely, basketball, track meets, football, band and dramatics. We became very competitive with other schools in our region and gained above-average recognition.

One of my top priorities was to achieve accreditation status for Washington High School from Southern Association of Colleges and Secondary Schools (SACSS). The accreditation process was a three year long and exhaustive process. The format required that we get organized the first year. Consequently, committees were organized and a consultant, Dr. Lawrence E. Boyd, from Atlanta University, was secured to coordinate our efforts and guide us through the evaluation process.

The self-study involved the appointment of major and minor committees in the following areas.

Major committees:
1. Steering Committee—Mr. Matthew Conyers, Chairman
2. Program of Studies—Mrs. Lillie R. Stansell, Chairman
3. Instructional Materials—Mrs. Hazel Daniels, Chairman
4. Health Services—Mrs. Lucille W. Hester, Chairman
5. School Plant—Mr. Theo Pittman, Chairman
6. Philosophy and Objectives—Mr. Matthew Conyers, Chairman
7. School and Community—Mr. Fred Daniels, Jr., Chairman
8. Student Activities—Mr. James L. Hester, Chairman
9. Guidance Services—Mrs. H. T. Harris, Chairman
10. School Staff and Administration—Mr. John R. Harris, Chairman
11. Statistical Summary—Mr. Earle B. Robinson, Chairman
12. Graphic Summary—Mr. Clyde Mackey II, Chairman
13. Individual Staff—Mr. Wellington O. Burrell, Chairman

    Minor committees:
1. English—Miss W. Richardson, Chairman
2. Mathematics—Earle B. Robinson, Chairman
3. Business Education—Miss Ruth Brown, Chairman
4. Vocational Home Economics—Miss Lucile Hardge, Chairman
5. Science—Irving N. Lewis, Chairman
6. Social Studies—Irving N. Lewis, Chairman
7. Vocational Agriculture—Fred Daniels, Chairman
8. Music—Wellington O. Burrell, Chairman
9. Health and Physical Education—James L. Hester, Chairman
10. French—George M. Koonce, Chairman
11. Student Evaluation—George M. Koonce, Chairman
12. Editing and Compilation—Mrs. H. T. Harris, Chairman
13. Dinner Meeting Program—Ear;e B. Robinson, Chairman
14. Industrial Arts—Theo G. Pittman, Chairman

15. Educable Mentally Retarded—Mrs. Kathryn Mitchell, Chairman
16. Parent Evaluation—Irving N. Lewis, Chairman
17. Hospitality—Miss Mattye Grimes, Chairman

The major focus was for the committees to carry out their assignments. One of the requirements of the self-study was to develop a philosophy and formulate objectives for the staff and faculty of Washington High School. The first philosophy was:

"We, the teachers of Washington High School, believe that our major concern is to develop individuals who will grow into self-directing, productive young men and women able to assume their responsibilities as American citizens.

"We believe that the home, the church, the school, and the community should cooperatively provide learning experiences which will aid in the development of such self-directing, productive citizens.

"Further, we believe that the school should provide opportunities for all youth to develop understandings, attitudes, and salable skills that make for intelligent and productive workers. The school should provide time in its daily schedule for activities that aid in the development of socially adjusted individuals; also, the secondary school should provide learning experiences in the various facets of the cultural heritage of the human race.

"Lastly, we believe that education is a continuous process; therefore, our entire curriculum should be designed to be effective as a basis for continuing education after the high school years as well as in meeting the needs of the school population."

The first objectives were:

"We, the staff of Washington High School, believe that the implementation of the above philosophy requires that the school provide arrays of learning and living experiences designed to foster in the student(s):

1. The knowledge and ability to understand themselves
2. The knowledge and understanding to examine, modify, and adopt moral as well as spiritual concepts that lead to a well-adjusted life
3. The development of background knowledge and skills required in the pursuit of higher learning
4. The achievement and maintenance of good physical and mental health
5. The knowledge and understanding needed in making choices of vocation in which they can succeed

6. The will and determined effort to raise the cultural levels of the school and the community
7. The understanding and appreciation and use of the "aesthetics" in the physical and spiritual environments
8. The ability and/or competence to understand, utilize, and conserve our natural resources
9. The development of the knowledge and competence to participate in democratic situations
10. The development of satisfactory competence in salable skills
11. The development of satisfying and acceptable qualities of social competence
12. The development of effective skills in self-expression
13. The full appreciation of and orientation to the major areas of the cultural heritage."

One of the requirements of the committee was that you look at the historical development of your school in the community. The committee charged with the responsibility of studying the history of how Washington High School evolved discovered that secondary education for Blacks in Early County was started December 18, 1875, when a school was opened in one of the African Methodist Episcopal Churches with Mr. E.H. Wilson as the teacher. The next reference on Black education was October 17, 1901, when it was announced that a "Colored High School" was to open in Blakely on the first Monday in November. Board for students could be found in private homes costing $4.50 to $5.50 per month. The tuition was $1.60 per pupil in advance for a term of 7 months. An entrance fee of $.50 per pupil was charged. In addition to this, pupils were required to bring a penny to help pay for wood and library books. Mr. William Oats was the principal with Mrs. Virginia Ross, first assistant and Mrs. Laura Hall second assistant. On June 22, 1903, a number of the leading Black citizens of Early County met in Blakely and organized for the purpose of establishing a Colored Normal and Industrial School in the city. Alonzo M. Stamper was the head of the project and he had in his possession twenty-eight acres of land which was to be used for the agricultural department. Washington High School was organized into a senior high school during the school year 1936–37 and functioned under the name of Blakely Colored High School. During this term and previous terms, the Blakely City Board of Education maintained the school, including the payment of the teachers' salaries and associated expenses. At this time the school had a very small enrollment served by one teacher and a teaching principal. The curriculum offerings were extremely limited consisting only of English, mathematics, general science and Latin.

At the beginning of the 1938–39 school term, the school was taken over by the Early County Board of Education. As a result, the high school expanded its course offerings to include vocational agriculture and vocational home economics. The name of the school was changed from Blakely Colored High School to Washington High School. No documentation exists as why it was called Washington High School. It could have taken its name from its location on Washington Avenue or from Booker T. Washington or perhaps it was named after the first president of the United States. The school grew under the administration of Mr. James T. Williams, Mr. Robert Rowe, Mr. Samuel Burton, and the able help of Miss Bessie Scott, the system curriculum supervisor.

Prior to 1945, Washington High School served only those students within walking distance or ones that provided their own method of transportation. Beginning with the school term of 1945–46 the first school bus transported pupils to the Washington High School resulting in increased enrollment. The charge to ride the bus was one dollar per student per week. It was several more years before free public transportation became available for Black students.

During the 1946–47 term, the curriculum offerings had broadened, the enrollment had grown and the personnel had increased but the length of school term was only eight months. During this term, under the administration of Mrs. K. P. Slaton, classes were held on Saturday in order that the students would have the benefit of a nine-month term. In the school year of 1949–50 as consolidation continued to progress, the high school department of the Early County Training School north of Blakely consolidated with Washington, which further enabled them to expand the curriculum offerings by adding typing. The course was initiated with one used typewriter and chair which was donated by a local law firm.

During the 1950–51 school term, as an outgrowth of the State School Building Authority, a survey team was organized of members selected from the three existing high schools, Carver, Kestler and Washington, and representative laity. Upon the completion of the committee's work, a reviewing team came into Early County to study the findings as a basis for determining present and future building needs. The team recommended the building of one high and two elementary schools. As a result, a high school, also called Washington, was constructed in Blakely, an elementary school for grades one through eight was built in Jakin, and what was to be an elementary school but functioned as an elementary and high school for six years was built in Damascus. All were occupied during the term of 1954–55. At this time Carver High School, in Jakin was consolidated with the Washington High School as recommended by the survey. However, it was not until the school year of 1960–61 that the Kestler High School in Damascus was consolidated with the Washington High School. Carver Elementary School and Kestler Elementary School served as feeder schools for the Washington High School.

The construction of these facilities represented significant improvement because all buildings were substandard and practically nonexistent prior to this time. The inadequacy of equipment and supplies had been an ongoing problem for Black schools. This need was addressed in large measure with the inception of Title III, Title V of NDEA, and Title I of Public Law 89-10. This act provided funds for instructional materials and equipment, library materials, and also included personnel both paraprofessional and professional.

The 1964–65 term was one of the most productive school years in that we organized for our self-study and this was also the beginning of our Title I programs. These programs were the most significant development during my entire professional career of forty years. Every department in our instructional program was upgraded. New programs included Headstart for preschoolers, summer programs for "at risk" students, a school nurse, transportation for students enrolled in summer programs, a language lab, and additional classroom teachers in the areas of math and reading. I do not have "hard data" to support the extent of the difference it made in our program, however, I am convinced that it was the greatest impact on our total program. Teacher morale was high and student motivation and interest increased tremendously. This program did much to address the cultural deprivation so prevalent in our school at that time. I do not know of any other program on the elementary and secondary levels that was so comprehensive.

Although Title I funds were not generally allowed for construction purposes we were able to get six new classrooms for our kindergarten program. This was definitely an exception to policy but our case was convincing enough to justify the approval of the construction. A major portion of the credit for what we were able to accomplish with Title I funds goes to Mr. Jimmy Hodge Timmons, who served as our first Title I coordinator for the school system. While serving in that capacity he displayed unusual imagination and creativity. Consequently, we were able to do some things that were not ordinarily allowed. It is also worthy of note that subsequently he was elected state senator for our congressional district and has done an excellent job while in that capacity.

It was at this point that the Early County Board of Education made a commitment to support our efforts by providing additional teachers, instructional materials and equipment. The local trustee board and I succeeded in getting the Early County Board of Education to approve the employment of an elementary principal for grades 1–6 for the Washington Elementary School at the beginning of the 1965–66 school year. The person that I recommended and the Board of Education approved was Mrs. Leona McWhorter from Meridian, Mississippi. Mrs. McWhorter had been a member of the faculty for four years. She taught first grade the first two years and second grade the third year. She was given administrative control of grades one through six and I was responsible for grades seven through twelve. However, I remained in the capacity of supervising principal of the elementary school. Mrs. McWhorter was a very valuable asset to me and served with distinction until the end of the 1969–70 school year. At the time of her appointment to the elementary principalship, the Carver Elementary School was consolidated with the Washington Elementary School bringing the total enrollment to 1655 and the professional staff to 53. From that time until we integrated in 1970–71, the enrollment remained above sixteen hundred and peaked at 1695 during the 1968–69 school year. Our professional staff numbered sixty nine for the 1969–70 school term.

Dr. Boyd successfully guided us through the process of becoming accredited and we were extremely proud and excited when the visiting committee spent the better part of three days in the Spring of 1967 on our campus making on-site observations and writing their reports. Highlights of the committee's report included the following commendations:

1. The Superintendent, Board of Education, school administration and staff are commended for recognizing critical needs and weaknesses.
2. The school consolidation has placed the students into fewer and larger school units providing for more efficient and effective educational program.
3. Encouraging the upgrading of the academic and professional status of the teacher personnel throughout the county.
4. The willingness to use Federal Titled Programs to provide materials, equipment and personnel.
5. Recognizing the pressing and immediate need for additional physical facilities.
6. The building of a Health and Physical Education building to be used in the Fall.
7. The purchase of additional land adjacent to the school plant to serve recreational needs and programs of the school and community.
8. The excellent rapport between all teachers; all teachers and administration; teachers and students.
9. The scheduling and handling of classes and activities.
10. The attempt to reach all ability levels.
11. The attempt to provide for differing ability-levels and vocational destinations.
12. The emphasis placed upon the use of multi-sensory instructional aids.
13. The large percentage of teachers who hold advanced degrees.
14. The well-equipped language laboratory.
15. The abundance of well equipped supplies in home ec., industrial arts and science.
16. On the job well done on the Self-study and the professional atmosphere.
17. The large enrolled PTA and the PTA being aware of the needs of the school.
18. For the desire and willingness to maintain "open channels" of communication between themselves and the citizenry of the county.

Our hard work culminated in the accreditation of Washington High School by the Georgia Accreditation Commission on the state level while it was also accredited by SACSS, Southern Association of Colleges and Secondary Schools. This was indeed a milestone in the status of Black education in Early County. Our graduates no longer had the disadvantage of being the product of an unaccredited high school. I still consider this one of my major accomplishments during my years in education and am extremely proud that I played a role in the pilot group which obtained accreditation for a Black school in Georgia before integration. An accredited Black high school in southwest Georgia was an exception instead of the rule. Another goal that I had set for my administration of the school was the erection of a physical education facility. Up until this point in my career there had never been any kind of provision made to address this crucial need. Consequently, it was necessary for our basketball games to be played out doors on a dirt court. It was a miracle that our players did not become ill as a result of exposure to the cold night-time temperature. In order to play these games, lights were strung around the court. Even though we were able to see well enough for the participants to play, it left a lot to be desired. Most of the spectators were courteous enough to pay to see our games. However, there were always those who would "slip through the cracks," so to speak, since we could not have a central check point.

We principals, trustee board and local P.T.A. consistently kept this critical need on the "front burner" of our list of priorities. Finally, this dream became a reality during the 1967–68 school year. It was fittingly named and dedicated to the memory of Miss Bessie Scott who gave twenty years (1937–1957) of exemplary service to upgrading the educational status of Early County in general and Negro education in particular. We were very appreciative of this long-awaited facility which included boys' and girls' dressing rooms, two classrooms, two offices, a concession area and bleachers to seat approximately 1,200. We were especially happy to show it off to our rivals in the Georgia Interscholastic Association. This culminated with our hosting the district and state basketball tournaments for Class A Black schools. These were indeed happy times for us in that our instructional needs were being met by Title I programs and our P. E., athletic and basketball needs by this modern facility.

Our next major endeavor was the introduction of football to our athletic program during the 1967–68 school year. We did not have adequate space to practice or play. However, an arrangement was worked out with the local post of the American Legion whereby we were able to practice on their baseball field. This arrangement proved very inconvenient, but we had at least made a beginning.

The second year was better as the Early County Board of Education purchased an additional fifteen acres of land adjacent to our school. A football field was developed and lights were installed which enabled us to play a limited number of home games. The program was terminated at the end of the 1969–70 school year due to the fact that our Board of Education desegregated the schools the following school term.

The decade of the sixties was characterized by an unusual amount of unrest in educational circles. This stemmed primarily from the concern of the forthcoming integration of the public schools. In Georgia, the Georgia Teachers and Education Association(Black) and Georgia Education Association (White) organizations were involved in a long drawn out process of negotiating a merger of the two professional organizations which took years to become a reality. This stems from the fact that primarily the White association did not want to share power with the members in the Black teachers association. Dr. H.E. Tate, executive secretary of GTEA, succinctly stated the problem in the annual GTEA convention on March 30, 1966 when he addressed the issue.

"When I look around and see an all-white Board of Education, an all-white Welfare Board and practically all other boards that have all-white members, despite the fact that one-third of our citizens are Negroes, I cannot help but know that it is not full representation and full democracy which those in power want to maintain, but full control.

"You, as educators, endowed with the ability and capacity with which to learn, perceive, direct and counsel must see that the efforts you have put forth in the past to teach American ideals, to seek justice and equality, to foster Christian principles and to accomplish the American dream, must not be in vain. You must continue to look until you see that, until every man, woman and child, not only in Georgia, but upon the face of this earth, has the same rights, the same opportunities and the same privileges as all other men, women, and children, there will be no real democracy and therefore no accomplishment of the American dream."

This was a period of extreme ambivalence for me because on the one hand I was fully committed to the concept of and rationale for integration, while on the other hand, I hated the reality that we faced in having to give up so much of what we had accomplished during my ten years at Washington High School. Commencement exercises that year were especially sad. My remarks to the graduates included the following:

"I wish to call attention to the fact that you represent the last class to graduate from Washington High School. I did a little research and found that the first class to graduate from this school was in 1934 and it consisted of only two members, namely, Mr. G. W. Fountain and Mrs. Juanita Threadcraft. You, the class of 1970, number 93. But you are the last. May you make it the best. YOU CAN; YOU MUST!

"Before awarding your diplomas, let us bow our heads for a special prayer.

"O God, in thy great mercy look upon the members of this graduating class, who have reached a new milestone in their experience, who will be leaving these halls of learning for wider service. Certify to them Thy will and reveal to them the divine blueprint for their lives. Make them willing to follow the plan that Thou hast ordained.

"As with the boundless energy of youth they undertake tasks difficult and challenging, help them to know that with Thee is the enabling power. As they wait upon Thee, may they mount up with wings as eagles, may they achieve in Thy strength, and in the last day receive the divine approval. Amen.

"And now, on behalf of the recommendation of the faculty and by the power vested in me by the Early County Board of Education, I am delighted to award you your diploma with all of the rights and privileges thereunto appertaining."

I am very thankful to have been privileged to serve as the last principal of Washington High School. In my opinion, we had indeed come a long way since that humble beginning in 1934 and certainly have a past to cherish and a future to fulfill.

Even though the school had to give way to change and hopefully progress, we have succeeded in organizing a very vibrant national alumni association with several local chapters. It's a real inspiration to me to see how some individuals are leading in trying to preserve and perpetuate the memory and ideals of Washington High School. The founder of the alumni association in 1973 was Pastor Bill Brewster. The association is chartered as a nonprofit organization and is registered with the Secretary of State for the State of Georgia. It is controlled and administered by a Board of Directors composed of not less than seven persons.

One of the primary goals of this association is to provide scholarship aid to deserving students who are enrolled in post secondary educational programs. Recipients must be in good academic standing in the educational institution in which they are matriculating. Many students have been able to continue their educational pursuits because of the financial assistance provided by this alumni group.

Mr. Lonnie B. Chester was our school superintendent at the time of integration and did an outstanding job facilitating a smooth transition from a segregated school system to a integrated one.

Under the desegregation plan there was to be one high school, one junior high school or middle school, and one elementary school. I had successfully completed twenty-one years of service in the school system at that time, which gave me seniority. I was given the option to be high school principal, junior high or middle school principal, elementary principal or assistant superintendent. It was a difficult decision for me. However, after much prayer, I opted to accept the junior high or middle school principalship. At the time, it appeared that in so doing I was getting the "short end of the stick." It meant that I was giving up the practically new physical education facility that it had taken so long to get. In its place I got the oldest physical plant in the school system including a shell, frame building which was a fire hazard. A major factor in my decision was the extent of extra curricular activities on the high school level, many of which were scheduled for Friday nights which presented a religious conflict with my observing the Sabbath from sunset Friday until sunset Saturday. I had faced this situation at Washington High School, so I decided that it was best not to become involved in another high school principalship. I have never regretted that decision.

The spring and summer of 1970 was a very busy time for the school system in that the White Early County Elementary School was moved to the Washington High School campus and became the combined elementary school for Black and White students. There was a vast amount of equipment and supplies to be shifted from one campus to the other. There were also numerous personnel changes made which required personal interviews with the personnel who would be transferred to another school. I was meeting most of these teachers for the first time, since there had been little dialog between Black and White teachers prior to that time. For some time our superintendent, Mr. Chester, had conducted joint meetings with all principals in the system, but not for the teachers in general.

Another concern that I had at that time was how I would be received in the White area of the town. Prior to this development, I had been "across the tracks," so to speak, and was not certain what I might expect. Nevertheless, I went about my work more or less routinely, without any overt negative response from anyone. For this I was especially thankful.

Even though I felt rather good about the level of preparation we had made in our efforts to make a smooth transition to a desegregated school system, I still felt just a little apprehensive. I suppose it was the fear of the unknown since we were "breaking new ground," so to speak. I really did not know what to expect. I couldn't help remembering how much we were giving up to achieve integration. Throughout my experience as a student in the school system and to that point in my professional career, we had been deprived of so many of the basic needs for a program of quality education. At the time of integration in 1970, most of these needs were finally being met, but by that time it was necessary to move on to what many Blacks thought would be the promised land, educationally speaking. In retrospect, that did not happen.

Before desegregation, Black children learned in an institution that, despite all the adversity it faced, succeeded entirely on the skills of Black adults who earned a deep measure of respect. The school was woven into the fabric of the community and was a sanctuary from the racial denigration that marked life outside it.

"The teachers were like an extension of your family," said Stephanie Esters, the black 1982 homecoming queen, whose older sisters attended segregated schools. "The whole issue of race wasn't there."

Integration changed all that, removing Blacks from top policy-making positions and raising racial questions about every faculty promotion and every student disciplinary action.

THE TEACHER

Lord, who am I to teach the way
      To little children day by day,
So prone myself to go astray?

I teach them knowledge, but I know
      How faint they flicker and how low
The candles of my knowledge glow.

I teach them power to will and do,
      But only now to learn anew
My own great weakness thru and thru.

I teach them love for all mankind
      And all God's creatures, but I find
My love comes lagging far behind.

Lord, if their guide I still must be,
      Oh, let the little children see
The teacher leaning hard on Thee.

               —Leslie Pinckney Hill.

CHAPTER 9

JUNIOR HIGH/MIDDLE SCHOOL
EXPERIENCES

1970–71 to 1988–89

At the time of my transfer to Early County Junior High School in June 1970, I was a little more than half way into my professional career, which spanned a period of forty and one-third years—March 1949–June 1989.

It may be of interest to note that it had been sixteen years since the U. S. Supreme Court declared "separate but equal" schools unconstitutional. This decision was rendered May 17, 1954, in the case of Brown vs. Topeka, Kansas. It was a landmark decision in that the U. S. Supreme Court said that such school systems were separate but unequal and that they, therefore, deprived the Black students of equal protection under the laws. Although the Court had decreed that public school systems would have to integrate, it was vigorously resisted even to the point that the National Guard had to be mobilized as was the case of Central High in Little Rock, Arkansas. Millions of dollars were spent in the construction of new school buildings for Blacks as a means of circumventing the Court's decree. In the end, the court prevailed; and many of these buildings set unoccupied today, in that they were not needed after the school systems were desegregated. They symbolize a monument to a way of life that has passed into history.

The politicians exploited the issue for all it was worth. In Georgia, it was Lester Maddox; and in Alabama, George Wallace, who was the most vocal, vowed, "Segregation now! Segregation forever!" When it was all over, the Court prevailed; and with a few notable exceptions, the transition was about as smooth as could have been expected under the prevailing circumstances.

When the time came to begin the new school year in 1970–71, I felt that I had done my homework and was ready to face the challenge

of making the transition from a dual school system to an inte-
grated/unitary system. Nevertheless, there was a degree of apprehension about how things would go.

During our week of preplanning, priority had been given to this
unique experience that we faced as we came together for the first time
as an integrated faculty. I strongly emphasized the need for everyone
to exhibit good human relations so that we could be good role models
for our students. In my opinion, this did much in creating and fostering
a climate or atmosphere conducive for effective teaching and learning.
I had chosen Mr. R.K. Sites, my former superintendent, as my assistant
principal and I was also fortunate to have a good and supportive
faculty consisting of 46 teachers, 27 of whom were White and 19
Black. By the end of our preplanning sessions, the consensus was,
"We're going to make it work."

The first day of school for the students went about as smoothly
as I could have hoped as our collective homework paid off. Homeroom
teachers distributed schedule cards to their students and after an
extended homeroom period of approximately twenty minutes, the
students attended their scheduled classes with a minimum of confusion and delay. I made a special effort to arrive at school well ahead
of any students and the faculty. We positioned ourselves at strategic
points to see that the students were under surveillance and adequately
supervised at all times.

I had placed unusual emphasis on making the first day of school
an enjoyable experience for everyone. In my opinion, this was extremely important since our students were having to adjust to a new
campus as well as a desegregated environment.

The majority of our parents did a super job in counseling their
children and admonished them to "go the extra mile" during the
adjustment and transition period. This, along with the collective
efforts of Mr. Lonnie B. Chester, Superintendent of Early County
Public Schools, building principals, and teachers, we came through
with flying colors. This is not to suggest that we batted a thousand and
everything was perfect. However, compared to the racial unrest and
disruptions experienced in some school systems, I felt that we had
much for which to be thankful. To God be the Glory, because we were
dealing with a potentially explosive situation; and the least bit of racial
agitation could have set off a chain reaction. I was totally committed
to feeding everyone out of the same spoon. I believe that by making

this known right up front and by stating in no uncertain terms that we would have only one school, this provided the framework for establishing policies that were not only fair, but in the best interest of all concerned.

I very vividly recall an applicant coming to me in the spring of 1970 and informing me that she would like to be considered for Mr. Sites' secretary. Mr. Sites had been designated to be my Assistant for the 1970–71 school year. As politely as I knew how, I explained to her that I was willing to consider her for the position; but, if hired, she would be school secretary as opposed to Mr. Sites' secretary. To have done otherwise, in my opinion, would have had the effect of continuing to function along racial lines. She was subsequently hired; and I am happy to say that she proved to be a loyal, dedicated, and supportive worker.

When behavior problems occurred, I did my utmost to insure that they were dealt with on a fair and objective basis. Extra effort was put forth to eliminate the possibility that race did not influence my decision in determining the appropriate action to be taken. Even so, there were times when I would find myself in a "no-win" situation when a problem involved a White student and a Black student. If I decided in favor of the White student the Black student and his/her parents would feel that I had done so because the student was White and vice versa. Happily for me, this was the exception rather than the rule. It wasn't long before students and parents alike respected the way I handled their problems and felt that I tried to be fair and objective regardless to the outcome.

I learned very early in my administrative career that a major portion of my work would consist of decision making. Consequently, I tried not to take it lightly; and in that connection I prayed for wisdom and understanding, and I am convinced that the Lord provided it. In retrospect, I am sure I made some bad decisions and some good ones. Nevertheless, once they were made, I stood by them. I did my best to avoid "shooting from the hip," so to speak. I found that when the situation would permit it, I would take a matter under advisement once I had the benefit of the relevant facts and make my decision later. This minimized the risk of making a premature decision, while at the same time improved my decision-making skills.

In my opinion, one of the most sensitive facets of the desegregation process was implementing the changes in our bus assignments.

The vast majority of our students were transported; and many of their parents felt reasonably comfortable with them attending an integrated school but did not want them riding on an integrated school bus. As a result of this situation, the buses were integrated on a more gradual basis. Fortunately, the fears that some parents had about their children riding on an integrated bus proved unfounded. The Early County Board of Education had already implemented a strict code of conduct for transported students. Mr. Chester was very supportive of his building principals. Therefore, we were able to stay on top of the situation, and we "played hard ball" with the few students who failed to observe the rules. In the process, we emphasized that riding the bus was a privilege and not a right and could be withdrawn if satisfactory conduct was not maintained. With very few notable exceptions, our students rose to the occasion and made a good adjustment; and I was extremely proud of them. In dealing with student behavior, you do not solve the problems once and for all; rather, it's an ongoing process. Even now more than twenty years after integration, there are isolated cases of bus conduct problems. Realistically, I believe that this will always be the case; but it is not a racial problem, just human behavior problems and should be viewed in that context.

For the most part, our school bus drivers did a fantastic job during the transition period and insisted that the students display appropriate bus behavior. In my opinion, they deserved much of the credit for things going so well during the adjustment period. Sometimes I feel we underestimate the importance and responsibilities of our school bus drivers. They are not only held accountable for maintaining order on their buses but, most importantly, for getting their students to and from school safely.

For whatever the reason might have been, there were White parents who were opposed to integration under any circumstances. As an outgrowth, these anti-integration forces formed the Southwest Georgia Academy, Damascus, Georgia. It is my understanding that the Early County Board of Education deeded the land and buildings of the Old Damascus Elementary and High School to this group for one dollar, just to make it legal. I have not tried to judge the motive of the parents who opted to send their children there. I might add that I support and defend till death their right to do so. Nevertheless, if their motive was to keep their children from having to interact with Blacks and other minorities, I feel that it was and is unrealistic. We live in a pluralistic society, and sooner or later we must all come together for the common good of all of us. From all indications, Southwest Georgia Academy has done exceptionally well academically, athletically, and in literary events. Presently, it serves a multi-county area and has an enrollment of approximately 291 students in kindergarten through twelfth grade. It's possible that, by this school offering an alternative to integration for those parents who were so adamantly opposed to it, most racial unrest was avoided. In that connection, I feel that it served a worthwhile purpose for parents who wanted another option. It served as a safety valve for parents who were not willing to send their children to an integrated school.

Many of the faculty members were former public school teachers, some of whom were retirees. A retiree from the public school system can draw his/her teacher retirement pension in addition to the salary from the academy.

The students are, to a large extent, from middle class and upper class families and are usually very talented. Therefore, the Academy often has a greater percentage of high achievers than in the public schools. I believe that this stems in part from the fact that their parents have to pay for their private education, as opposed to being free in the public schools. However, we know that this is a myth, because in reality there is no such thing as a "free lunch"; someone must pick up the tab.

In my opinion, another reason for the higher level of achievement is that a private school can afford to be more selective about the students admitted; whereas, in the public schools everyone must be admitted, so long as he/she maintains satisfactory conduct. Many such students lack motivation and do not strive to perform anywhere near their level of ability. Also, parents who sacrifice to send their children to private school are paying for their education over and beyond the taxes that they pay for public schools; therefore, they demand more from them. In my opinion, there is a higher level of parental support and involvement on the part of parents who send their children to private school. In public school I know for a fact that many parents never came to the school until there was a problem involving their child. This placed the child at a significant disadvantage that he/she would not have if the parent were more supportive of their efforts.

Southwest Georgia Academy is not by any means unique in its existence; rather, it is part of a whole network of private schools, usually referred to as academies, that sprang up throughout the southern states as a means of circumventing the U.S. Supreme Court's decision outlawing segregation in public schools. Many of them are no longer in existence due primarily to decreasing enrollment, which made it impossible for them to generate enough income to keep afloat. In many instances, their programs were substandard, due in part to a lack of official standards that had to be met by such schools. As a result, most any group could open a private school and stay in business as long as they could maintain sufficient parental and financial support to justify its existence.

In the case of S.G.A., I believe that it is here to stay since it has the benefit of very strong and solid financial and parental support.

Prior to the 1970–71 school year, only five Black students had attended a White school in the Early County school system. These students were: Alvetta Moses, her brother, Thomas Moses, Alice Pittman, Lawrence Ford, and Annie Unice Jackson. These students were admitted under the "freedom of choice" policy that was in force for several years after the Supreme Court ruling in 1954 and prior to actual desegregation in 1970 of remaining school systems that had not integrated prior to that time.

Under this policy, each student was given a "Freedom of Choice" form, usually in the eighth or ninth month of the school year to take home to their parents or guardians. The names of all the schools in the system were listed on the form. The parent(s) or guardian(s) was to check the name of the school that he/she wanted their child to attend the next school year. The child subsequently returned the form to his/her homeroom teacher who in turn submitted it to the building principal. The building principal submitted all forms to the system superintendent, who checked them very closely to see what choices had been made. Upon the completion of this process, the form was returned to the school in which the child was enrolled and placed in his/her permanent record folder.

In my opinion, many parents felt intimidated by the form in that they were afraid that they might lose their jobs if they signed the form for their child to go to one of the White schools. For that or whatever other reasons there might have been, the five above-mentioned students were the only Black students to attend an Early County White school. I consider it worthy of note that those five students still rode the Black school buses to the Black school, Washington High School campus, and were transported to the White school, Early County High School, in the Washington High School van. At dismissal each day they were transported back to the Washington campus to link up with the assigned Black bus for the return trip home. Although one or more White school buses passed their homes each day, this practice was continued until the beginning of the 1970–71 school year. To my knowledge, this arrangement was never challenged by the concerned parents.

It is interesting to note that even though the Early County public schools were desegregated in 1970, it was not until twelve years later that the Early County Board of Education became integrated. I do not have an explanation for the long delay. Nevertheless, this body has remained integrated with one to two Black members out of a total of five. At first they were appointed by the Grand Jury; however, all members are presently elected by the voters.

Another major task that I faced after transferring to the middle school was that of getting the school accredited by the Southern Association of Colleges and Secondary Schools. I had gone through this process in my former position as principal at Washington High School and knew first hand how exhaustive and demanding it could be. Washington High School accreditation was transferred to the newly established junior high.

I decided against tackling such a major task until we had gotten settled into the routine of things, which included students adjusting to a new campus, a new faculty having to develop rapport with each other and with me, and parents adjusting to a new school. Prior to the beginning of the 1970–71 school year we only had elementary schools and high schools. Consequently, the major thrust of the first year of integration was to get through the transition period as smoothly as possible. In my opinion, we succeeded in accomplishing that objective.

Early in my second year (1971–72) at the middle school, I organized the faculty in committees for our self-study. This is the initial step in the evaluative process. The major committees included the following:

1. Steering Committee, Mr. Judson Cooper, Chairman
2. Philosophy and Objective, Mr. Jimmy Mathew, Chairman
3. School and Community, Mr. Roscoe Nash, Chairman
4. School, Staff and Administration, Mrs. Othell Evans, Chairman

5. Major Education Commitments, Mrs. Dwayne Davis, Chairman
6. Design of Curriculum, Mrs. Mary Berzett, Chairman
7. School Plant, Mr. Fred Daniels, Jr. , Chairman
8. Learning Media Services, Miss Beauty Lewis, Chairman
9. Student Services, Mr. Terry Pitchford, Chairman
10. Parent Evaluation, Mrs. Odelia Bowman, Chairman
11. Student Activity Program, Mrs. Herdisene Harris, Chairman

In addition to the major committees the following minor committees were appointed:

1. English, Mrs. Betty Henderson, Chairman
2. Math, Miss Glynda Mills, Chairman
3. Vocational, Mr. Judson Cooper, Chairman
4. Science, Miss Mattie Grimes, Chairman
5. Social Studies, Mr. Jimmy Mathews(?), Chairman
6. Reading, Mrs. Melba Daniels, Chairman
7. Health and Physical Education, Mrs. Dwayne Davis, Chairman
8. Foreign Language, Mrs. Odelia Bowman, Chairman
9. Editing and Compilation, Mrs. Odelia Bowman, Chairman
10. Educable Mentally Retarded, Mr. Johnny Henderson, Chairman
11. Hospitality, Mrs. Sylvia Carter, Chairman
12. Dinner Meeting Program, Mrs. Mary Brezett, Chairman

Dr. Lawrence E. Boyd, from Atlanta University, had been our consultant when we went through the laborious process during my tenure at Washington High School. I had been extremely well impressed with his expertise and the excellent rapport that he developed with the faculty, students, paraprofessionals, parents and the support personnel. With this in mind when I needed a consultant to guide us through this in-depth process at the middle school, his name immediately came to mind. I was elated when he accepted the invitation to steer us through the yearlong process. I might add that in addition to working with me on the evaluative process in my schools, Washington High School and Early County Middle School, Dr. Boyd had also been my professor at Atlanta University and was my major advisor for my master's thesis and my oral. He was indeed a mentor for me.

Our self-study went extremely well, culminating with the visiting committee spending the major portion of three days on our campus, March 19–21, 1973.

Following is a historical statement that I consider germane:

The Early County Junior High/Middle School is relatively young, having just come into being in the fall of 1970. The creation of the school stemmed, in large measure, from many hours of deliberation on the part of the Board of Education, Superintendent, principals, teachers, students, and parents in an attempt to find what promised to be the most effective plan of shifting from a dual system of education to a unitary system. It was in this context that the Early County Junior High/Middle School emerged. Since its inception, significant strides have been made to develop a relevant program for the community it serves.

By the end of my service at the middle school, we had conducted two additional self-studies applying the junior high evaluative criteria in 1973 and maintaining our accredited status. Subsequent studies were directed by Hubert A. Hutcherson, a retired school administrator who had streamlined the self-study, thus making the process somewhat less difficult. In the 1983 evaluation the middle school criteria were applied thus enabling our school system to have one of the first Southern Association accredited middle schools.

Another noteworthy experience that I had while at the middle school was to be chosen by Mr. David Rivenbark, high school principal, as the commencement speaker for the 1984 Early County High School graduating class. The following are several excerpts from that address:

"It was with a great deal of reservation and reluctance that I accepted the invitation to speak to you on this momentous occasion. However, with a good bit of persuasion and after consulting with the Lord, I decided to do my best. I invite you to pray with and for me that I may be able to say something during the time allotted me to cause these young people to think on their way and to face the future courageously. I assure you that I am both honored and humbled as I endeavor to fulfill this responsibility.

"Having made my decision to speak to you, the next most difficult task was to decide what to say, because there is so much that I would like to say that probably should be said, but cannot say it because of time constraints. There is so much bad news in the world today, such as the conflicts in Central America, the Persian Gulf, Lebanon, drug abuse, and the arms-race between the super powers, to name a few. We are told that we already have enough missiles and other nuclear weapons to destroy our civilization several times over, but we continue to develop more.

"However, I decided not to spend my time discussing these issues. I was interested to know something about the success of this class in terms of dropouts. So, with the assistance of the central office staff, I researched it and discovered that in first grade (1972–73) you started out with an enrollment of 196. Your enrollment hit the "high water mark," so to speak, when you were in seventh grade with an enrollment of 239. Two hundred twenty-eight of you started out as ninth graders during the 1980–81 school year. I understand 149 of you are graduating today.

"Concerning the matter of dropouts, it was revealed that a total of 96 of your classmates dropped out or met the definition of a dropout as defined by the Georgia State Department of Education. A dropout as defined by the State Department is a student who leaves a school for any reason except death before graduation or completion of a program of studies and without transferring to another educational program. It is interesting to note that three of this number occurred in elementary school, thirteen in middle school, and eighty in high school.

"What are the implications stemming from these findings? Well, among others they suggest: (1) These young adults are without salable skills. (2) They are going to find it very difficult to survive in the job market. The first question after the blanks for name and address on most job applications forms is, "Do you have a High School Diploma?" A young person without one has a permanent sentence to a limited life. (3) Their earning power is approximately 68 percent lower than what it would have been had they "hung in there" as you, the graduating class of 1984, have done. (4) The farther up the educational ladder we climb, the more competitive it becomes. I congratulate you for your perseverance and stick-to-itiveness.

"Before I continue, let me commend your parents for being so supportive and encouraging when you needed them most....

"In case you haven't already discovered it, it's a new ball game for you; and it is a complex, mean world out there waiting for you. What are you going to do about it? Will you be part of the problem or part of the solution? Whatever you do, I plead with you to not take a 'hands off' attitude and stand by and do nothing as these cherished freedoms continue to erode...."

"I recommend that you set some goals for yourself, because if you don't know where you are going, you're not likely to get there...."

"You deserve to be commended for your post high school plans. According to information made available to me from the high school guidance office, eight of you are planning to go to vocational technical schools, sixty to junior and senior college, thirty-three into the military, five into the world of work, and forty-seven are undecided. So, I commend you for having planned ahead...."

"Another very important part of success in life is to learn from your setbacks or failures. When you examine the lives of successful people, you'll find they have gone through the same kind of experiences on the way to success. They were willing to get into the arena, to try their best, and to profit from their mistakes...."

"Remember, life is what you make of it—not what you let it make of you...."

"A noteworthy quote is: Life's battles don't always go to the stronger or faster man; But soon or late the man who wins is the fellow who thinks he can...."

"When you start to think that something is impossible, I want you to remember this story, a true story, of David Hartman's impossible dream. This David Hartman should not be confused with ABC morning show host. This David Hartman lived in Havertown, Pennsylvania. He was born blind. He wanted to become a medical doctor, a psychiatrist. He believed he could help rehabilitate people with problems similar to his. When he asked his dad what he thought about his dream, his father said, 'You'll never know unless you try.' How about that? What wise counsel! It would have been so easy for him to have said, 'Son, I don't know about that, maybe you ought to consider something else since you are blind.' Instead, he simply said, 'You'll never know, unless you try.' "

"David finished high school, was graduated Summa Cum Laude with a 3.8 average, out of a possible 4 points. Even before graduation, of course, he had applied to medical schools. Nine turned him down. And while David waited, discouraged, the tenth school, Temple University School of Medicine in Philadelphia, considered his application. The assistant dean in charge of admissions told the other members of the admissions board, "David Hartman already is doing impossible things. I think we should see how far he can go."

"They agreed. And David Hartman was admitted to medical school. It was tough. His fingers had to "see" for him whenever possible. He learned to take notes on a recorder during the six lectures each day. Then came the acid test in his third year. He began working with real patients.

"David learned to rely on nurses and the patients themselves for what he could not see. He found he could use a stethoscope very skillfully. He had developed very highly his sense of touch. He learned to listen to what he heard.

"On May 27, 1976, David Hartman received his M.D. Degree. Later, when he was honored for his achievement, he said, 'My dad was right. You'll never know unless you try.'

"Years before that happened, there was another youngster from Georgia, born poor and Black, blind from the age of seven, left motherless and so grief stricken that he had to be force-fed, recovering only to experience the death of his father a year later. But you know something, he said, 'I'm never going to beg.'

"As a teenager he worked in bands, singing and playing the piano, arranging music, and earning three dollars a night. Then the day came when he caught a bus from Jacksonville, Florida, to Seattle, Washington, and found a job as an entertainer. He was on his way!

"Today his record sales have exceeded the two million mark. He has two music publishing companies, a record production business, and a management firm, grossing over two million dollars a year. His name is Ray Charles.

"And if his life story is not impressive enough, let me tell you what he said after recording his hit song, "America the Beautiful."

"He said that he had a reason for doing that recording, and this is it: 'America is the greatest country in the world. We have a lot of things that need to be changed and a lot of things we have to accomplish. But when we travel to other places outside of the United States, you realize how great this country is.'

"I cannot overemphasize that we still live in a country where you can make it if you try; and as David Hartman's dad told him, 'You'll never know unless you try.'

"Finally, in the words of the wise man Solomon, 'Don't let the excitement of being young cause you to forget your Creator. It's wonderful to be young. Enjoy every minute of it, do all you want to, take in everything, but realize that you must account to God for everything you do—remember that youth, with a whole life before it, can make serious mistakes.' Ecl. 11:9–10 and 12:1. (The Living Paraphrased Bible.)

"If my dear wife were still with us and had any input when I was organizing my thoughts, she, in all probability, would have wanted me to tell you to be somebody—to be all that you can be. Further, she would want me to remind you as the United Negro College Fund Commercial says, 'A mind is a terrible thing to waste.'

"I realize that my time has expired, but I must reiterate that: (1) The opportunities seized by the few were available to the many. (2) You can make it if you try. (3) You will never know, unless you try.

"I conclude by challenging you, the graduating class of 1984, that you have an important responsibility in keeping alive the real American Dream, in holding high the torch of freedom as you reach out for others, and helping to lead the way to a brighter future.

"May the Lord richly bless you, I love every one of you, my prayers go with you!"

The main focus of my last five years at the Middle School was the fine tuning of the Middle School concept that we had previously implemented. In my opinion, we experienced outstanding success in our endeavors; and I was very pleased with our accomplishments.

We consistently sought to upgrade our academic program; and at the time of my retirement, our performance in the areas of writing, reading, and math skills was equal to or greater than our Educational Planning District. In my opinion, this was a very noteworthy accomplishment that resulted from a team effort on the part of our professional staff.

Another humbling experience that I will share briefly was the special retirement program presented for me as the final day of the 1988–89 school year. The greatest surprise was that all seven of my surviving siblings were present. I had no idea that this was going to happen, and it was even more special when it took place on a happy and joyous occasion without anyone being ill, without a life-threatening condition, or at someone's funeral. I was almost overwhelmed by it. With the exception of my oldest son, Mike, his wife, Enid, and their boys, Matthew and Joel, all of my children and grandchildren were present. I know for certain that had they been in the states, they would have also been present. Instead, they were in South Africa, serving the second year of a six-year term as missionaries at Bethel College, located in the Transkei area.

In addition to my immediate family, there was a host of parents, friends, former teachers who had worked with me, and well-wishers who just came to express their appreciation and be a part of the celebration. I shall always remember and cherish that very special event. In my opinion, the song writer, J. B. F. Wright, vividly expressed my feeling in these words: "Precious memories, how they linger, how they ever flood my soul—in the stillness of the midnight, precious sacred scenes unfold."

I was the recipient of many gifts, congratulations, accolades, and best wishes for a happy and fulfilling retirement. I deeply appreciated all of them. However, there was one in particular that I especially treasured so much so that I decided to share it with you. It's what I consider to be an expression of gratitude from Bob Kornegay, one of the middle school faculty members. It is as follows:

"Dear Mr. Harris,

"Tributes in the form of group-sponsored accolades are both fitting and well-deserved. I join the collective masses in sincerely wishing you all the best and congratulate you for remaining so dedicated, for so long a time, to the task in which you have so admirably performed.

"However, I would be remiss in not offering a little something of myself, on a personal level, in the best way I know how. It is here, with the written word, that I offer my own tribute.

"You, sir, are quite special to me for a number of reasons, not the least of which is the fact that, quite simply, you are you. I know dozens of people from all walks of life who would learn a helluva lot about being a human being were they only afforded the opportunity to know you as I do.

"Professionally, you are the only "boss" I have ever had and a major reason for my remaining 15 years in a line of work that may well not be my true calling. Frankly, I will never be ranked among the most dedicated schoolteachers you have known, but I have done my best and felt successful largely because I have had a superior with the instinct to let me teach the best way I can. I break a lot of so-called "tried-and-true" educational rules and feel most comfortable when I am ad-libbing. Call it going with the flow or "winging it," if you prefer.

I wonder if anyone other than a John R. Harris will be willing to cut me enough slack.

"You were also a major influence in my decision to remain a teacher after those first few tough years when neither you nor I honestly figured on my staying in the profession. By neither discouraging nor encouraging and allowing me to work it out on my own, you helped make the decision, if not an easy one, at least one a bit less difficult to arrive at. Uncanny how you always seemed to know how to handle me, huh?

"Above all else, Mr. Harris, you have always been willing to consider my side of an issue, whether you agreed or not. You have a real talent for that. Most of us cannot say the same for ourselves.

"I remember, and chuckle over it now, that right after we lost Mrs. Herdisene, one of my first thoughts was, "Oh my, who do I have now to act as a go-between in my dealings with Mr. H.?" Well, as it turned out, I survived and quite well, too.

"Specifically, there are dozens of other reasons why working with you these past 15 years has been a major chapter in the Life and Times of Bob Kornegay. Listing them one-by-one in this well-meant but quite-inadequate salute is really not necessary. As a principal, you know as well as I what you have done for me. Just know, too, that I am just as grateful for these that remain unmentioned as I am for the ones touched on previously.

"Now, forget your being my principal for a moment and consider what you mean to me in another, far more important way. In the same fashion that teachers are encouraged to take an interest in their students, you have shown genuine interest and concern in my life beyond the confines of the classroom. That is not only rare, but almost unheard of in an employee/employer relationship.

"Not only have you been willing, but have gone out of your way to share my happiness, my sadness, my dreams and ambitions. You have applauded my successes, large and small. Frankly, there are members of my family who couldn't care less about my achievements. You care and don't have to. That is the most wonderful caring of all.

"I will conclude, sir, by telling you what I have already told others. I do not relish the thought of returning to Early County Middle School next fall to find someone other than John R. Harris occupying that familiar chair. Like the little boy said to his mother when she was demanding that he eat his broccoli, "I'll eat it, but danged if I'm gonna like it!"

"As for yourself, please don't allow retirement to become a negative phase of your life. Get out there and live! You have paid your dues many times over. You deserve it. And do it with yourself in mind, too. Think about YOU for a change and enjoy your life to the fullest.

"Well, this ol' soapbox has gotten too rickety to stand on any longer. I'll climb down now and leave additional accolades to others so inclined. I have no doubt that you know my feelings even had I not attempted to relate them here. But just for the record, let me once and for all say, in sincerity and unashamedly, I love you.

"You will be missed."

      Bob Kornegay

      ...Lives of great men all remind us
      We can make our lives sublime,
      And, departing, leave behind us
      Footprints on the sands of time;...

      A PSALM OF LIFE
      —Henry Wadsworth Longfellow

CHAPTER 10

SUPERINTENDENTS WITH WHOM I SERVED

1949–89

MY SERVICE WITH MR. R. K. SITES

Mr. R. K. Sites was my superintendent when I began my professional career in 1949. However, my interaction with him was somewhat limited due to the fact that most of his administrative policies for the black schools were delegated to Miss Bessie Scott, the Jeans Supervisor.

It was during his service at the Middle school that I really got to know him. I must admit that when I was informed that he was to be my assistant principal, I had some rather strong reservations and was somewhat apprehensive as to how it would work out. I was delighted that my reservations proved unfounded. I could not have hoped for an assistant who would have been any more loyal and supportive during our turbulent years of adjusting to an integrated school system. In fact, I consider his service with me in his capacity as assistant principal, one of the most positive things to happen to me during the transition period. He consistently went beyond the call of duty in doing what he could in helping to develop a quality program at the Early County Middle School. He was a very good role model, a very strict disciplinarian, and an exceptionally good algebra teacher. He stuck with me through thick and thin throughout the ubiquitous changes that we were experiencing at the time.

In my opinion, Mr. Sites' career was even more noteworthy when placed in perspective. He had come to Early County from Irmo, Richland County, South Carolina, in the mid-nineteen thirties. This made him "an outsider," so to speak, but he was still able to capture the votes for superintendent. He demonstrated his leadership qualities as superintendent and was able to hold the position of assistant principal with equal ability. At the time of integration, he already had more than thirty years of teaching experience, as opposed to my twenty-one years of service at that time. He was not only a leader but also could be a follower. While serving in the Early County School System, he endeared himself to the hearts of many people.

His teaching career included service in the following Early County Schools: Union, Hilton, Jakin, Blakely Union, Early County High School, and Early County Middle School. Twelve years of his service was in the capacity of Superintendent of Early County Public Schools. In addition to his teaching and administrative duties, he also found time to coach basketball and football. At the time of his retirement in 1974, he was serving as my assistant principal of Early County Middle School.

MY SERVICE WITH MISS ANNIE GRIER

My next superintended was Miss Annie Grier who served for four years during my service at Kestler. After serving her four years she apparently retired or did not work in the school system.

MY SERVICE WITH MR. LONNIE B. CHESTER

Throughout my entire professional career I believe that the one person who contributed the most towards my success was Mr. Lonnie B. Chester. He came to Early County from Dawson Springs, Kentucky, in 1951 and spent the remainder of his life as a loyal and dedicated educator in the Early County school system. During this period he served with distinction as a classroom teacher, baseball coach, principal, and superintendent of Early County public schools. Not only was he a capable and dedicated educator, but a Christian gentleman and a genuine friend. He was also an exceptionally good role model and leader. During his administration of the public schools of Early County, beginning January 1961, he was usually the first one in his office, which was located in the county courthouse, and the last to leave. In my opinion, he earned every cent of his salary.

I enjoyed working with Mr. Chester, and I especially appreciated the supportive role that he played in behalf of my administration while at Washington High School and Early County Middle School. I could always count on him being there when I needed him. It was never too late or too early to call him if the situation necessitated it.

Whenever I needed to be away to attend committee meetings for my church, personal business, or for any other reason, he always encouraged me to go and to take as much time as necessary. Of course, I tried not to abuse the privilege; but it was a good feeling to be able to go without him ever exhibiting any negative response.

Another reason that I enjoyed my years of service with Mr. Chester was his philosophy about permitting the building principal complete control over the day-to-day operations of his school. If a parent called him or went to his office to complain about a school-level problem, he would listen very politely, after which he would explain that it was a school problem and would have to be addressed by the concerned building principal. It didn't take very long for the parents to learn and accept his administrative style. Thereafter, parents knew that they would have to consult with the building principals pursuant to school-level problems. The end result, in my opinion, was that the parents gained a greater degree of respect for their child's principal; and better rapport was established between the parent(s) and the principal.

Mr. Chester was always trying to make things better for the students and employees for the Early County School System. One noteworthy example was his tireless efforts to a local supplement. He was indeed happy when it became a reality and gave it to the personnel in the form of a Christmas bonus. It was greatly appreciated by all concerned and did much to boost the morale of the recipients.

Mr. Chester was a strong advocate of the pursuit of excellence. Under his leadership our students made significant gains in the areas of language arts and math. I consider it worthy of note that teachers, principals, and curriculum directors from surrounding school systems came to observe first hand the specific things that we were doing to motivate our students to make such significant gains. They were so favorably impressed with what we were doing that some of the school systems adapted/ adopted our programs.

Mr. Chester really put our school system on the map, so to speak. To keep our momentum going he utilized the services of consultants on the local, regional, state, and college/university levels. In addition to aforementioned consultants, specialists from several publishing companies were invited to give classroom demonstrations, which enabled the teachers to improve their expertise. By taking advantage of these resources, we were able to keep abreast of the changes and innovations that were taking place in our academic disciplines.

The officials in the State Department of Education from the State Superintendent of Schools right down to the various chairpersons for the many departments knew Mr. Chester and held him in very high esteem. Many of them he knew on a first-name basis. His rapport with them was so good that if there were any available funds around, Early County would certainly get its fair share. Indicative of his success in this area were the major building and renovating projects that took place during his tenure of office. They included the following:

1. Construction of six new classrooms for the Washington Elementary School.
2. Construction of Bessie Scott Health and Physical Education building for the Washington High School.
3. Construction of the 9th grade wing for Early County High School.
4. Construction of a new vocational wing for Early County High School.
5. Construction of a new band room for Early County High School.
6. Installation of air conditioning in the Elementary School and the Middle School
7. Renovation and expansion of the media center for the Middle School.

The cost of the projects amounted to several millions of dollars. However, because of Mr. Chester's perseverance and the respect that the officials in the State Department of Education had for him, he was able to get them for the citizens of Early County for only a fraction of the total cost. He was very pleased with his accomplishments in this area. On the one hand, he was very sensitive to the economic status of the tax payers of Early County and put forth every possible effort to avoid raising the local tax millage. On the other hand, he wanted the very best facilities for the students of Early County. Consequently, he explored every possible source of available funds; and I might add that his batting average was very good. The citizens and students of Early County are still enjoying the benefits of his labor and will continue to do so for years to come.

I am especially indebted to Mr. Chester for his very unselfish act of recommending to the Early County Board of Education that the new media center at the Early County Middle School be named in my honor. The Board accepted his recommendation; and on Sunday, March 15, 1981, the ultra modern facility was dedicated in my honor. It was a humbling as well as a joyful experience for me, to say the least. I could not help wondering whether or not I was deserving of such special recognition. I feel that this could very well have been the high-water mark of my professional career. While it is not uncommon for someone to have a building, a street, or some other fitting tribute named for him/her it usually occurs after his/her, death. The fact that it happened in my lifetime is why this tribute meant so very much to me. I thank the Lord first of all, then Mr. Chester, the members of the Early County Board of Education, teachers, and parents for having bestowed such a distinguished honor upon me. I could not help but reflect on the difficulties and hurdles that had been overcome at that particular juncture of my professional career. This stemmed from the insatiable desire that my mother had instilled in me to learn even if it had to be accomplished under adverse circumstances. I can truly say that the race is not to the swift nor to the strong but to him who holds out and endures to the end. My words are inadequate to express my thanks and appreciation because I would rather have the media center named in my honor during my lifetime, than all of Early County after I have passed on. I pray consistently that I will always be worthy of such a unique recognition. My family also deeply appreciated this kind gesture; it is priceless and will always be cherished as one of our fondest memoirs. The Early County Board of Education, through Mr. Chester's leadership, secured a $250,000 grant from the State Department of Education for this project. The local system's share of this enterprise was $50,189. It has been almost ten years since this facility was constructed, and even now it is equal to or superior to any middle school media center in this southwest Georgia educational planning district. In my opinion, this speaks well for the foresight that Mr. Chester and the Board of Education exhibited in sponsoring this project. The Lord blessed me to do another eight years before my retirement in June 1989.

In addition to the many admirable traits that I have already mentioned about Mr. Chester, I would add that he was very patriotic. In this connection, he volunteered for the U.S. Navy at the age of 17 and experienced combat in World War II.

As long as I served with him, he always gave 110 percent of his effort for whatever the cause might have been. This continued until the very end, which came unexpectedly on August 24, 1981. He was in Atlanta at the time on school business, as he frequently was, when he suffered a massive heart attack. He was rushed to Crawford W.

Long Hospital, where efforts to save him were unsuccessful. It is worthy of note that my niece, Beryl Michelle, was a member of the ICU team who tried to resuscitate him. It was indeed a sad experience for me when I received the phone call to inform me of his passing. It was just like the passing of a member of my family. It really was a traumatic experience for the school system, staff, students, and parents. I remember his stopping by my office before leaving for Atlanta that day for an informal chat. This was almost a routine of his and he appeared upbeat and very happy as we parted. We had no idea that we were seeing each other for the last time in this life. At the time of Mr. Chester's demise, he was serving the first year of his fifth consecutive four-year term of office as superintendent of the Early County public schools. It is interesting to note that I served with him longer than any other superintendent with whom I worked during my entire professional career.

We not only had lost our capable and beloved superintendent of our public schools, but a loyal, dedicated friend, and citizen as well. His passing created a void that, in my opinion, has been extremely difficult to fill.

The vocational wing at the Early County High School was named in Mr. Chester's memory. It is also worthy of note that a scholarship has been founded in his memory. It is called the Lonnie B. Chester Scholarship Fund and is awarded to a deserving high school graduate from Early County High School each year. A committee reviews the applications and conducts a brief interview with each applicant. Several criteria are applied in the selection process, including academic standing in the class and the financial needs of the applicants. The amount of the scholarship is usually $500.

In retrospect, Mr. Chester was the only Early County school superintendent to die while in office during my forty-year educational career.

Fortunately, the school system was able to make a reasonably smooth transition. The Early County Board of Education appointed Mr. Robert May, Title I Coordinator at the time, as interim superintendent to serve until a special election could be held to elect a successor to serve out the remainder of Mr. Chester's term. When the special election was held, Mr. Ray Knight was elected and was sworn in as our new superintendent. Prior to his election to this office, Mr. Knight was principal of the Early County Elementary School. It is also interesting to note that he and Mr. Chester had been housemates when they moved to Early County in 1952. They were both bachelors at the time. Subsequently, they both met and married Early County ladies.

Mr. Knight took over the leadership of our school system under rather adverse circumstances. However, Mr. Chester had been extremely well organized and businesslike. Consequently, Mr. Knight, with the able assistance of Mr. May, was able to keep everything "on an even keel."

MY SERVICE WITH MR. RAY KNIGHT

I was not personally acquainted with Mr. Knight until the spring of 1970, at which time we were beginning to do our homework for integration of the school system at the beginning of the forthcoming school year. He was coaching basketball at Early County High School at that time. He had succeeded in developing an outstanding coaching record for himself, which included a state championship team in 1964. As a result of his coaching success, he had excellent name recognition and was highly respected in the school system.

The 1970–71 school year was his first year as an administrator. His position was assistant principal of the Early County Elementary School, a position he held until Mr. Joe Cannon's retirement in 1980. Upon Mr. Cannon's retirement, Mr. Knight became principal of the Early County Elementary School. He remained in that position until he was elected to succeed Mr. Chester as superintendent of Early County public schools in 1981.

Prior to Mr. Knight's election to the office of superintendent, our paths crossed only seldom, primarily at periodic administrative meetings. Nevertheless, my impression of him had always been very favorable; so I did not experience any major difficulty in adjusting to his style of leadership. In my opinion, he always tried to be fair and professional in dealing with his subordinates.

I considered him to have been an excellent role model for his building principals. He demanded and expected much from us, but he always set a good example by carrying his share of the load. Consequently, I enjoyed my years served during his administration.

In many respects he seemed to have shared much of Mr. Chester's philosophy. This resulted in somewhat of an extension of Mr. Chester's agenda. The school system benefited from the smooth transition that Mr. Knight was able to make when he took over the reins of leadership for our school system.

During Mr. Chester's administration, he had envisioned the time when the central office would have its own building with adequate space to accommodate the staff. This was a very deserving priority due to the fact that the office space in the court house was very inadequate. When he became superintendent, the office consisted of only one room, which meant that there was a complete lack of privacy for professional conferences and discussion of business matters. Mr. Chester did partition off one corner for privacy; this helped tremendously, even so, it left a lot to be desired.

Mr. Knight was keenly aware of this problem and gave it top priority when he became superintendent. As a result of the importance placed on this matter, a new central office building became a reality in 1985. It is located on the rear of the middle school campus, some distance away from the street and under the shade of several big oaks. The major portion of the construction was done by students enrolled in the high school building and construction classes under the direction of Mr. John Pritchett. This project proved to be a very rewarding experience for the students by providing them an opportunity to get hands-on practice in the areas of carpentry, electrical wiring, plumbing, and masonry. It was also a tremendous financial saving for the Early County Board of Education.

Many dignitaries were on hand for the dedication and open house, including our state school superintendent at the time, the late Dr. Charles McDaniel. It is interesting to note that this facility could have very well been built during Mr. Chester's administration, but he believed in putting the needs of the students first and himself last. Consequently, he allowed the project to "stay on the back burner," so to speak. It was indeed a happy experience for me when this facility was completed.

Another of Mr. Knight's priorities was the building of a new health and physical education building to replace the old frame gym at the middle school. The old, substandard facility had been a major concern of mine ever since my transfer to the middle school in 1970. Being a frame structure, it was highly combustible and a major fire hazard. I constantly prayed that it would never catch fire while it was occupied. There was no way that it would have passed the state fire marshal's inspection if they had enforced all of the codes. However, because of its age, they allowed us to continue the use of it until a replacement could be erected. The exterior reminded one of a barn. As best as we were able to determine, it was built in 1935. I am convinced that it would have burned like paper in the event that it had caught fire. Fortunately, the Lord blessed; and it did not burn, and we were spared such a potential tragedy.

The winter months were very difficult since it was practically impossible to maintain a comfortable indoor temperature. As a result of this problem, we did not require our students to dress out for their physical education classes.

In retrospect I applaud the physical education teachers who worked in the old facility for the excellent job that they did under such adverse circumstances. They improvised and did their best with what they had. In my opinion, they developed and maintained a fantastic program.

It is not my purpose to be overly critical of the old building because it did serve a very worthy purpose. Many of our former students and parents have very fond memories and sentimental feelings about it. Consequently, there were mixed emotions when the time finally came for it to be demolished and ground was broken for the new building.

As the new facility was nearing completion, my thoughts turned towards a deserving person for whom it should be named. It was not long before my mind settled on the name of the late Mr. R. K. Sites. There were many reasons for this choice, including the following:

1. He had been my superintendent for several years; in fact, he was superintendent when I came to Washington High School as principal in 1960.
2. It was during his administration and through his leadership that our first Black school buildings were built. This was very significant because the need for school buildings for Black students was statewide. Nevertheless, he succeeded in getting the first building in the second congressional district to be built by the newly formed state school building authority. The project included an elementary and high school for Blakely, an elementary school for Jakin (Carver) and an elementary school for Damascus (Kestler). As stated earlier, I had the privilege of serving as principal in all three of those schools,

3. He had served as assistant principal of the Early County Middle School for four years.

   Hopefully, the preceding highlights of the life of the late Mr. R. K. Sites will explain why he was my choice to be recommended as the most deserving individual for whom the new physical education facility should be named. Mr. Knight, our superintendent at the time, concurred with my recommendation and subsequently presented it to the members of the Early County Board of Education, who took it under advisement. The input from parents, community civic leaders and teachers was solicited. The responses were overwhelmingly in favor of the proposal. At that point the Early County Board of Education approved the action. Consequently, on June 6, 1985, the new modern health and physical education building for the Early County Middle School was dedicated to the memory of and outstanding services rendered to the Early County School System by Mr. Sites.

   During Mr. Knight's tenure of office as superintendent of our school system, the pendulum began to swing away from the old junior high school concept to that of the middle school concept. In many instances, the process consisted of little more than the change of the name from a junior high school to that of a middle school. However, in our situation, we researched the problem by reviewing the current literature, visiting other middle schools, and bringing in consultants from the State Department of Education and colleges/universities within the state. At the conclusion of this process, it was clearly established that it was not possible to convert from a junior high school concept to a pure middle school concept with the current number of teachers. In order for us to continue the pursuit of the objective, it was necessary that we have the full support of Mr. Knight, our superintendent and the Early County Board of Education. Fortunately, they saw wisdom in the proposal and gave us the green light to go forward in making the transition to a pure middle school.

   Benefits to be derived from becoming a pure middle school included the following:
1. The teachers work together as teams.
2. Each team of teachers would have a common planning period.
3. All students would take exploratory courses during their three years at the middle school.
4. The dropout rate would hopefully be reduced,

5. Teachers would have a greater degree of flexibility within their respective teams.

6. Parent/teacher conferences were more effective since all of the concerned teachers could meet with the parent(s) in one setting. The parents appreciated not having to make more than one trip for their child's conferences, especially if they lived a long distance from the school or if they had to take time away from their job.

Making the transition to a pure middle school was a long and demanding process. Nevertheless, the professional staff and I worked very diligently to meet the criteria as set forth by the State Department of Education for a pure middle school. You can only imagine how overjoyed we were when our efforts were finally rewarded and we were designated as a pure middle school. The accomplishment of this status enabled the Early County Board of Education to receive a $100,000 incentive grant, which had the effect of "putting the icing on the cake," so to speak. I look at the realization of that objective with a great deal of pride and satisfaction. It was the culmination of the best efforts of our middle school professional staff, our superintendent, Mr. Knight, and the Early County Board of Education. I am indeed happy that the Board of Education and Mr. Knight had confidence in our ability to achieve such a noteworthy objective. I was also pleased that we were one of the first schools in our educational planning district to earn such recognition.

At first the teachers were not very comfortable with the changes. It is more or less an established fact that we all possess a certain amount of resistance to change, even if it is for the better. Therefore, I expected and respected their feelings; however, it did not take long for them to make the adjustment. In my opinion, they were overwhelmingly in favor of it by the end of the 1988–89 school year. I consider the successful implementation of the middle school concept to have been the most innovative educational change to be made during my entire tenure as middle school principal.

The parents and students also made an excellent adjustment to the change. This was very rewarding and fulfilling when their apprehension and anxiety were taken into consideration.

My years of service during Mr. Knight's administration were very productive and fulfilling; and I have nothing but praise for his leadership during my years of service with him. I ended my forty year educational career under Mr. Knight.

A MEASURING ROD
That best portion of a good man's life,
His little nameless unremembered acts
Of kindness and of love.

—William Wordsworth

CHAPTER 11

FAMILY TRAGEDIES

As previously mentioned in an earlier chapter, my parents lost two daughters as a result of severe burns, the first being their oldest child, Dorothy, December 7, 1930, who was four years old at the time. The second loss was their seventh child, Juanita, April 1, 1939, who was just four months short of her third birthday. I cannot remember Dorothy since I was only three years of age at the time of her death. If we had any pictures of her, I do not recall having seen them; however, my parents stated that she was a very beautiful child with a radiant personality.

At the tragic death of Juanita, I was twelve years of age and can remember the experience very vividly. I was not at home when the accident occurred. Nevertheless, I remember her body being at home afterwards. This was before we had undertakers in our area. Several of the neighboring mothers volunteered to prepare the body for burial. My dad made the trip into town on our one-horse wagon and purchased a coffin for her burial. I can still remember him returning with it, the neighbor men unloading it, carrying it into the house, and placing Juanita's severely burned body into it. As I recall, her body remained at home that night and was laid to rest the following day beside her older sister. I am sure Dorothy's body remained at home also; I was just too young to remember the details. The circumstances surrounding Dorothy and Juanita's death were almost identical in that each time my mother was doing the family laundry. This was before the advent of the mechanical washing machine, and the weekly laundry for the family was a major chore for my mother. The routine involved drawing water one bucket at a time from an open well to fill the wash pot and three large tin tubs. My dad would draw the water, fill the tubs and the wash pot, and kindle the fire around the wash pot to heat water. The remaining details were done by my mother. It is worthy of note that the well, the tubs, the wash pot, and the clothes line were located across the county road from our house, a distance of approximately 150 feet. On wash days, my mother would leave my siblings in the house attended by one of the older children while she did the washing. Before leaving, she would always charge us as emphatically as she could not to play in the fire. Nevertheless, being young children, we were naturally inclined to mischief and yielded to the temptation to disobey.

Our house was heated with an open fireplace, and my mother felt that it would have been too cold for us if the fire was not allowed to continue to burn. Apparently, she never realized the potential danger that it posed.

The washing required several hours of hard work on the part of my mother, starting with the soaking of the clothes in very warm soapy water. The soap was usually the homemade variety and was called lye soap. After soaking for approximately one hour, the clothes would be placed in the wash pot that was about two thirds full of boiling soapy water and allowed to boil for about one half hour. In addition to the homemade soap, the boiling water in the wash pot contained two or three tablespoons of lye. When the clothes were removed from the wash pot, they were placed on a large block, about three feet high and one and one-half feet in diameter. We called it a "battling block." The clothes would then be beaten with a board that we called a "battling stick." It was about 4 inches wide, three feet long, and 1 inch thick. The clothes would be turned after every few strokes of beating. At the completion of the beating process, the clothes would be dumped in a tin tub and hand washed "piece by piece" on a rub board. Upon the completion phase of the washing, the clothes were placed into another tub for the first rinse and finally into a third tub for the final rinse.

After the clothes had been through the complete washing process, they were hung out on an outdoor clothes line to dry.

It is obvious that the family wash was a very laborious process and required many hours of hard work on the part of my mother. It was not unusual for the weather to be cold and windy. Such were the circumstances on the days when Dorothy and Juanita suffered their fatal burns. I do not know whether or not it was by coincidence, but in each instance my mother was doing the family wash; and the prevailing circumstances were almost identical.

As best as we have been able to determine, they were playing in the fire that was burning in the open fireplace and their clothing accidentally caught on fire. Before my mother was able to rescue them, they had sustained third degree burns which proved to be fatal.

It was a tremendously sad experience for my siblings and me and even more devastating for my parents, especially my mother. In fact, I am not sure whether her emotional scars ever healed completely, even though her strong and enduring faith enabled her to bear the excruciating pain.

The year of 1939 was also disastrous for us in another way; namely, flooding rains drastically reduced the yield of our crops. At harvest time the fields were so wet until we could not get the mules into the peanut field to plow the peanuts up. The few that we were able to save had to be pulled up by hand as we stood in water at least ankle deep. As a result of such unfavorable weather, the quality was very poor.

The cotton crop was just as much of a failure in that the excess rainfall had given the boll weevil a heyday, and they took full advantage of it. The little that we were able to salvage was of very poor quality as a result of the adverse weather conditions.

In retrospect, I believe that the year of 1939 was the most devastating that our family ever experienced. This is not to suggest that there were not other tragedies. Christmas for us that year was very bleak as we were trying to cope with the trauma of Juanita's death and the most devastating crop failure that we had ever experienced. However, the Lord sustained us.

The next tragedy occurred April 29, 1968, when my brother Charles was killed in a senseless accident caused by a drunken driver. It was on a Monday morning and due to recent rains over the weekend, it was too wet for farm work until later that day. Therefore, Charles had gone into town to take care of a few business details, including a stop at the Bank of Early, before returning home. While returning home, his pickup truck was hit on the driver's side by a pulpwood truck, at what is known as "Rick's Crossing." The driver of the pulpwood truck had been to the woods to work, but was too intoxicated and was returning home at the time of the accident. He and my brother Charles were both killed, all because of this driver being under the influence of alcohol.

I was at work at Washington High School, when notified that the accident had happened. Norma, his wife, and my mother were substituting at the school that day. As I recall, Norma accompanied me to the emergency room at Early Memorial Hospital. When we entered, it was evident by the sad expressions on everyone's face that Charles was dead. Nevertheless, the administrator of the hospital broke the silence and said that they were sorry and they had done everything possible, but he did not make it. In addition to other injuries, he had sustained a broken neck. His body and that of the pulpwood truck driver lay on separate gurneys covered with white sheets. It was only the saving power and enduring strength of the Lord that sustained me when I raised the sheet and saw Charles' lifeless body as Norma and I stood by doing what we could to encourage and strengthen each other. I had been so cruelly and unexpectedly bereaved of my oldest brother and she of her husband of eleven years.

Suddenly, Norma had become a young widow with five children to raise, their ages ranging from eleven to two.

I do not remember exactly how we broke the news to my parents, because there was no easy way. Having already experienced the tragic deaths of Dorothy and Juanita, I can imagine that it was like reopening an old wound before it was completely healed.

With the Lord's help, we survived the trauma of his passing; and he was laid to rest on May 1, 1968. He was right in the prime of life at the time of his premature death, being only thirty-seven years of age.

He and daddy seemed to have had more in common than the rest of us boys. I suppose it was because Charles had chosen farming as his career, whereas the others were in other professions. The Lord had indeed blessed his farming endeavors, and he was indeed a "rising star" as a young farmer. He had been able to acquire most of the modern equipment that he needed for his operation, including a cotton picker. I do not want to exaggerate, but I feel safe in saying that he was the most progressive and successful young black farmer in Early County at the time of his death.

In addition to trying to recover from his unexpected passing, there was the additional problem of cultivating and harvesting the crop that he had planted prior to his death.

Many neighbors and friends rose to the occasion and helped in whatever way they were needed. Although, it was not by any means what it would have been had Charles lived to finish what he had started.

William, my youngest brother, was a senior agronomy major at Ft. Valley State College and upon graduation helped out for awhile. I will have more to say about him later.

Charles was a prudent businessman and left sufficient resources to pay off all of his financial obligations. Norma was able to build a nice modern house for the children and herself. I know that we would have preferred having Charles with us; but since that was not to be, I am thankful that Norma and the children were adequately provided for and did not have to resort to welfare assistance.

I am sure that Charles would be happy with the accomplishments of his children. Specifically, Tony, his first born, spent several years in the U.S. Navy. Regretfully, his marriage failed; however, he and his wife, Lottie, were blessed with five lovely children, one of whom died as an infant. As of 1994, the four surviving children are doing fine and range from grades seven through eleven. It may be worthy of note that there is a set of twins in this group of children.

His second child, and only daughter, Beryl, received her bachelor's degree in nursing from Florida State University in Tallahassee, Florida, and is a registered nurse. After working for several years in the ICU at Crawford Long Hospital in Atlanta, Georgia, she met and married Dr. Christopher Vaughan. He is an Internist with a very lucrative practice in Atlanta, and they are the proud parents of two boys.

Keith, his third child, received his bachelor's degree in mathematics from Oakwood College, Huntsville, Alabama, after which he served as a student missionary in Haiti for almost two years. Upon the completion of his service in Haiti, he enrolled in the Theological Seminary at Andrews University in Berrien Springs, Michigan, where he earned his Master of Divinity degree. In 1989 he enlisted in the U. S. Army and graduated from Officer's Candidate School on January 25, 1990. It was quite an accomplishment, and Norma and all her children were blessed to be on hand for the occasion and spend a few hours together. Three of the surviving uncles, Benny, Woodrow, and myself, also attended. Pastor Fred Daniels, Jr. was also present and offered his congratulations and encouragement.

Eric, the fourth child, received his B.S. degree in Agricultural Education from the Ft. Valley State College and has completed several years as a Vocational Agriculture teacher in the Early County School System. In addition to his teaching duties, he is striving to keep the family's estate on a sound financial footing. Specifically, he is establishing pine trees on a major portion of it and has the remainder of it leased out to Shelton and Tony Bruner. He also manages the cows for me, and we share equipment. He is a very valuable asset to all of us and for me in particular. He is married to Willie Mae Smith; and they are the proud parents of one son, Quinton, and a daughter, Erica.

Shawn, the youngest of Charles and Norma's children, graduated from Tuskegee University, Tuskegee, Alabama, in the class of 1992. He has completed four years in the U.S. Marines Reserve program. He received his commission as a Second Lieutenant in the U.S. Army. He is married to Carla Hemphill from Seattle, Washington, who is currently enrolled in medical school at the University of Michigan. They have two boys. He also has another son, Shawn Andre Harris, Jr.

In spite of Charles' untimely death, the children have done well; and I, as their uncle, am proud of their accomplishments and pray that they will ever strive to walk in the straight and narrow way.

A corporation in Charles's memory, CRH Enterprises has been formed. It is still small, but growing and is on a sound fiscal basis at this time. Its potential is great, and I encourage the family's wholehearted support and cooperation with its endeavors.

Norma has remarried but still maintains a close relationship with the Harris family.

William, my youngest brother and my parents' youngest child was our next family tragedy. Before graduating from high school, he fathered one child, Larry. While in college he met his wife, Linda Jones. She was a nice young lady from a very prominent and respectable family. They were married; and to this union one son, Kevin, was born. Unfortunately, this marriage failed; and they were divorced while Kevin was still a baby. In my opinion, this was not only a personal tragedy for William, Linda, and Kevin, but the entire Harris family. We loved Linda; and I firmly believe that if William had met her only halfway, their marriage would have succeeded. Linda's parents took Kevin and her to their home and subsequently legally adopted Kevin, and Linda remarried.

Upon graduating from Ft. Valley State College in 1968, William decided to take over the operation of Daddy, Charles and my farms. We were excited about the possibilities of being able to take over where Charles had left off. However, this was not the case, due primarily to the undesirable life style that he had acquired by that time. I am reluctant to say that he had become an alcoholic, but he did have a very serious drinking problem. Unlike Charles, he did not have any real difficulty obtaining adequate financing for his operation but was not prudent in meeting his fiscal obligations. The situation continued to deteriorate until several businesses swore judgment against him, and his grain combine was repossessed.

On Sabbath, June 1, 1974, Herk and I had traveled to Huntsville, Alabama, and worshiped at the Oakwood College Church. It had been a very happy and fulfilling day; and Herk's brother Ben and his family from Chicago were also there, which heightened the degree of our happiness and excitement. While still enjoying this "mountain top" experience, I received an urgent telephone call from the Early County Sheriff's Department, which stated that William had been killed in an automobile accident earlier that day. This was devastating for me; but my major concern was for my parents, who had already been bereaved of three of their children, all as a result of fatal accidents. As soon as we could regain our composure, Herk and I started our long trip home, which was approximately a six to seven hours' drive. We arrived at my parents' home around midnight that following night, where we found them sitting on the front porch along with several of my sisters and neighbors. As soon as I entered the house, someone quietly informed me that my parents had not been told about William's death. The rationale was that it would have been easier for them to accept it if I were the one to break the news. As I mentally tried to put everything in perspective, I concluded that there simply was not an easy way to tell them. I simply said to them that I was sorry but William had been killed. I could only imagine the anguish they must have felt as they accepted the reality of the tragic loss of a fourth child, their youngest at that. My brother James was in Seoul, Korea, at the time on active duty with the military; however the Lord blessed him with traveling mercies, and he was able to arrive safely and share in our sorrow. On Wednesday, June 5, 1974, we laid William to rest beside our brother Charles. At the time of William's death, he was married to Mrs. Lilla Cummings. There were no children born to this union; however, she had two daughters of her own, Tina and Venus Cole. I really feel that I grieved more for my parents than for myself. They had been blessed with twelve normal children at birth, six boys and six girls; and now they were bereaved of four of them, two girls and two boys. Only the Lord was able to sustain them and see them safely through such a devastating period of their lives.

William and Charles had three things in common, namely, they both died in tragic automobile accidents, and they both left crops that had been planted and had to be cultivated and harvested. As had been the case with Charles, the neighbors and friends were very supportive. However, William had named me as executor of his estate; and I thought that under the circumstances, it was better to get Hunter Farms to complete the year's operation. The Lord blessed, and everything was successfully completed for the crop year. Another comparison between Charles and William that is worthy of note is their ages at the time of their death. Charles would have been thirty-seven his next birthday, November 23, 1968; and William would have been twenty-nine on his forthcoming birthday, July 29, 1974. Both had been cut down at the prime of their life. Even now there are times when I find myself wondering how much different things might have been had they lived. However, in reality, I know that only the Lord knows; and I console myself with the fact that He knows just how much we can bear, and He will never leave us or forsake us.

His property was located in the Rock Hill Community, a distance of approximately fifteen miles from us. I was very much concerned about the possibility of theft and vandalism; but the Lord blessed, and Brother Jimmy Snipes and his family were in need of a more adequate place to live and were happy to move in within a few days following William's death. I am especially appreciative to them for the very special interest they took in maintaining the house and watching out for unauthorized trespassing on the farm.

Larry and Kevin, William's children, are young men now. Larry finished high school and was a very good athlete with exceptional baseball potential and hopes he may one day get the opportunity to play professionally. He presently drives an eighteen wheeler for Winn Dixie. Kevin has graduated from Fort Valley State College with a B.S. in Agriculture Education like his dad. His grandparents have done a super job as surrogate parents, and I am very optimistic about Kevin's future success.

In 1977, our family experienced another crisis; namely, Herk's niece, Rhondda was stricken with cancer. Since she has a journalism degree from the University of Georgia, I thought it would be better if she shared this traumatic experience in her own words. She entitled this ordeal, "Share my Sadness, Share my Joy."

Tumor...cancer...another operation...another hospital...pathologist knows specialist in New York...Sloan Kettering Cancer Center...I've never been to New York...Empire State Building...Statue of Liberty...Twin Towers...sightseeing...No, wait...cancer...tumor...

"I got all I could see. I'm not a specialist."

Why did you keep me here so long without telling me? I thought everything was OK. Cancer?

"You've got to snap out of it, Rhon." Tears began to flow down my cheeks. Daddy took my hand in his. "Please, don't take it so hard."

I'm going to New York! What can I buy my friends? I can go shopping at Macy's and Bloomingdale's. And I can finally meet Mamma's sisters. I wonder if there're any cute guys up in New York? Cancer...tumor...synovial cell sarcoma only strikes teenagers. Oh, it can't be too serious...just another thing that has to be done. I've got to get back home so I can find a summer job. Hope we won't be gone long.

Eight days earlier, I had never been a patient in a hospital. Our family doctor had suggested that I see a surgeon after examining an unusual lump in my stomach.

Dr. Naso took one look at the lump and said, "I'm going to put you in the hospital immediately, today, this afternoon. Go home, get some clothes and check in at the admitting office at Mercy Hospital. I want to operate as soon as possible."

Hospital? Today? Operation? But isn't this thing only supposed to be a hernia or cyst? What's the rush? Why's everyone so anxious to get me in the hospital?

"Would you like a private or semiprivate room?" the receptionist called from the front office.

"Uh, um, private, I guess." I have to go to the hospital today. Oh, Mamma and Daddy are gone to Florida. They didn't leave a number where we could reach them. Maybe they'll call. They always call. It will be OK. It can't be serious.

"You're only seventeen? We'll need your parents to sign the consent form for your operation." The secretary looked around the waiting room for my parents.

"Uh, my parents are out of town. They're class sponsors on a trip to Orlando, Florida. My brother's here. Can he sign the papers? He's eighteen."

"No, I'm sorry but we have to have a legal parent or guardian sign. Don't worry. We'll contact your parents somehow. Just go ahead and get settled in your room."

I called every Day's Inn in Orlando, but could not locate my parents. A few hours after I'd given up calling, the telephone rang.

"Rhon? Mamma. What's the matter, baby?"

"I'm in the hospital, Mamma. They want to operate on me. Did you give 'um permission? They wouldn't let Donald sign the papers even though he's eighteen. How's your trip going? Did ya'll go to Disney World yet? What motel are you staying at? We had such a hard time trying to find you. When are you coming home?"

But mother answered none of my questions. "How are you feeling? What did the doctor say?"

"Oh, I'm OK, Mamma! They just want to do a little operation to get this lump out. They say it's probably only a hernia or cyst— probably a hernia. You know how I used to lift those heavy boxes and pans working in the cafeteria. Believe me, it's nothing serious."

Nothing serious! And then the nurse came in.

"Have you ever had an IV before?"

"No. I don't even know what an IV is!"

"Well, I'm gonna stick this little needle in your arm—it might sting just a bit. We have to put it in so we can give you fluids and blood to replace those you'll lose during the operation."

After the IV was in, they wheeled me into the operating room.

"Breathe deeply. This gas will put you right to sleep."

I drew a deep breath. Choke…gag…the lights above the operating table grew dimmer. And then I was back in my room.

Need some help to the bathroom. I pressed the buzzer for a nurse. A few moments later a male nurse appeared, bed pan in hand. Oh no. No male nurse is gonna help me on to a bed pan.

"You wanna use this?"

"No. Help me to the bathroom."

I stumbled into the bathroom. Just as I got back to the bed, I crumpled to the floor.

"Hey now, little girl. Next time you'll have to use that thing," the nurse chuckled as he lifted me gently into bed. "Here, careful now. Just rest. You'll be all right."

I was unaware of the passing of time. Pain...pills...sleep...nurses taking my blood pressure...bandages changed...then a familiar voice.

"Hey look at you, girl, up here in a private room. How ya doing?" Daddy and Mamma hugged me tightly.

"Mamma! Daddy! when did ya'll get back? I'm just fine, a little sore. I'm ready to go home."

"Have you lost any weight," Mother smiled as she winked.

"No, of course not! The food's pretty good, and I didn't lose my appetite. How's Monika 'nem? I haven't seen anyone since I've been in here."

We chatted a few minutes. I was reluctant to see them leave, yet relieved...so tired...sleep.

A few days later as I stood watching out the window for Mamma and Daddy to bring Sabbath dinner, someone knocked at the door. I jumped in bed and pulled the covers over my head.

"Hello, Ms. Robinson?"

"Yes, that's me." I peeked from under the blanket.

"I'm here from the church, visiting the sick and shut-in this afternoon. Mind if I sit down?"

"No, go right ahead." Oh no, what am I going to talk about? I don't even remember ever seeing him at church.

The young deacon never uttered another word. Occasionally our eyes met—we'd smile, then continue in zombie like silence.

After about an hour, he left.

"Been nice visiting with you. We'll be praying for you. Have a nice evening."

Oh man, I hope no other deacons decide to pay me a visit. We just moved to Charlotte. I don't even know hardly anybody!

While visits from strangers were awkward, Mother's were filled with solemn moments.

"Rhondda, I want you to listen to this: 'For I am persuaded that neither death, nor life; nor angels, nor principalities, nor powers; nor things present, nor things to come; nor height, nor depth; nor any other creature shall be able to separate us from the love of God which is in Christ Jesus our Lord.'

'And we know that all things work together for good, to them that love God, to those who are called according to His purpose.'

"You believe what God has promised, don't you Rhon?"

119

"Of course I do, Mamma! I know how to claim God's promises." Why does Mamma keep reading me these texts? Something must be up. No, it can't be. Dr. Naso would have said something by now. But they've kept me here so long—almost two weeks! Nothing can be wrong. They wouldn't keep me in suspense that long.

But they did. A rare tumor, Dr. Naso? Cancer? No, this can't be happening to me. And before I knew it, we were on our way to New York.

In the hospital at home, I felt like a normal patient. In New York at Sloan Kettering Cancer Center, I became Case A, Room 1620.

"We've quite a number of interns interested in your case since your cancer is so rare. We'd like for you to come down this evening to one of our classes and answer a few questions."

"Sure, I'll come down." Nothing better to do. I'm getting so tired of sitting around or having tests run. I wish they'd hurry. I have to get back home soon.

As they wheeled me into the lecture hall, I wished I had stayed bored up in my room. About 200 interns sat waiting to inspect the next case—me.

Several gathered around the table. And then the questions began

"About where was the tumor located?"

"Right below my belly button, on the left side."

"Approximately how big was it—like a lemon, an orange?"

"About the size of a lemon."

"Did you have much pain?"

"No, not until recently."

"When did you first discover the growth?"

"Back in November, 1976."

"You've had one operation already?"

"Yes, back in Charlotte at Mercy Hospital."

"And you'll be having more surgery here?"

"Yes, Wednesday, I believe."

The young interns poked and jabbed my incision, then scribbled notes on their clipboards.

"That will be all, Ms. Robinson. Thank you.

"You're welcome." Anytime! Anytime at all!

The following afternoon, I met my surgeon.

"Hello, I'm Dr. Shui, and I'll be doing your surgery tomorrow. We're going to have to take some more tissue and muscles out around the area where the tumor was, and we'll also have to remove the lymph nodes in your left leg. Your leg will swell some. You will have to wear special support stockings and elevate it for at least an hour every night. But don't worry, we'll have you discoing again in no time!"

"I don't disco."

"Well, swim, skate—whatever! We will be putting a plastic sheet in your stomach area to fill the hole that will be left from taking the muscle and tissue out. There's nothing to be afraid of. The cancer hasn't spread to anywhere else in your body. That's why we must take your left lymph nodes out—it would go there next, get in your blood stream, and just go all over. You were very lucky."

Lucky? Ha! I wonder what my leg will look like? I wonder if I'll be able to sing again—they're taking out so much muscle. Oh God, please take care of me. My life is in your hands.

Daddy sat close to Mamma, his arm around her shoulder. Mamma's cheeks were wet with tears. Why is Mamma crying so? She acts like this thing is so serious. Oh, Mothers are so sensitive. I should be the one crying.

As the orderlies wheeled me out of the room, Mamma sobbed in Daddy's arms. Mamma acts like she's never gonna see me again. I longed to comfort her as I waved goodbye.

Outside the operating room, they wheeled me next to a little Spanish lady who lay crying on her wheelie. I turned and smiled, but before I could comfort her, I fell asleep.

A sharp pain shot through my stomach as I tried to roll over on my side. My eyes adjusted to the bright lights. A nurse came by. She gently slid a long needle out of my arm.

"Your operation was a success. You're in the recovery room. We'll be taking you back upstairs a little later this morning."

She bandaged my arm and walked away. I struggled to call her back. No words came out. Mamma! Mamma! Somebody get my Mamma! I cried until I slept again.

"How are you feeling this morning?" I opened my eyes. My doctor stood by my bed. I was back in my room. "Here, let me take this tube out of your mouth."

The doctor grabbed the end of the tube and pulled faster and faster. Where is the end of this thing? Seems like its all the way down in my stomach! Hurry doctor! It hurts, it hurts!

"Now that wasn't so bad was it? Feel any better?"

I closed my eyes and tried to sleep. Just get out of here and leave me alone. Can't you see I'm in pain?

A few days later as the nurse unbandaged my leg, I remembered the doctor had warned me it would be a little swollen. But as I peered down at my swollen mass of flesh, I was convinced that I would never walk again. It will never go down. I'll never be able to walk again. I'm gonna lose my leg. Oh, just let me sleep!

But sleep only brought nightmares. Suddenly I am back at school, walking up to my friends in the cafeteria. Just as I reach them, I fall flat on my face. I struggle to stand up again. My friends laugh and refuse to help me. I felt my body lurch up as I slipped back into consciousness. I couldn't even move when I was awake, yet the fear of not being able to walk again made my whole body jump as I fell in my sleep. I drifted off to sleep again.

A new doctor awakened me.

"Hello, my name is Dr. Zorvio. I'm here to talk to you about the chemotherapy you'll be getting in a few days. The chemicals have several side effects. They'll make you very sick. You'll throw up a lot. We have some medication to help keep you from vomiting, but it doesn't help much. You'll still throw up a lot, anywhere from a day to a week. The chemicals affect everyone differently, but they make everyone sick. You'll vomit a lot. You'll also lose all your hair, and you'll probably have to wear a wig. Oh, your hair will grow back; but after each injection, it will all fall out again until you get off chemo completely. Well, Dr. Magill will be here to talk with you later today. I probably won't see you again. I'm being transferred to a hospital in California. I wish you the best of luck."

Before I could whisper any response, he left me, alone. Wait! What's happening? No! Stop! Lose all my hair? Vomit continuously for days, even weeks? Lose *all* my hair? This can't be happening. I'm a Senior. I'll be graduating this year. Doesn't he understand what that means? No hair—a wig my Senior year? What will the guys think? No guy will want to date a girl who wears a wig! Lose my hair? No! No! I just can't do it! I will not take chemotherapy!

Later on that afternoon, Mamma walked in smiling. "How's my girl?" Her smile vanished as she saw my tears.

"Mamma!" I reached out my arms. The more I thought about losing my hair, the harder I cried.

Mamma held me tightly as I sobbed on her shoulder. "Lord, please help my poor baby, " she cried. As my tears slowed to a trickle, she invited me to pray.

"God," I cried, but could speak no further. I can't even pray. God has forgotten me. He doesn't even care about my suffering. I don't even know Him anymore.

****

I had only been home a few weeks from New York when all my hair fell out. My left leg had swollen about two inches larger than my right one. I had begun to gain back the weight I had lost. My family didn't seem to understand that I wanted to suffer alone.

But one Sunday afternoon as I sat alone in the house thinking about the immediate experience past and the year and one-half of chemotherapy that lay in front of me, I finally wanted to talk with someone, anyone. But I was alone.

Why me God? I can't understand why You picked me to suffer. What have I done to deserve this? My left leg swells so I can hardly walk. My hair's gone. The chemo makes me sick. I'm so scared. I could have died. I still might die! What if they didn't get it all? I haven't even finished high school! Lord, more than anything, I'd just like to feel like a normal person again.

Epilogue

I've been to New York—too many times! I saw the Twin Towers from my hospital window. I saw the Empire State Building too—from the car window on our way home.

Today I look out on a Fall campus four years after I learned that cancer was a word used to describe me. I am pursuing a Communications major. A scar on my abdomen and a swollen left leg remind me of my illness. However, there are less visible scars that are taking longer to heal.

By the end of most days, my leg is so swollen I can barely bend it. I hardly ever have enough energy to accomplish everything I have planned.

I battle fear—that the cancer might come back; that my leg will swell so much that I'll lose it; that people are staring at my leg wondering why it's so big.

There are times when I wish I had died from cancer.

I am still searching for answers to my question. I have found few, but I have learned to pray again and have also realized that people do care about me. On the rare occasions that I do share the sadness my experience has left me, I can begin to share my joy.

My joy—for being alive in spite of the pain I know I'll be experiencing each day; for having a head full of hair again; for learning to love and trust those around me; for sharing....

So, share with me my sadness, and I'll share with you my joy.

      by—Rhondda Robinson

My dad lived approximately three and one-half years after William's death. Nevertheless, it was almost that life was never the same. He passed away on January 26, 1978, at the age of seventy-seven and was laid to rest on Sunday, January 29, 1978, beside his two sons Charles and William.

My mother lived approximately four and one-half years after the death of William. However, the quality of her life left a lot to be desired in that she had become senile. Her mental state was often confused and she had to be kept under very close surveillance or she would slip away and get lost. It was difficult for me to see her in such a state of deterioration, much of which I believe stemmed from the trauma she had experienced in losing four children in fatal accidents.

It was very demanding on me in that they, mother and daddy, required around the clock care for several years. Finally, I was able to arrange for a nurse, LPN, to come to the house to give mother a bath, comb her hair, and take care of any other personal needs that she might have had. I would go over every morning before going to work and give daddy his bath, shave, and dress him. The only exception was on a weekend when my brother, James, would relieve me. Through it all, Nellie, Annette, and James cooperated with me by coming on weekends and relieving me. I am sure that my other sisters and brothers would have done likewise had they been closer. Nevertheless, the Lord blessed and it finally came to a point that my sister, Nellie, and her husband, Brother Uzziah, decided that our parents needs could be better addressed if they had them in Thomasville with them. I was especially pleased that they were willing to take on such a major responsibility. However, it was a sad experience to see them get into the car for the trip to Thomasville. Although they did not cry or physically resist, I believe that they had a premonition that they were leaving home for the last time. Once they arrived in Thomasville and got settled into Nellie and Brother Uzziah's home, they seemed to have accepted the situation without any significant overt unrest. It was much more convenient for them to see the doctor there than it was in Blakely.

My brothers, sisters, and I had more or less made a commitment not to put them in a nursing home. It was indeed difficult, but I thank the Lord that He enabled us to fulfill that commitment. As it turned out, they never returned home; and Nellie and Brother Uzziah looked after them until the very end.

When I consider the adversity that my parents experienced in rearing such a large family of us, it is obvious to me that the Lord still blessed them with longevity. They both had reached the age of seventy-seven at their death, thus realizing the Lord's promise of three score years and ten.

I thank my parents for the sacrifices that they made in behalf of my siblings and me. I believe they would be proud of the accomplishments of their descendants which include:

1—cardiology technologist
2—chemical engineers
1—clinical psychologist
5—commissioned officers
1—C.P.A.
2—farmers
2—foreign missionaries
1—guidance counselor
1—hair stylist
1—industrial engineer
1—lawyer
1—legal staff supervisor
2—noncommissioned officers
6—nurses
1—nurse practitioner
1—occupational therapist
2—ordained ministers
1—pharmaceutical representative
5—physicians
1—principal (elementary, middle school, highschool)
1—professional truck driver
2—pulpwood and plywood workers

9—teachers

1—telephone staff administrator

To God be the glory, great things he hath done. Our family does indeed have a past to cherish and a future to fulfill.

On November 29, 1983, our family was dealt another devastating blow by the unexpected passing of my wife, Herdisene, affectionately known as "Herk." I have gone into more detail in another chapter.

In 1987, Naomi, Rhondda's mother, succumbed to cancer. Her teaching career began in Blakely, Georgia. From 1970–1985 she taught church school in the South Atlantic Conference. She loved young people and often adopted young couples, her children's friends, students, and other youngsters and treated them as her own. She and Herk were especially closely knit to each other in a Christian bond of love.

Our most recent family tragedy was Herk's brother's wife, Marie, who succumbed to inoperable brain cancer on October 15, 1994 at the age of 58. At the time of her death she was Vice Chancellor at the University of Illinois in Chicago.

Even though the experiences were traumatic, I realize that such tragedies were not unique to our family and I take comfort in the thought,…"Weeping may endure for a night but joy cometh in the morning" Psalm 30:5

God hath not promised
Skies always blue,
Flower-strewn pathways
All our lives through;
God hath not promised
Sun without rain,
Joy without sorrow,
Peace without pain.

But God hath promised
Strength for the day,
Rest for the labor,
Light for the way,
Grace for the trials,
Help from above,
Unfailing sympathy,
Undying love.
                    —Annie Johnson Flint

CHAPTER 12

LIFE WITH HERK

As stated in an earlier chapter, I escaped service in World War II, in that it ended before I was called up, even though I had already had my preinduction physical. However, on November of 1950 during my second year of full-time teaching, I was drafted into the U.S. Army as a result of the Korean Conflict. I was stationed at Ft. Jackson, South Carolina; and even though I did not realize it at the time, the Lord was leading and had arranged for me to be assigned to Fort Jackson. While I was stationed there, I went to the Adventist Church located on Henderson Street. At that time, I became acquainted with the young lady who would later become my wife, Herdisene Theresa Robinson, better known as Herk. For several years I had sought guidance from the Lord in my choice of a life companion. In that connection, my favorite text was Proverbs 3:6, which states, "In all thy ways acknowledge Him, and He shall direct thy paths." Herk was not my first girlfriend, but I could tell in no uncertain terms that she was, indeed, the answer to my prayers. It was a case of love at first sight.

It all started when I attended church the first Sabbath and was invited to dinner with Herk's parents. This was a part of their hospitality routinely extended to servicemen that attended their church. I was somewhat homesick at the time, and to be able to visit in their home and to have dinner did much to offset the homesickness I was feeling at the time. Imagine my pleasure when I saw their beautiful daughter, and we found that we shared many of the same interests. This stemmed largely from having been brought up in a Christian home environment where she did not attend movies, dances, or night clubs as many of her peers. This is not to suggest that her parents were overly protective of her, rather she seemed inclined to a very conservative life style. I was pleased that we had so much in common when it came to moral and spiritual values. She was in her junior year at Benedict College studying to become a teacher.

Our relationship continued to blossom; and on Sunday, August 19, 1951, we were united in holy matrimony by Elder P. H. Morgan.

She was nineteen at the time, and I was twenty-four. Herk was born and reared in Cayce, South Carolina, which is on the south side of Columbia, the capital of the state of South Carolina. She was the only girl in her family and was second in a family of five. This was her senior year at Benedict College in Columbia. I promised her that I would be supportive of her efforts to complete her program. Consequently, she remained in school and graduated in the spring of 1952 with a B.S. degree in Business Education.

While Herk was finishing her senior year, I lived with my parents and continued my duties as principal at Carver Elementary and High School. My car traveled the many miles between Blakely and Columbia that year on weekends and holidays. When Herk finished school, she moved to Blakely; and we lived with my parents for two years until our house was completed. She helped my mother with the cooking and household chores; so, she made a smooth transition into our home and never seemed to have a problem with managing a career and duties at home. Herk had a wonderful and warm personality and became a part of the family very quickly. She was more like another sister to my siblings, and this rapport continued throughout her life.

The following fall she was given a position in the school system and taught typing and math at the Carver School in Jakin. I had been transferred from the Washington High School to this school, and she was a member of my faculty. From that time forward, she consistently served as "my right hand" professionally, both in school and at home.

Herk was born and reared in the city but made a very smooth transition to our rural environment. We were married for three years before our first child, Michael, was born, with Cheryl and Wayne following during the next three years. Eventually, the Lord blessed us to buy a farm, located on the Cedar Springs highway where we later built our house. We were able to occupy it on October 19, 1955. Mike was our only child and had just started walking a few weeks earlier, being only about fourteen months of age at the time of occupancy. Our fireplace was open and he would back in and out of it without his head touching and would laugh with much excitement. In fact, that was his favorite past time for several weeks.

We did not necessarily realize at the time when we made our decision to rear our children in a rural environment that it was, indeed, a blessing. The Lord was leading all the time; and, as a result of that decision, they never developed the habit of being out at night and frequenting places of amusement that were of a questionable nature. Being on the farm meant there were always chores to be done, and the children were very positive about that facet of farm life and would always promptly pitch in whenever they were at home. We were fortunate to have cows and horses on our farm, and many happy hours were spent horseback riding on "Dixie" and "Silver."

Her rapport with the children was fantastic; they were more like brothers and sisters than mother and children. We worked hard to enable our family to come up to the standard the Lord has set for it. In my opinion, Herk did much to make our home happy and bright. We tried to make our home a place of love, a place where the angels of God would abide. In my opinion, the Lord rewarded our efforts; and I am eternally grateful for the important role that Herk played as mother of our children.

Herk enjoyed living and brought much joy and sunshine into the lives of those with whom she came in contact. She was indeed a servant of God and a friend to man. Her favorite pastime was to go on Main Street in downtown Columbia and window shop. Oftentimes I would drive her up town, park the car, and wait for her in the parking lot while she enjoyed her favorite activity. When she returned to the car, sometimes she would have a few items; other times she would not, but the thrill of the experience was nonetheless diminished, even if she had not made any purchases. It was what she derived from this experience that mattered.

Herk was extremely talented and versatile and excelled as a typist, pianist, teacher, school counselor, Sabbath School teacher, and church treasurer. Whatever she did was done with enthusiasm and dedication. Her philosophy was that if a thing was worth doing at all, it was worth doing well. Whenever it was necessary for me to have to call upon her to do a particular task, I could rest assured that it would be done effectively and efficiently. The Lord blessed us to work together in the school system for more than twenty-nine years.

The Lord also led in another facet of our lives; namely, the education of our children. We kept them with us, Herk and me, through grades 1–8. This was during the period of the school integration controversy, and freedom of choice forms were distributed to the students in the spring to ascertain whether or not there were any students interested in transferring to Early County Elementary School and Early County High School, the White schools at that time. When our children expressed an interest I was told that on the one hand it was o.k.; but on the other hand, however, there was a feeling on the part of the superintendent and the chairman of the Early County Board of Education that since I was principal, it would send the wrong signal if our children transferred to the White schools. Specifically, it was felt that the impression would be given that I did not feel that the school that I headed as principal was good enough for our children. It was at this point that the children became interested in going to our church academy. Forest Lake Academy, Maitland, Florida, was the choice. Mike was the first to go, and we were pleased with the adjustment that the Lord enabled him to make. Herk and I always tried not to do for one what we would not do for all three of them. Consequently, we made the sacrifice to send all three of them to Forest Lake for grades nine through twelve. We had reservations about them going away to a boarding school at that age, but the Lord blessed and they made an excellent adjustment. Hence, we avoided the potential controversy over their going to the White schools; and they were blessed with experiences that they would have been unable to get had they remained in the public school system. All three were in the band in Early County with the main performances held on Friday nights, thus creating an ongoing conflict with our Sabbath observance. In addition to these problems, the children, Cheryl and Wayne, were subjected to pressures stemming from being the principal's kids. At the time, they handled things themselves for fear of making the situation worse by telling me. If I had to discipline a student, there were times the student would take it out on the children, especially Cheryl. They enjoyed pulling her "pigtails." Finally, she asked Herk to fix her hair a different way so that it would not be so easy for her peers to pull. There was also a problem when they received special recognition, as different ones would imply that they only received it because their dad was the principal. Going to the academy required a major financial commitment, but the Lord blessed; and I am thankful that Herk and I allowed Him to lead us in what was a crucial decision for us. To God be the glory!

Another joyful experience for her was that all three of our children were able to go to England and West Africa for two tours with the Last Generation, a singing, witnessing group from Forest Lake Academy, under the direction of Pastor Les Pitton and Mr. Richard Lake. These experiences were especially enriching for our children, and we praise the Lord for them.

Not only was I blessed with a jewel as a wife for me and mother for our three children, but her family was special, also. I do not believe that I could have been blessed to marry into a family that would have been any more accepting and supportive of me. It was more like being born into the family.

My father-in-law, Granddaddy, was a role model for me and a very special Granddaddy for the children. Even though he did not have the benefit of a high school education, he was very intelligent and creative. Michael, Cheryl and Wayne adored him and were always fascinated by the stories he would often tell them about his experiences in the "old days." He possessed poetic ability; and on one occasion, after one of our visits with him and my mother-in-law, Other Mother, we were saying our goodbyes, and Cheryl said that she would see him in the summertime. This inspired him to write a poem by that title. It is as follows:

SUMMER TIME

The Christmas Holidays were cold and drear,
And wintry winds blew in from northern clime;
But I was undisturbed and did not care
Because your smiles were warm as summer time.

You showered loads of sunshine in our home
And made us happy with your childish play.
Your Mom and Dad and brothers, too, had come
To visit; but YOU "stole the show" each day.

You asked me questions, sat upon my knee,
Rode on my back, and laughed as children do;
You sang and prayed, said grace, and followed me
Around so much that I kept playing, too.

You whispered to me as you went away
Words that to me were music so sublime;
"Granddaddy, I am going home today,
But I'll come back to see you summer time."

Dear little girl, so sweet and full of cheer,
At every thought of you my joy-bells chime:
No matter what the season of the year,
When YOU are near it's always SUMMERTIME.

Herdisene (Herk) and the author on their 25th wedding anniversary

He was always making toys, bicycles, motor scooters, or something that he felt the children would enjoy. Most times when we visited their home he would have a new and exciting creation for the children. He even built a play house for Cheryl and towed it all the way from Columbia, South Carolina, to our house, a distance of approximately 375 miles. In addition to his special attributes as a very special Granddaddy, he also conducted a very successful religious radio program for a number of years.

Another skill that he possessed was that he was blessed with a mechanical mind and was one of the best diesel mechanics in the area. He could fix most things and always had his personal cars equipped with special creative devices that would thrill the children, including his CB radio. His "handle" was Book Man; and the children, especially Mike, enjoyed talking with him on the mobile unit and Mike on the base unit.

A company publication, *Around the Rocks* featured Herk's father in 1959 and has the following to say about him:

"Benny Robinson, automotive mechanic for Weston & Brooker, first revealed his talent when, as a boy in New Brookland, Columbia, he repaired watches that his father's friends brought to him. He joined the company in 1920 at the age of 14 as a waterboy. Successively, he became a helper on the jackhammer drill, worked on the tripod drill, broke rock, and loaded skip by hand. One day during World War II, when help was scarce, Mr. Weston asked him to help grease the trucks.

"Benny had learned mechanics by working on all kinds of machinery. His ability came to light on the truck-greasing job; and he was elevated to automotive mechanic, a position he has held ever since.

"Benny was married in 1929. He and his wife, Thelma, have four sons and one daughter. All five were graduated from college. All are married except one son, who is an Air Force sergeant in Newfoundland. The Robinsons have lived for the last 30 years at 1507 Hopkins Street in Cayce.

"We asked Benny about his hobbies, and he mentioned bird watching. When he used to report every morning to Mr. Charlie Simons, a bird lover, they compared observations on the birds they had seen. He said that his real hobby was radio. He has been assistant pastor of his church 25 years, giving special attention to mission work. For some time he broadcast sermons over WNOK every Sunday.

"But we suspect that Benny's major hobby is writing. He has written an unpublished autobiography. After interviewing him for *Around the Rocks*, we asked him to call us if he later recalled any events of his life that we had overlooked. A few days later we received a letter from him, including the following paragraphs which speak eloquently for his writing ability and recount a most interesting personal experience: 'Upon reaching school age, but being unable to attend, I turned to everything I could find that carried pictures or printing, with a keen desire to learn. Before I was eight, I could read the Bible and newspapers, and write quite well. When I was ten, I picked cotton for an old lady who paid me off with some old school books her children had studied. These I studied, along with my old papers and magazines, spreading them out before the fireplace, reading by the firelight. I kept my books in an old grocery box that my father gave me to sit on. Before I was fifteen, I was hired as waterboy by Weston & Brooker Company; but my quest for knowledge did not end there—it still continues.

" 'As I take this retrospective glance over the long road over which I have come, and then view in contrast the educational advantage that our children enjoy, I am humbly grateful to God for my past experiences and profoundly grateful to those who have made our educational institutions what they are today.' "

Herk was very fond of her father even though there were periods of frustration when she could not get him to do what she thought he should. A case in point was for him to renovate the old house or buy a new one; he was indifferent to both ideas in spite of her pleading and crying. Her greatest desire was for her parents to have a comfortable place in which to live. The Lord blessed; and in January 1965, she was able to purchase a home for her parents, thus fulfilling a lifelong dream. This was her way of expressing her appreciation to her parents for the many sacrifices that they had made in her behalf. Even though she had strong feelings about some of her father's beliefs and attitudes, she loved him dearly. Her favorite treat was for her father to buy her a banana split, which she enjoyed immensely. This enjoyment for this little gesture on the part of father continued throughout her adult years.

I also loved and admired her dad to whom I refer as Granddaddy in this book. He was a man of principle; and I respected him, whether or not I agreed with him.

In the case of my mother-in-law, Other Mother, I do not believe anyone could have been any more loving and caring than she. Her hospitality extended to me and the family while in her home was fantastic. We enjoyed many delicious meals served on her table. She made a point of knowing all of our likes and dislikes and went out of her way to see that they were accommodated.

One of the extra special things that she did was to baby-sit for us on a live-in basis while the children were growing up. I know that this was a tremendous sacrifice for her. Nevertheless, she did it and did it willingly, for which I am eternally grateful.

She still remembers all of our birthdays and special occasions. She and Granddaddy were blessed to attend the graduation exercises of all three of the children when they graduated from Forest Lake Academy. They also had the opportunity of attending the weddings of all three of the children.

Herk was especially close to her brother Earle; in fact, she said that when they were growing up, they promised each other that they would live in the same location when they became adults. This became a reality in 1961 when he and his wife, Naomi, accepted positions in our school system. Earle taught math in Washington High School, and Naomi taught first grade in the Washington Elementary School.

They moved to Blakely from Spartanburg, South Carolina, in the summer of 1961 and began their teaching assignments at the beginning of the 1961–62 school year. They were very capable in their respective fields and were highly respected by students, teachers, and parents. Not only were they a tremendous asset to our educational program, but to our church as well. Earle served as Sunday School superintendent for several years, during which time our Sunday School experienced vibrant growth and genuine fellowship. Naomi was more active with our Adventist Youth program and kept the youngsters involved in some phase of our church's program designed especially for them.

After being in the area for awhile, they purchased a mobile home and located it just across the street from the campus.

This was an especially happy period of Herk's life, because in addition to having her brother Earle nearby, she also had developed a very close bond of friendship with Naomi.

I do not believe that they could have been any more caring and loving to each other had they been blood sisters. Thus, it was a sad experience for us and especially for Herk when they decided to move to Atlanta in the summer of 1970 and begin teaching church school. Earle taught on the high-school level of the Berean Academy, and Naomi continued to teach first grade. The Lord richly blessed their work in church school. Even though the distance was greater, we still found a way to be together on weekends. Earle later became principal of the academy and provided exemplary leadership while serving in that capacity.

After our children had become adults, her health began to fail; but she faithfully fulfilled her duties and responsibilities until the very end.

She and I celebrated Thanksgiving 1983 in Atlanta at the home of her brother, Earle, and his wife, Naomi. Earle had gone to Columbia and picked up Granddaddy and Other Mother so that we could all spend the Thanksgiving holidays together. We had a very delightful time and returned home the following Sunday, cherishing the precious memories of a very fulfilling and rewarding Thanksgiving holiday celebration. We resumed our professional duties on the following Monday. On the way home from school, Herk stated that it had not been a good day for her. I asked her if she wanted to go to the doctor, and she said that she felt it would be o.k. to wait until her appointment on the following day. I trusted her judgment, and she experienced a reasonably restful night. The following morning she decided to remain at home until time to go for her doctor's appointment, which was in Dothan, Alabama.

I called her frequently throughout the day, and she assured me that she was no worse. She also talked with Cheryl via telephone, who at the time was teaching freshman nursing students at Loma Linda University, Loma Linda, California. From their conversation, Cheryl had no reason to feel that there was any emergency or life threatening situation. Meanwhile, I left school in the early afternoon and returned home to get Herk and take her for her doctor's appointment, which was scheduled for 4:30 EST. Upon my arrival at home, I found her dressed and ready for the trip; all she lacked was putting on her all-weather coat. I assisted her in getting it on, after which she made a few steps towards the door and collapsed. She became completely limp and nonresponsive. I managed to get her back on her bed and called our local doctor; however, he could not come at the moment but told me to call the EMT at our local hospital, Early Memorial. They responded immediately, but it was too late. She never spoke another word or gave any indication that she experienced any severe pain. We were certainly not prepared for such an unexpected and traumatic event.

In my opinion, the most difficult task I have ever had to perform was that of calling the children and conveying to them the sad news that their mother had so quickly and unexpectedly expired. It was just as difficult for me to have to call Granddaddy and Other Mother and tell them that their precious, one and only daughter was no longer alive. This seemed almost impossible after the recent Thanksgiving celebration that we had just shared with them at Earle and Naomi's house in Atlanta.

Naomi was the most emotional of all the members of the family that I had to call and break the news of Herk's passing. Nevertheless, the Lord sustained her, and she was able to cope with it.

This was not the first time that I had experienced the death of a family member, having lost four siblings and both parents prior to that time. Nevertheless, it was not nearly as intense as having lost my beloved Herk. Through it all, the Lord sustained us.

Her parents, brothers, Michael, Cheryl, Wayne, Mike's wife Enid, Wayne's wife Marilyn and little Matt, our only grandchild at that time, all arrived at our house safely. We supported and comforted one another as best we could. I felt so helpless when Herk's parents came in that there was really nothing I could do. Herk had been such a loving and special daughter for them, and now she was gone. Those were difficult days, indeed, for us; but we took comfort in the fact that we hope to meet her again in the earth made new, where there will be "no more death, neither sorrow, nor crying, neither shall there be any more pain: for the former things are passed away." (Rev. 21:4)

The children and I shall always be indebted to Wayne's mother-in-law, Mrs. Mahabee who had not said anything to me about her coming to be with us during our period of grief. However, when I met the children at the Atlanta airport, she was already there; and upon her arrival at our house, she more or less took charge and saw that meals were prepared and anything else that needed doing was done in a very organized and professional manner.

Another thing that enabled us to survive the trauma of the sad and unexpected experience was the tremendous outpouring of love and sympathy on the part of neighbors, friends, co-workers, and colleagues. They were fantastic.

Herk's passing occurred on my fifty-sixth birthday, November 29, 1983, so that all subsequent birthdays have been mixed with joy and sadness.

I have never been more proud of Mike, our first born, than when he gave his mother's eulogy. I know that it was probably the most difficult sermon that he will ever be called upon to preach. I assured him that we did not want him to feel pressured into it. Nevertheless, he felt that with the Lord's help he could do it. The Lord blessed in a mighty way; and even though he almost choked up at one point, it was beautiful and a fitting tribute to his mother. Everyone who witnessed it was moved and amazed at the way the Lord blessed in what must have been a difficult situation for him.

On Friday, December 2, 1983, we laid Herk to rest in the Greene Cemetery, which is located within sight of our house. It was approaching sunset as we bade farewell. Precious memories! Oh how they linger! The epitaph on her grave is "...she hath done what she could..." (Mark 14:8)

The trauma of Herk's passing exceeded anything that I have ever experienced, and there have been times when I had difficulty understanding it. Then I concluded that the Lord blessed her to see all three of the children reach adulthood and see the birth of our first grandchild, little Matt. On the other hand had her passing occurred when the children were minors, it would have been so much more difficult. When I put it in that context, I thank the Lord that He allowed us to have her as long as He did. The thirty-two plus years that the Lord blessed Herk and me to share each other's lives were not perfect but were as close to it as I believe is realistically possible on this earth.

She had the joy of seeing Mike get his Master of Divinity from Andrews University, Berrien Springs, Michigan, and Cheryl her Master of Nursing from Rush University, Chicago, Illinois. She also had the pleasure of seeing Mike receive his first call into the gospel ministry by the Central California Conference as associate pastor of the Palo Alto Church, Palo Alto, California. It was our pleasure to visit him in California and attend camp meeting at the Soquel campground.

Unfortunately, she passed away without seeing Wayne graduate from medical school. Nevertheless, we are thankful that..."all things work together for good to them that love God, to them who are the called according to His purpose" Romans 8:28.

I thank the Lord for the very special mother that Herk was to all three, Michael, Cheryl, and Wayne. She was always there when they needed her. The Lord blessed her to see them all graduate from elementary school, academy, college, graduate school, and the theological seminary. She was also blessed to see the boys happily married and to be present at the birth of our first grandchild, little Matthew.

The Lord blessed the children, Herk's parents, and other relatives to return safely to their several places of abode, where the grieving and healing process continued.

Her peers and the professional staff at school loved her as a confidant, as well as a genuine friend and colleague.

The parents of the students loved and respected her for the very special interest that she manifested in and the genuine concerns shown for the well being of their children.

Her students respected and admired her and were saddened by her death. She always displayed a warm, friendly, and congenial personality to each child. The following is a sampling of some of the comments written by students upon hearing of her death:

"I will always remember her smile."

"Mrs. Harris meant a lot to me because when I came to Early County Middle School this year she made me feel like I was very welcome here."

"She was the one that talked me into doing my best."

"She would help me when I didn't understand my homework. She was like a best friend to me."

"I remember Mrs. Harris the most for understanding people problems."

"I hope that I will be as concerned and understanding to others as she was to me."

"She wasn't on the job just for the money. She was on the job because she cared."

"No matter what your problem was, Mrs. Harris was always there to help you with it."

"She would always wave to me whenever she saw me."

"She was like a school mother."

"She didn't hate anybody. She treated all kids the same way."

"She was always more concerned for others than herself."

"When I was in the sixth grade, I did something real bad; and she told me she should call my mother, but she didn't. Instead, she just talked it over with me and told me what to do about my problem."

"I will remember Mrs. Harris for all the times when I was hurting. She gave me something to stop the pain."

"She is the person you would want your child to grow up around."

"When you needed your pants sewed, she was glad to do it."

Former students were especially appreciative of her invaluable assistance with college admission information. They also were indebted to her for helping them to believe in themselves so that they could be the best in their chosen endeavors. I can truly say that she was one who was always willing to go the extra mile.

At the time of Herk's passing, she was already in the process of coordinating Cheryl's and Phill's wedding plans scheduled for Christmas Day, not knowing that she would not live to see them carried out. Consequently, we were faced with a difficult decision. We fully realized that the dead knoweth not anything. However, we felt that if it were possible for her to know it would have been her desire for the original plans to be followed through to completion. With this thought guiding us, we decided to go ahead with the original wedding plans.

Many of the ladies on my faculty at the Early County Middle School, along with my sisters, took over; and it was an overwhelming success.

The only noteworthy problem that we encountered was the extremely cold weather. In fact, it was one of the coldest periods ever experienced in our area. In spite of the severity of the cold, Herk's parents, brothers, our children, my brothers and sisters, other relatives and friends all came and returned safely.

Phill's adopted parents, the Caspers, came from Oregon in their motor home and provided much encouragement and support. Specifically, they sponsored the meal for the participants after the rehearsal, the evening before the wedding.

Elder Les Pitton and his wife Joni, from Washington, D.C., where he was serving as Youth Director of the North American Division of Seventh-day Adventists, came for this special event. He sacrificed quality time away from his family and children so that they could be with us. Elder Pitton performed the wedding ceremony as he had previously done for Mike and Wayne and their brides. I am personally indebted to him and Joni for the very special interest that they took in all of the children while they were at Forest Lake Academy and even now after they are out and striving to establish Christian homes of their own.

. The Lord blessed; and our prayers for a successful wedding in spite of our recent loss of Herk, were, indeed, answered in no uncertain terms.

I am convinced that life for all of us, the children, her mother, brothers, and relatives will never be the same. Nevertheless, "…let us press toward the mark for the prize of the high calling of God in Christ Jesus." (Phil. 3:14)

It has been eleven years since Herk passed away. I do not know whether or not it was coincidental, but it happened on my fifty-sixth birthday. I thank the Lord for every birthday that He blesses me to experience. However, since she has passed, I can't celebrate my birthday without reliving the trauma that her sudden and unexpected passing caused. Nevertheless, I appreciate more and more as time passes the invaluable contributions that she made as my wife and professional colleague. Also, I thank the Lord that he blessed her to be the mother of my children. I have experienced a great deal of loneliness since her passing and sometimes think that I should seriously consider getting married again. But that is a very difficult decision. Therefore, I feel that I should trust in the Lord as I did when He led me to Herk. I have discussed the idea with the children, and they are very supportive of my feelings about the matter and say that they will respect my decisions. Of course, they share my belief that Herk was unique, and I will not find another. Therefore, I find myself coming back to the inspired counsel found in the Bible (Proverbs 3:6), "In all thy ways acknowledge Him, and He shall direct thy paths."

MY TASK

"To love someone more dearly every day,
To help a wandering child to find his way,
To ponder o'er a noble thought and pray,
And smile when evening falls—
    This is my task.

To follow truth as blind men seek for light,
To do my best from dawn of day till night,
To keep my heart fit for His holy sight,
And answer when He calls—
    This is my task.
And then my Savior by and by to meet,
When faith hath made her task on earth complete,
And lay my homage at the Master's feet,
Within the jasper walls—
    This crowns my task."
        —Maude Louise Ray

CHAPTER 13

RELIGIOUS/SPIRITUAL LIFE

I was fortunate enough to have grown up in a Christian home atmosphere. My parents, at that time, were A.M.E. Methodists and taught my siblings and me the basic fundamentals of Christianity. We did not have family worship on a daily basis; however, they would call us together before breakfast on Sunday mornings for a devotional consisting of Bible verses, the twenty-third psalms, prayer by one or the other of my parents, and the recitation of the Lord's prayer. If there was singing, most times it was "Blessed Assurance," my mother's favorite.

We attended Sunday School on a consistent basis and learned the doctrines of the Methodist church.

In 1935, our family was introduced to the fundamental beliefs of the Seventh-day Adventist church. This resulted in a very dramatic change in our spiritual life because we learned for the first time that Saturday was the Sabbath, as opposed to Sunday. Also, we learned that pork was unclean and, therefore, not fit for human consumption. Another revelation was that the Bible taught that we were to be baptized by immersion, rather than sprinkling, as was the custom in the Methodist church. The principle of tithing was also taught, which meant that ten percent of our income (increase) belongs to the Lord. After much soul searching and agonizing over the matter, my parents, my oldest sister, Nellie, and I embraced the teachings of the Seventh-day Adventist church.

My mother never wavered and remained steadfast until her death.

My dad, on the other hand, was in and out of the Adventist church; however, I am happy that at the time of his death, he was a member, also.

My sister, Nellie, married a Methodist minister, C.M.E.; and decided that, in order to be a supportive minister's wife, she would need to be a member of his church.

I have remained a member of the Seventh-day Adventist church since becoming a member in 1935. This is not to suggest that I never strayed away from the path of righteousness. However, I remembered the precious promise recorded in 1 John 1:9, which states, "If we confess our sins, He is faithful to forgive us of our sins, and to cleanse us from all unrighteousness." I thank the Lord for this promise and for what it has meant in my life.

At an early age, I made a commitment to make the Lord first, best, and always in my life; and it has made all the difference. In my opinion, whatever success I have been able to achieve can be attributed to this stabilizing influence in my life.

My parents were severely criticized by their fellow church members for leaving the Methodist church. Some even predicted that they would be back. Their comments included the following:

1. "It does not matter what day we observe, so long as we give God a day."
2. "You could not survive without eating pork."
3. "The seventh-day Sabbath was for the Jews and not for us."

For several years we did not have a church building. Consequently, we met in the homes of the few members who had joined this church. At that time, the total number of homes represented was no more than four.

Finally, it was decided that a church building should be built; so, my Dad, Uncle Melva, and the other men in the church pooled their resources and bought for $25.00 an acre of land for the first church site. The location was approximately one half mile from our house. Afterwards, the men cut logs from trees donated by them and hauled them to the saw mill where they were sawed into lumber. The portion to be used for the exterior was planed. The other necessary materials were also donated.

This group possessed very limited expertise in the field of carpentry. Nevertheless, the Lord blessed their efforts, even though the finished product left much to be desired. It consisted of one room including a pulpit, a homemade heater, a 55 gallon drum adapted to that purpose. The benches were homemade and very uncomfortable. At that time, electricity was not available in rural areas; therefore, the building was without it, as well as indoor toilet facilities. It's obvious that it left a lot to be desired, but we were happy and rejoiced anyway because we knew that the Lord's presence was with us; and this made all the difference.

Even though it was ever so humble and plain, we received some very special blessings during the time we worshiped in it.

Soon after occupying the church building, Elder J.B. Mallory came to our area and conducted a series of evangelistic meetings. He used visual aids to illustrate the highlights of his sermons. Since we did not have electricity in the church, he improvised by connecting his projector to the battery on his car which was a Model A Ford. This was a very exciting and fascinating experience for us. Many people from the community attended out of curiosity to see the pictures on the screen. It was a unique experience for us, and it added a new dimension to his sermons, especially those about the prophecies of Daniel and Revelation.

During Elder Mallory's tenure of service, he was accompanied by his wife and two daughters. He played a trumpet or coronet exceptionally well, and this was a most exhilarating and fascinating experience. He also had many of his songs on slides, and we were able to sing them from the screen.

Elder Mallory was succeeded by Elder Matthew Green, who was a recent graduate of the Oakwood College, a two-year program, Huntsville, Alabama. He came to Blakely via of the Trailway Bus and was met at the bus station by my dad. This was before we were able to afford a car or truck; so, the trip from the bus station to our house was made in my dad's buggy or wagon. Elder Green was very energetic and down to earth. He lived with us for much of the time and would work in the fields with us, doing whatever jobs that had to be done. We accepted him as just another member of the family. He had a very dynamic preaching style, and we were tremendously blessed as a result of his ministry. It was during this time that my sister, Nellie, and I were baptized.

As time progressed, the R.E.A. provided electricity to rural areas; and we wired the old church building and connected the current, thereby providing lights as well as current for audio visual aids. We also discarded the old homemade heater and installed gas space heaters.

It is interesting to note how my Aunt Fannie and her husband, Uncle Melva, became Adventists. Pseudonyms are used but with that exception, the scenario remains the same and was composed by their daughter, Odessa. It is as follows:

"As the sun sank into the western sky, in the distance, its crimson glow once more reminded Esther that another hard work day had slipped into eternity leaving her with lots of thoughts to crowd her already tired mind. However, there was one thing that continued to cause her anxiety, and that was the strange messages which had been told to her by a new preacher from another town. It seemed that no matter how hard Esther tried to forget, the more they troubled her.

"Barefooted, she slowly walked in the fresh deeply plowed earth that felt soft and cool to her hot feet. Fred, Esther's husband waited for her at the other end at the wide-open field where they both had been working. After meeting one with the other, they began their long walk home hardly speaking a word.

"It was early spring, and the countryside was heavily decorated with lots of colorful wild flowers. The cool evening air soothed their tired body. Soon they arrived home, their four small children greeted them. Esther busied herself in the kitchen preparing the evening meal, which consisted of fresh vegetables, homemade bread, and pork meat. After supper was finished and the kitchen was tidied, the family sat around and talked for a few hours. Then it was time for bed. The children and Fred retired for the night, but Esther wanted to read her beloved Bible. She sat by the dim flickering light that shone from one small lamp on the table. 'At last,' Esther thought to herself, 'I can read some of those scriptures that the new preacher left for me.'

"As she read, it seemed strange to her that she felt confused, because her preacher had been teaching just the opposite of what she was reading. 'I wonder which preacher is right?' Esther said. After a few hours, the light had burned down too low for Esther to read any more. So she went to bed and her troubled mind was at rest.

"Every day Fred and Esther worked very hard to cultivate their crop of peanuts, corn, and cotton. More and more they listened to the teachings of the new preacher, but she couldn't convince Fred to believe the strange religion the same as she did. Therefore, it was a hard battle going on inside of Esther and she was determined to be the winner.

"Very soon, spring gave way to summer, crops were harvested, and summer slipped into fall. Finally, winter stole away the cool friendly autumn air, and beautiful colors, replaced them with "Ole Man Winter."

"Since the seasons had changed and taken on new forms, Esther's life also changed. Only her change was a secret between herself and God. You see, Fred and Esther didn't talk too much about the strange religion because it condemned too many of the things that they loved to do. And one of those things was 'bootlegging.' Fred and Esther made hard liquor and sold it to the neighbors, Esther and Fred didn't drink it. That small illegal business earned them extra cash for the family.

"Later that winter, Esther began to tell her sister, Charlie Mae, and her husband about the strange religion. At first, they laughed and made fun of Esther for even listening to such 'trash' as they viewed it. But sooner than they both realized, they were hooked. Now, Esther had someone else to talk to about the strange religion. Never before had they even heard that you should go to church on Saturday instead of Sunday. But stranger than that! Whoever in the world said that you couldn't eat pork had to be crazy. After all, that was the main stay of poor people. (So they thought)

"As time passed on, Esther began to do a lot of praying and deep serious thinking. One day, she decided to tell Fred that she would no longer help him make 'moonshine.' He almost fainted from anger! He didn't say but a few words. "I don't care, I'll do it by myself!" But all along Fred had felt the Holy Spirit, too. But he was playing tough. Not too many months followed before Fred gave up his business, too. His decision made Esther very happy.

"One day Fred came home from work, only to hear that Esther had decided to keep Saturday instead of Sunday. At first, Fred was very angry, but not for long. He followed Esther and so did her sister, Charlie Mae, and her husband, Rufus. Well things went along pretty good for awhile, so they thought. People in the neighborhood began to call Esther and the rest of her family names such as 'them Seven Days.' They would say, 'Look at those crazy folk hauling their little children up and down the road trying to preach that foolish religion to us and our children. Just let them keep up that mess. Very soon they'll be carrying sacks on their backs begging for food.' But you know, those accusations didn't bother Esther and her family one bit. They never had to beg for food and they kept telling people about the strange religion.

"Late that summer, Fred got another shock of his life. He arrived home a little after Esther. And she met him at the door with a smile and said, 'Fred I got rid of all the lard and pork meat that we had and I replaced it with cooking oil, flour, meal, and other foods that's better for us. God said we must eat only the clean foods that he had made.' Before Esther could say another word, Fred spoke in a loud angry voice and said, 'Woman, are you crazy? Have you lost your mind? How are we going to feed all these children now?' Esther simply said, 'We ought to obey God rather than man. The earth is the Lord's and everything that's in it. I'll never worry about having food on my table.' With that statement Fred rushed outside.

"That very night Fred had a strange dream that really frightened him. The next day he told Esther about it and she told him that God was showing him that all the things that he had heard and read about concerning the strange religion was true. And that God wanted him to love Him and keep His commandments. Even at that point, Fred wasn't willing to give his heart to Christ. However, Esther continued to pray for him.

"Late that fall, one evening at dusk, Fred and Esther sat quietly on the front porch listening to the frogs croak, crickets sing, and a whippoorwill's lonely call, and felt the gentle breezes blow. Many thoughts were running through each other's mind. But neither bothering to tell the other about their decision, as far as the strange religion was concerned.

"Finally, Fred broke the silence. He told Esther that he could no longer fight against the Holy Spirit. He wanted to be a Christian along with his wife and children, because they had always formed a habit of doing things together, so why should we be different now? Esther was both shocked and happy at what she had heard. She didn't know the right words to speak, so tears ran down her cheeks and a lump formed in her throat. That very moment, the two of them decided to follow Jesus together.

"A few months later, in 1935, Fred, Esther, Charlie Mae and her husband, Rufus, were baptized into the Seventh-day Adventist church. In the years that followed, Fred and Esther were blessed with ten children. One is sleeping, waiting for Jesus to come. The other nine children including their husbands and wives are all members of the Seventh-day Adventist church.

"Today, Fred and Esther are the only survivors of the original little company of the first converts in their hometown. Although Esther, her sister, Charlie Mae and her husband, Rufus, sleep in Jesus, most of their children and grandchildren are still members of the Seventh-day Adventist Church. They long to see Jesus so that he can be reunited with his loved ones, never to part again.

"Fred and Esther have given over 50 years of their faithful and willing service to God. Now he waits patiently for Jesus' soon return to gather together all of His saints and take them to their heavenly home. I want to be in that number. What about you?

"*Esther and Fred are pseudonyms for Brother Melvin and Sister Fannie Powell Calvary S.D.A. Church, Blakely, Georgia."

It is also worthy of note that many of our neighbors/friends were convinced that the beliefs of the Seventh-day Adventists were Biblically sound. Nevertheless, they rationalized by saying, that if the Sunday keeping, Methodist beliefs were good enough for their grandparents and parents, they were good enough for them. As a result of that attitude, very few accepted or joined the Adventist church.

After worshiping on the old church site for twenty-eight years, it was decided that it was in the best interest of all concerned to relocate. The original suggestion came from Elder Warren S. Banfield, who was serving as our conference president at the time. We saw wisdom in his suggestion; and my wife Herk and I gave the land for the new church site. This action took place in 1963, during which time Elder Charles Cheatham was our pastor. He possessed more than usual building skill and was able to take over and coordinate the building project. Since my wife Herk, the children, and I were in Lexington, Kentucky, where she and I were attending summer school, we gave Pastor Cheatham the key to our house, where he lived until the job was completed.

This structure was over 25' by 40' and was built out of concrete blocks. It consisted of a sanctuary, pulpit, restrooms for men and women and a Sabbath School room. The front of the building was brick veneer. It also had exposed beams; and for the first time, we had custom-made pews. At that point, we had a thermostatically controlled gas heating system that was equipped with a blower to provide for an even distribution of heat. This system was very much superior to the old homemade heater and the gas space heaters used in the old church, but it had a serious drawback in that it was very noisy. After several years, we were able to replace it with a heat pump, which was capable of heating and cooling. Soon after the completion of this sanctuary, we erected one of our denominational church signs, which still stands today.

The rationale for relocating the church to its present site was that the Cedar Springs highway runs right in front of it. Because of the Georgia Pacific Paper and Plywood Mills, located in Cedar Springs, it is probably the most heavily traveled road in the county. Also, it makes it easily accessible for someone coming in for the first time.

Even though our church has always been small, we have tried to be involved in many facets of the conference program. Hence, in 1968, we went forward in faith and purchased a new 12 passenger club wagon van. This enabled us to:

1. Transport non-Adventist children to Vacation Bible School.
2. Take our youth to the federation held throughout the state.
3. Take the members to camp meetings.
4. Take our youth to Junior and Senior Camp.
5. Sponsor a van ministry for our members who needed to be transported to and from church.

This was a major undertaking; but I am convinced that, with the Lord's blessings, there is no limit to what can be accomplished.

I can truly say "To God be the Glory, Great things He has done." From the church's humble beginning, we have produced:

1. Two medical doctors.
2. One nurse practitioner.
3. One ordained minister.
4. Several teachers.
5. At least two registered nurses.
6. At least one Licensed Practical Nurse.

In 1982, the Lord inspired us to expand again, by adding a new sanctuary, foyer, pastor's study, baptistery, rest room, and Sabbath School room. The original part of this facility was converted into a fellowship hall, thus making it possible for us to accommodate pot luck dinners, Sabbath School classes, extra seating at funerals and other special occasions. Presently, the entire facility, old and new, is centrally heated and cooled.

In 1988, it was decided that our original 1968 van was no longer mechanically dependable. After much prayer and soul searching, we located and purchased a 1987 Ford, twelve passenger van that is serving us very dependably and is keeping our van ministry vibrant.

In addition to our van ministry, we are involved in the following outreach programs:

1. nursing home—Sabbath afternoon, 3:00 p.m.
2. prison ministry—Sabbath afternoon, 3:45 p.m.
3. Regional Youth Development Center—Sabbath afternoon, 3:45 p.m.
4. Radio program, Voice of Prophecy.

It has been my desire to be a faithful steward over whatever the Lord has entrusted me and by letting my light shine in this part of the Lord's vineyard. Through it all, the Lord has been good. He blessed me to serve several years on the South Atlantic Conference Executive Committee, under three presidents, Elder W.S. Banfield, Elder R. L. Woodfork, and Elder Ralph Hairston. I was also blessed to serve a five-year term on the Executive Committee for the Southern Union Conference of Seventh-day Adventists.

I am reminded that the Lord expects His people "to be the head and not the tail." It is in that context, that I am able to appreciate the marvelous manner in which the Lord has blessed our feeble efforts.

Our physical plant is plain and simple, but no comparison to what we started with more than fifty years ago. This church, as an institution, has meant more to me than any one thing, outside of the influence of my Godly parents. It has been a stabilizing influence in my life, thus enabling me to be a faithful steward in whatever my Christian duty might have been.

There remains much work to be done, and I have dedicated the remainder of my life to doing whatever I can to help those in our area who are still groping in darkness to come into the marvelous light while the door of mercy still lingers.

The following quotation has been and still is a high standard for me to obtain. Nevertheless, I have consistently striven to be such a man. With the Lord's help, I shall continue to press on towards the mark of the high calling in Christ Jesus.

"The greatest want of the world is the want of men—men who will not be bought or sold; men who in their inmost souls are true and honest, men who do not fear to call sin by its right name; men whose conscience is as true to duty as the needle to the pole; men who will stand for the right though the heavens fall."

Education, p. 57; *Colporteur Ministry* p. 54, E. G. White.

CHAPTER 14

MIKE AND ENID

John Michael, "Mike," Harris, our first son, was born September 2, 1954. He was an excellent baby and did not keep us awake at night. He was always pleasant with a smile on his face. We, as most parents, thought he was wonderful, the smartest baby, in our opinion, and probably the future President of the U.S. He was very lovable and adventurous. He had a very close relationship with his Grandfather Robinson, who had a C.B. radio; and Mike enjoyed being able to talk on the radio. Grandfather Robinson made him a little car out of an old gas tank that had been discarded at his job. When it was finished, it looked much better than the ones in the stores. It even had a horn. It was a very special gift for Mike, as he valued it even more because his Grandfather had made it for him.

In our house, we never taught Mike to believe in Santa Claus. I remember the tremendous letdown I had when I found out that there was no such thing as the jolly little man that brought gifts on Christmas Eve. We didn't want to spoil Mike's love for Christmas and all that the season really means. All went well with our gift giving until the year that Mike was about six. On this particular Christmas, Mike had been begging constantly for a cowboy hat and western guns and holster set. We were not really in favor of this gift because of sending the wrong message and seeming to condone violence. We had communicated this to Mike. Out of desperation, Mike decided to try Santa. On our visit to the Mall, he begged to talk to Santa so relentlessly that we finally consented. Needless to say, the only gift he wanted from Santa was the cowboy hat and western guns and holster set. When we heard this, we felt that we should relent and allow him the pleasure of receiving something that he desired so much. We were never sorry, for it definitely didn't make him a violent person; and the pleasure he received that year from this gift was worth our bending a bit.

Mike loved horses. Wherever we drove, he called everyone's attention to the horses in the fields. He read books, and his happiness knew no end when we provided him with a horse that Mike named

151

Dixie. Dixie, in turn, had several foals and gave Mike much pleasure in his growing up years. He became a very good rider and made trips to his Grandfather Harris' house frequently. He was conscientious about the upkeep of the horse, and she was always well groomed.

Early in his life, while still in elementary school, he had set his goal for the ministry; and nothing ever, even for short periods, changed his mind about his life's calling.

While in elementary school, Mike was an excellent student. He was a favorite of the teachers; and if he ever needed discipline, it must have been a very light transgression, as I never had to deal with him or did anyone tell me that he needed discipline. I know that, at times, Mike and our other children wished that I was not the principal, as my discipline of a student may sooner or later fall on their shoulders with unpleasant results; however, they did little complaining to us as they must have thought that this was the natural occurrence for having a father as a principal. Mike was consistently on the honor roll and received many awards for scholarship. Children being children, a few would always spoil their awards by saying that they only received them because I was principal. This actually hurt me more inside than it did the children; so, we always went out of our way to make sure that our children were more deserving of whatever recognition they received than their peers. Even though some of the memories are not pleasant, in retrospect, I believe that they contributed much to their character development. When Mike went to the sixth grade, he became very interested in band; so, we bought him a cornet, the instrument he decided he would like to play. He loved the cornet and became very proficient with it. He became so good that he was allowed to play in the marching band. All in all, Mike had a very exciting, rewarding and successful elementary-school experience.

The next year was a year of changes for our family as Mike was making the transition from seventh grade to high school. As stated before, Early County was in the first stages of integration. At the time that Mike would be in high school, there was a system of "freedom of choice" of schools in the system. Only a sampling of Black students chose to attend the White high school. Mike was interested in transferring to the White high school but it was communicated verbally that it would seem that if Mike attended the White high school, it would send a negative message of the quality of the Black school and its education, of which I was the principal. Mike, being the adventurous person that he is, became interested in our church school academy in Florida. We visited the school while at our annual church meeting. We were very impressed with the school and what it had to offer in education, but we did not want our family separated at such an early age. With reluctance and mixed emotions, we sent Mike to Forest Lake Academy in Maitland, Florida, approximately 325 miles away. To this day, I still have the picture of our Mike, standing in front of the boys' dorm door, with tears in his eyes, until we faded from sight in our station wagon. It was difficult to have our family separated at this age; but Mike, although homesick from time to time, made a tremendous adjustment and came to love the school, its activities, and especially the commitment that the school had made for spiritual growth.

Mike was the only Black student in his ninth grade class and in his dormitory. He made a very smooth adjustment to this situation and to being away from home for the first time. There were periods of homesickness, but he did not allow it to overwhelm him. The home leaves scheduled for every six weeks were a welcome relief. We made many trips to and from Forest Lake by the time of his graduation; however, we did not mind it, even though it was approximately a six-hour drive each way. We would usually leave after breakfast on Sunday morning and arrive back home around ten or eleven p.m. By the time he became a senior, we arranged for him to take our 1967 Ford Country Squire station wagon.

Mike graduated from Forest Lake in 1972 and chose Andrews University, Berrien Springs, Michigan, for his freshman year. The fact that he was so fond of snow influenced his decision to enroll in that institution.

Mike has always been somewhat adventurous; so, he spent his sophomore year at Newbold College in England. After going to school in England for a year, he then attended and graduated from Southern College in Collegedale, Tennessee, in 1976.

During the summer of 1976 and until October 1977, he spent as a student missionary in Norway. While there he worked with pastor Henryck Jaworskie and assistant pastor Age Rendolen, where he performed general pastoral duties. He also participated in an evangelistic meeting conducted by Elder Rolf Kvinge, Union Evangelist, in Trondheim, Norway. The Lord blessed his service in Norway, and he gained sufficient mastery of the language to enable him to give devotional messages, work with the Missionary Volunteer planning committee, and conduct prayer meetings.

After returning from Norway he entered the master's program in religion at Andrews University. Upon his completion of his Master of Religion degree he entered the Seminary at Andrews University where he earned his Master of Divinity degree.

After having been blessed with a loving Christian wife myself, I prayed consistently that the Lord would bless the children with spouses that would be sincere Christians and an asset to them in their chosen endeavors.

In 1979, while enrolled in the Seminary at Andrews University Mike met and fell in love with a beautiful young lady, Enid Pekeur from Cape Town, South Africa. Enid had met and worked with a team of American missionary doctors, Doctors Elton and Rita Stecker and Doctor and Mrs. Lewis Hart, while serving in MaLawi, South Africa. These doctors were favorably impressed with her work and felt that she possessed unusual potential if it could only be developed. They were impressed enough to sponsor her to come to the U.S. and attend Andrews University. The Lord blessed her while there; and she was successful in earning her B.S. degree in nursing, thus enabling her to become a R.N. The Lord blessed Mike's relationship with Enid, which culminated in their marriage on September 14, 1980. It is interesting to note the events that led Enid to the U.S. and Andrews University and subsequently to our son Mike's acquaintance. In my opinion, it is best described in Enid's own words as quoted below:

"It was in the 1960's during my high school days that I dreamed of one day becoming a missionary for God in a foreign country. I dreamed of sharing the gospel of Jesus Christ with people in a country different from my own. Perhaps this desire or dream to become a missionary came from being impressed by all the wonderful mission stories that were presented in Sabbath School week after week during my early childhood years.

"The year was 1969. I was a new employee at the Good Hope Conference of Seventh-day Adventists, working as an assistant in the accounts department. Imagine my surprise when the president called me into his office one day and informed me of a 'call' that had come via a letter addressed to him requesting my services as a missionary to Blantyre, Malawi, Southeast Africa. I can still remember being asked whether I had anything to do with engineering such a call, as it was specifically for me. The letter was read to me and I can still remember very clearly some of its contents: '...that Miss Enid Pekeur (my maiden name) be released as soon as possible to serve as medical receptionist at the Malamulo Blantyre Clinic (which became the Adventist Health Center later).'

"I tried to convince my president that I had nothing to do with engineering such a call but that I was definitely interested in accepting the call. He recommended to me that I pray about it; and only if the Conference Executive Committee agreed, would they release me. This was proper procedure and following protocol, although I realize now that at that time I was too young and excited to understand all the 'red-tape.' My president reminded me very sternly (I thought) that they could have 'blocked' the call. That is, they didn't have to tell me about it at all; and perhaps I never would have known about it otherwise. By this time I was excited and was ready to tell my friends. I was cautioned not to say a word to anyone until the committee had voted upon it. I did tell my parents. My father's immediate reaction was 'NO.' He was not about to send his daughter to a place where there were riots and people killing each other. It had just been a couple of years since Malawi had gained its independence from Britain; and, of course, he (my father) reminded me of the unrest in that country. Nonetheless I had already decided that I wanted to accept the challenge.

"A few days later I received word from my president that it had been voted for me to go to Malawi. I can still recall him saying 'Enid, now you can stand on the rooftop and shout to everyone that you are going to Malawi. We are sorry to lose you.' I was so happy and excited. I started processing all the necessary documents to obtain a passport. My father threatened that he would tell the authorities not to give me a passport. I kept on praying. Months passed and still no passport. I was beginning to wonder whether my father had, in fact, informed the passport office not to issue my passport. Finally it arrived. Then a work permit had to be obtained. It was on the night of February 12, 1970, that I left Cape Town on this new adventure headed for Blantyre, Malawi. I had never seen the place. Nor had I ever seen pictures. I was given no job description. Fortunately I knew of two ladies from Cape Town, who were working in the same clinic; but their term of service had ended, and they were getting ready to return home. I was to replace one of them as medical receptionist/secretary. I don't remember feeling scared or afraid that I might have made the wrong decision. At age 19 I felt quite confident with myself. Little did I know at that time that this was the start of an experience that would change my whole life. That was just the beginning of a whole new world for me. I had committed myself to the regular two-year mission service program as policy had it for single workers at that time.

"When my two years ended I returned to my home in Cape Town, but I was not satisfied. I had returned to work at the Good Hope Conference office again but felt impressed to return to Malawi. After spending two months in Cape Town, I went back to Malawi and served an additional five years. It was during those last few years in Blantyre, Malawi, that I decided to continue my education and to pursue the nursing profession. I wanted to do nursing in an Adventist institution but didn't know where. Cape Town doesn't have any Seventh-day Adventist hospitals where I could do my nurse's training. Somehow word about my desire to educate myself as a nurse had reached the ears of one of the doctors for whom I worked at the clinic. She called me in and encouraged me to pursue my goal. She asked me if I had thought about studying in the United States of America. That thought hadn't really occurred to me because I had heard from American missionaries how costly things (especially education) were in America. During all this time, I had been corresponding with an American doctor and his wife with whom I had also worked in Blantyre, but they had left permanently. We had become good friends while they were in Blantyre. Being the youngest one on the mission compound, I felt like I was part of their family. I had written and told them that I was about to finish seven years in Malawi and that perhaps I would do some touring. They wrote and invited me to come to the United States. In fact, their offer went further. They suggested that if I could raise my plane fare to travel to the U.S., then perhaps if I wanted to study, they could help with my tuition. This came as a complete surprise! I mentioned this to my doctor friend, the lady who had asked me if I had thought about studying in the United States. She made another proposal or offer. She and her husband (I was working with both of them at the time) would be willing to help with my airfare if I would be willing to accept the offer made to me by the couple in California. Here was such a wonderful opportunity. Two dedicated, missionary minded couples who were willing to invest in me. All this was just beyond me. I sat there in my doctor friend's office not knowing what to say. I remember saying,'No, I can't accept this, I've never had anyone do such great things for me.' I just couldn't believe that some kind people would do something like this for me. I was aware of the high cost of education in the United States. My first reaction was a 'No' answer. I knew I would probably never be able to pay back all that would be spent on me during my stay in the United States of America. My friend graciously encouraged me to accept the offer that they and the other couple were making. She kindly reminded me that they and the other couple really wanted to do this, but I was not used to this; and my mind was in a spin. It took me a little while to get myself together and accept the offer.

"Once again God was working. He had great things in store for me and my life that I knew very little of. I left Malawi in May, 1977, after serving seven wonderful years in mission service. My job had not been easy. Most nights I would leave long after everyone else had gone home. Fortunately, I was single and had few responsibilities at home. My apartment was upstairs from my workplace; so, this worked out very conveniently. I was dedicated to my work. I loved my work; I loved the people. We were a happy family of dedicated workers.

"It wasn't long after I returned to Cape Town that I received word from my lady doctor friend and her husband who had also returned to the United States permanently after serving for about 13 years in Malawi. They called to let me know that my flight arrangements had been made and that the air ticket was on its way. I still couldn't believe what was happening to me. My very ill father had been glad to see me home, but again he seemed reluctant for me to cross the Atlantic Ocean.

"August, 1977, came very quickly. I was once again leaving home. This time I didn't know how long it would be before I would return. My father was too ill to see me off at the airport. A close neighbor friend came over to console him. He wept bitterly. This too was a difficult time for me, for in our hearts we knew we may never see each other again. Yet, life must go on. I left with mixed feelings but confident in knowing that God was in control and that He was the One that had made this whole experience possible.

"I spent a few months in Dunkirk, New York while waiting and preparing to enter Andrews University, Berrien Springs, Michigan. I had worked with several Americans in Malawi and had gotten used to their lifestyle, way of talking, customs, etc. In fact I had begun to adopt some of their ways of life. Now that I found myself living in this great country, everything seemed different. I missed the quiet peaceful mission life and the friendships I had been blessed with in Malawi. That closeness and security, the warmth and dedication of our mission family that I had enjoyed in Malawi was now being replaced by fast-moving traffic, strangers wanting to know about South Africa and its politics, food that was strange to my palate. I began to realize that life is like writing a book. We write a chapter and it closes. Then on to the next chapter. This was happening to me. Everyone I met seemed friendly and nice. January, 1978. Andrews University. It was winter and snowing heavily. This was my first experience with snow. It was fascinating but soon became tiring and I longed for blue skies and sunshine. Winter time does not lend itself to making new friends. I found myself getting very lonely. I kept busy with my books and studies. My basement apartment was cozy and warm, but this, too, was a new experience. The small windows soon got covered with snow. I felt like a creature hibernating for the winter. I knew several folks at Andrews University from Malawi and from my own country, but we all kept busy with our own programs. Summer brought with it more things to do, another work experience with Charlotte Hamlin in the Health Department and exciting work with Lifelong Learning, new friends. I was writing yet another chapter in my life's book.

"January, 1979, found me much more prepared for the cold of winter. I had completed one year at Andrews University and felt quite comfortable with my surroundings. I enjoyed studying in the James White Library. The reference section especially seemed a safe, secure place. Even though it wasn't always quiet, the same people seemed to occupy the same areas. I was one of them. One day I was sitting at one of the desks minding my own business and preparing for a religion class. I was greeted by a young man looking over my desk. I can still hear him say, 'Hi, I'm Mike' as he introduced himself to me. He was so friendly and wore a nice smile. We started speaking. I felt as if I had known him all my life. Strangely enough, I had not noticed him before; but after that day, I seemed to see him more frequently in the reference section of the library. We became friends. There was lots to talk about. He was interested in my missionary experiences, and here for the first time since my arrival in the United States was someone who was willing to spend time to listen to me and what I had to share about my life's experiences. Little did I know that he had traveled quite extensively in Europe and more recently in Norway. Had even been to West Africa! (My continent—must have been during the time that I was in Malawi). It was only after I had practically exhausted sharing my experiences that I discovered that he had even more to share. I discovered this quite by accident one day while hearing him talk to someone on the phone. He was speaking in Norwegian! I started asking questions about his experiences. They were fascinating experiences. Our friendship continued to grow. We saw each other quite a bit. We enjoyed eating lunch together in the cafeteria and studied together in the library. We always had lots to talk about and share.

"One day later that year Mike invited me to accompany him to his parents' farm in Georgia. I was so excited. I had always wanted to see an American farm. I couldn't wait. When the time came late in the summer, we traveled together with some friends. I had not seen Georgia before. It was hot! The people spoke with a different accent. In fact, I had difficulty understanding the accent of some of Mike's relatives. Sometimes he had to translate for me. I felt embarrassed. But they didn't seem to mind. 'Have you ever seen a snake in the wild?' This was a question that one young relative asked me after he learned that I was from Africa. I kept saying, 'Excuse me.' 'Excuse me,' until after about the third time, Mike had to interpret for me. That holiday was one of the best I've had. I shall never forget it. I felt like I was back with my very own family. When I met Mike's grandmother affectionately known as 'Other Mother,' I thought I was with my own mother. I didn't feel like a stranger at all, except for when I opened my mouth to say something, my way of speaking sounded strange to my ears, how still to theirs?

"This was the beginning of a lasting friendship not only between Mike and me but also with the whole Harris and Robinson family and their friends and relatives, as well as my friends and relatives. Our friendship grew and developed into a binding, permanent relationship when we committed ourselves to each other on September 14, 1980. Although my family were unable to attend our wedding and to personally meet Mike and his family, God sent another opportunity our way for Mike to get to know my family through a mission appointment in Butterworth, Transkei, which is one of the homelands in South Africa.

"As I look back over the past few years I can see God's leading in every aspect of my life. He has opened many doors of opportunity.

Some doors were closed but always God was there, leading and guiding me even in my personal life. As I reflect on the circumstances that brought Mike and me together, I am assured in knowing that God in His wisdom and might made it all possible by allowing someone from Cape Town, South Africa, and someone from Blakely, Georgia, U.S.A., two different continents separated by a large body of water, to be joined together as one.

"What else can I say, but 'To God be the glory, great things He hath done.'"

Enid's American parents hosted the wedding, which was held in Hot Springs, Arkansas. This was our first wedding, and much excitement and enthusiasm prevailed. Granddaddy and Other Mother, Herk's parents, drove down to our house from Columbia, South Carolina, the Thursday preceding the wedding. This was about an eight-hour drive for them.

We were up well before daylight the following Friday morning for the long drive to Hot Springs, Arkansas. Pastor Raymond Baker was our pastor at the time; and Herk, Other Mother, and he rode in his car, and Granddaddy and I followed in our 1974 Ford pickup, which was equipped with a camper shell. We drove all day, only stopping for periodic rest stops and to buy gas. We arrived in Hot Springs just a little before sunset on that Friday afternoon. After a few phone calls to get directions, we arrived at the home of the Steckers. Their warm hospitality was very much appreciated after our long drive from Georgia.

We enjoyed a delightful Sabbath with our fellow believers in the Hot Springs Seventh-day Adventist Church on Saturday, with the wedding rehearsal following the Vesper service that night.

In a way it was somewhat of a homecoming even though we were away from home, since Cheryl and Wayne were also there. We visited with each other well into Saturday night, after which we received some much needed rest.

The following morning, Sunday, was beautiful; and the wedding went off without any noticeable "slip-ups." I am sure Enid would have appreciated having her biological parents present, but her American parents were fantastic and were the next best thing.

Enid also has another special friend, Melody Glass, presently residing in California whom she knew from Malowi. Melody is a registered nurse who served with the Steckers and came back to the

U.S. with them at the end of their mission service. A very strong bond of friendship exists between Melody and Enid. In fact they are more like sisters and she served as Enid's Maid of Honor. Melody allowed Mike and Enid to use her car for their local driving before the wedding and for their honeymoon.

We, Other Mother, Granddaddy, Pastor Baker, Herk, and I , began our long trip home after the reception and arrived at our house before day that Monday morning. All of us returned in Pastor Baker's car so that Mike and Enid could have the use of our pickup camper for their trip to our house after their brief honeymoon.

Enid had not graduated from her nursing program, and Mike was still studying for his Master of Divinity. Consequently, they both returned to Andrews University at the end of the summer and resumed their studies.

Before completing his Master of Divinity, Mike received a call from the Central California Conference of Seventh-day Adventists to serve as associate pastor of the Black Seventh-day Adventist church in Palo Alto Church in Palo Alto, California. After serving there for three years with the pastor, Elder Jones, he was assigned to pastor the churches in Modesto and Merced, California. He was very successful in this assignment. While in the Modesto/Merced churches, the Lord blessed them with two sons, Matthew Allan born August 18, 1983 and Joel Andrew November 9, 1985.

The Lord wonderfully blessed Mike's ministry in California and I was blessed along with Cheryl, Wayne and Marilyn to attend his ordination service held in the Hacienda convention center in Fresno, California September 27, 1986. It was a very moving and solemn occasion that brought tears of joy to my eyes. My only regret was that Herk did not live to see it.

After his ordination Mike accepted a call to serve in the mission field; specifically, he assumed the position as religion teacher and interim pastor at Bethel College, Butterworth, Transkei, South Africa. This was a six-year commitment, and the Lord is blessing his efforts as he tries to carry out his duties and responsibilities. While I supported Mike's decision to go into mission service, I had mixed emotions about what problems he and his family might encounter under the apartheid system of government in South Africa; however, I came to the conclusion that the Lord was just as able to protect them over there as He could here in the U.S.A. I had mixed emotions as I bade farewell to Mike, Enid, Matt, and Joel as they boarded the plane in Albany, Georgia, to begin their long journey to their assignment in the Lord's service in South Africa. On the one hand I realized that it was possible that we were parting for the last time. On the other hand, because of the vast distance, I realized that our visits would have to be limited to their two-year furloughs. Enid was to serve as school nurse along with various other duties.

Mike's assignment in South Africa made it possible for Enid to be near her family, who still resides in Capetown. The distance from the college to Capetown is approximately 850–900 miles. Even so, it is much closer than being here in the U.S. She was away from home for years before returning. Her father passed away during the time she was in the United States. It was not economically feasible for her to return for his funeral. Fortunately, her mother is still living; and she, along with Mike and the boys are able to spend their Christmas holidays with her mother each year.

Enid is proving to be a very loving and capable minister's wife and a very good mother for the boys. I especially admire the success she is having in home schooling their boys. The Lord moves in a mysterious way, His wonders to perform. Only He could have brought Mike and Enid together. I am sure that Enid's American parents, the Steckers and the Harts, are proud of her and the way that she has allowed the Lord to lead in her life. Their faith and confidence in her have been richly rewarded.

The Lord has abundantly blessed Mike's ministry since being at Bethel College. He was involved in an evangelistic meeting during the summer of 1989, and the Lord blessed him with fifty baptisms.

The college is striving to become a satellite for Oakwood College, Huntsville, Alabama, and has possibilities for becoming a very strong institution of higher learning in that part of the Lord's vineyard.

During the fall of 1991 there was a good bit of turmoil and unrest at the college. One of our General Conference officers visited the campus for a first-hand assessment of the overall controversy. Upon the completion of his investigation, he informed Mike that he did not have to remain in the situation. Officially he informed him that there was a position open for an associate pastor in the General Conference area and that he would be happy to recommend Mike for the job. This was a very attractive offer and would have solved a lot of problems for Mike, but he turned it down on the grounds that he thought that he should finish what he had started. As much as I wanted Mike and his family back in this country, I was proud of his decision and his commitment to his mission.

In the spring of 1992 Mike was appointed to a new position, namely the Director of the Home Study International program for that area. This is a correspondence program with headquarters in Hagerstown, Maryland, and offers courses from kindergarten on through the graduate level. The program that Mike directs addresses the educational needs of the local pastors who have not had the opportunity to obtain college or seminary training.

Presently the Lord is continuing to bless Mike and Enid's endeavors, and they have both made exceptionally good adjustments to their situation. During the month spent with them in 1993, I discovered that many of my concerns were unfounded. I am very proud and supportive of what they are striving to do.

"To accomplish great things, we must not only act but also dream, not only plan but also believe."

—Anatole France

CHAPTER 15

CHERYL AND PHILL

Cheryl, our second child, and only daughter, has been as close to a perfect daughter as parents could realistically hope for. This has been consistent from babyhood to the present. Unless there is something that I am unable to recall, she never had to be disciplined for being naughty or disobedient at home or at school. Older people especially love Cheryl because of her kindness and special interest shown in them.

Another one of Cheryl's attributes is her singing ability; while she is not a professional, she really blesses my soul when she sings. Many others have expressed a similar attitude. Maybe it's because she puts so much expression and feeling into her singing. I always look forward to her singing when she is at home and has an opportunity to worship with us.

Cheryl and her mother shared the same birth date, January 20, and had extremely good rapport with each other. In fact, their relationship was more on the order of sisters rather than mother and daughter.

The Lord has blessed her with the ability to express her feelings with clarity. The following is a sampling and tells about her experiences on one of her overseas tours with the "Lost Generation."

"A Little Love From London

"Attending Forest Lake Academy was one of the most rewarding experiences that our parents could have provided for us. While there we met our lifelong friends, Elder Les and Joni Pitton. The Pittons were responsible for coordinating an evangelistic singing tour to Europe for our choral group, 'The Last Generation.'

"This experience provided a unique opportunity for us to grow in our personal relationship with God through the process of sharing His love with others. The following is an example of one of those memorable experiences:

"We arrived at the children's school in East London an hour early—quite an unusual feat for a group like ours, which managed to

164

get lost at least once on any trip. The school was surrounded by huge walls and two large iron gates that made it appear like a jail. The playground was only a small area of cement. My mind flashed back to my elementary years where a nice playground and plenty of hide-and-go-seek room was the least we could expect. How could anyone possibly go to school here? Oh, well, my task would be to show that Jesus loves, and I love, too.

"At the front iron gate stood a toothless old man, the keeper, I presumed. His stooped position and snow-white hair made him appear like Rip Van Winkle. My fairy-tale opinion was soon changed as I heard him snarl at the children for coming to the gate to look at us. Not only did he snarl, but he swung out to strike them. I was mad!

'Don't yell at them!' I mentally rebuked. 'We're here to love them. Don't hold them back.'

"But when millions of tiny hands wanted to help us carry in the equipment, I soon wished that he would hold them back. Little girls tugged at my long dress, and the boys wanted to know if the 'Miss' was from America. In their uncontrollable excitement, questions spilled out of their mouths,

'Do you know the Jackson Five?'

'No.'

'What about Donnie Osmond?'

'No.'

'Is David Cassidy from your town?'

'No.'

'Don't you know anybody?'

"The closed door brought a welcome silence. I couldn't help but laugh as I thought of the children associating *me* with movie stars. Peeping out the window, I saw other members of the group stumbling slowly through the human maze trying desperately not to drop the equipment. They looked funny. The children seemed to fight for attention; and with an aching heart, I realized that they were starving for love. I prayed that God would guide us.

"Les, our pastor, went to check with the headmaster to make sure everything was okay, while the rest of us got the equipment set up, the guitars and bass tuned, and a host of other last minute preliminaries. Where we were singing was about the size of two classrooms, but there were no chairs. Les came back and informed us that everything was all set. We were giving three half-hour programs. The first program was to the first and second year students. It would start in 10 minutes. We had prayer; then, all that was left to do was wait. The minutes dragged.

"With the sounding of the bell came the rows of children. Each wanting to get out of line but being restrained by the guiding figure at the end of the row. Under their breath, our guys remarked about the beauty of the teachers, while we girls shot them reprimanding looks. Finally, everyone was in and sitting in Indian-like fashion on the floor. The children's whispered questions soon had the room sounding like a beehive. This all stopped when the headmaster stepped forward. He raised his hands in an authoritative yet fatherly manner. I could see the children respected him, for the room had suddenly become quiet. Then he spoke.

'Children, today we have visitors from America. Would you like to welcome them?'

"An enthusiastic 'Yes' was the response, dressed in the splendor that can be found only in 200 children's voices.

"Then, let's tell them 'Good morning.' Again in the same sing-song fashion came our greeting. The headmaster spoke again, 'Children, the funny-looking obstacles in front of our singers are called microphones. They are used to make their voices louder so that even Bobby, in the last row, can hear.' Sounds of disbelief escaped from their lips. We smiled. '*But*, children, the microphones are rather expensive and if broken would cost a lot of pounds to fix. So no one comes past this line, understand?'

" 'Yes, sir,' they replied. This time a bit of awe tinged their voices.

" 'Very well, then. Let us begin.'

"Now it was our turn. Myrna played the lively introduction, and we began singing 'The Happy Side of Life.' I have experienced few greater thrills than singing to children because they love ya, no matter who you are. Their eyes continually give you the assurance that they are listening. Their smiles, some toothless, others sprinkled with cavities, and a few perfect sets, made our spirits rise to the outer limits of space. Each group of children loved the songs we let them sing with us, and many heard of Jesus for the first time.

"At the end of the program the headmaster again came forward. At the raising of his hand, the room was silenced. We didn't even dare to speak. He spoke, his voice so typically British, yet so marvelously kind.

'Did you enjoy the program?'

"The cries of 'Yes!' rose in a not-so-uniform manner. Nevertheless, he seemed pleased.

" 'Then let us in a more orderly manner, thank them for coming.' A unison chorus of 'Thank-you' responded. 'Would you also like to give a clap?' Instantly, thunderous clapping bombarded our ears, and we were so happy. The headmaster went on to make the usual dismissal remarks while we got in conspicuous places where we could greet the children. At the end of his comments we suddenly found ourselves crushed by children of all shapes and sizes, wanting our autographs. I couldn't believe it, and at first thought it a joke. However, their persistence soon changed my mind. I thought my hand would fall off from writing so quickly, but I enjoyed every minute of it. Questions still flooded me. 'Are you *sure* you don't know Donnie Osmond?' 'Are you rich?' Then I became aware of a persistent tugging on my dress. I looked down, and there I found a short-haired, seven year old little girl. She was one of those who had sprinkled cavities.

'Miss! Miss!' she yelled persistently until I quieted her by giving my full attention.

"Her voice became a whisper, and I could feel her becoming embarrassed. She spoke again. 'Miss (pause) do you mind if I kiss you?' Her brown eyes pulled me to her. How could I resist? Perhaps this is what God's love is all about. In Jeremiah 31:3 He tells us that 'I have loved thee with an everlasting love: therefore with loving kindness have I drawn thee.'

"Oh, God, thank you for bringing me all the way to London for yet another taste of your love."

Cheryl's rapport, kindness and love of children are very evident in this essay.

While doing her Master's degree in her nurse practitioner's program, the Lord blessed her to spend two quarters here in Blakely working under the direction and supervision of Doctors Eugene Giles and Lowell Justice. They, along with the office staff really fell in love with her and gave her a very special party upon the completion of her work. Even now, they continue to follow her career and how she is doing in general. Dr. Giles' mother worked on the staff at that time, and Cheryl was the only one she would allow to give her certain tests while there. Many of the elderly patients referred to her as "my doctor."

The Lord has richly blessed her; and upon her graduation from Rush Presbyterian University, Chicago, Illinois, she was given a teaching position at Vanderbilt University, Nashville, Tennessee. She remained in that position for two years, during which time she taught freshman nursing students.

Following her work at Vanderbilt, she served in a similar capacity at Loma Linda University, School of Nursing, for approximately two years. It was at this juncture of her life that she got married and relocated to St. Louis, Missouri, where her husband Phill was attending graduate school in economics at Washington University.

Shortly after getting settled in St. Louis she was given a position at Jewish Hospital in February, 1989, during which time she was primarily responsible for the operations of Employee Health. Subsequently, this expanded to include the management responsibilities of the Employee Health/Infection Control Department.

While serving in this capacity, she was honored by being selected for the annual Meritorious Service Award in 1988. She was chosen Employee of the Month at Jewish Hospital in July, 1988; and the following excerpt was published in the monthly *Employee Up-Date*:

"Cheryl Wa-Ndambi, June's 'Spotlight' employee, believes in the value of people and the power of love. 'If there is one thing I try hard to do as I go about my work,' she says, 'it is to reinforce the importance of remembering that each one of us is special. We have to let others know that we can do a good job, and we have to retain our pride in the process.'

"Wa-Ndambi, R.N., MSN, manager of Employee Health and Infection control for Jewish Hospital, gives physical examinations to most new employees and is usually the person workers see if they become ill or are injured on the job. She also educates employees about infectious diseases and the procedures for protection from undue exposure.

"Wa-Ndambi is the recipient of the Hospital's 1988 Meritorious Service Award, which annually goes to an employee whose work activities 'transcend the normal job description,' noted David A. Gee, Hospital president, at the recent employee recognition program. With a willingness to help others, she actively participates in Hospital functions. Two years ago, Wa-Ndambi asked to take part in the Hospital ceremony memorializing Dr. Martin Luther King, Jr. She says remembering King reinforces positive opportunities for change through the power of love. She offered the homily and a song.

'Cheryl's contribution to the ceremony must be noted,' says Robert Jewell, assistant vice president. 'She is one of the kindest and most thoughtful individuals Jewish Hospital is fortunate enough to employ. She lives the spirit and philosophy exemplified by the life of Dr. King.'

'I cannot say enough good things about Cheryl,' says Barbara Tarantola, manager of patient relations. 'She goes out of her way to exhibit caring for others.'

"Phyllis Jackson, coordinator of the Employee Assistance Program, agrees. 'She'll give you the dickens when you deserve it, especially when it deals with your health, but you always know she cares.'

"Gee also cited her as a role model for everyone, and especially for minority employees. Wa-Ndambi says she seizes the opportunity to speak up for employees whenever possible.

'Sometimes minority employees will come to me when they have a problem on the job,' she adds. 'If necessary, I will intercede on their behalf with their supervisors, and at other times I try to offer the moral support they need.'

"A graduate of Andrews University in Michigan and Rush University in Chicago, Wa-Ndambi practiced and taught at Vanderbilt University in Nashville, Tennessee, and at Loma Linda University in California before coming to Jewish Hospital in 1984. Her husband, Phillip, is a financial analyst, and they are the parents of nine month old Jessica Kristine."

I was very proud of Cheryl's outstanding recognition and wished so much that her mother could have shared this experience with me. The Lord has richly blessed her in all of her endeavors. Jessica Kristine was born September 15, 1987 and at that time was my one and only granddaughter. In order to be able to spend more quality time with Jessica, Cheryl resigned her position at Jewish Hospital in the summer of 1989, after which she accepted a position on the faculty of St. Louis Community College at Meramec, where she taught freshman nursing students.

In 1991, Cheryl, Phill, and Jessica relocated to the Chicago area; and she has a part-time position as adjunct faculty/nursing instructor at the William Rainey Harper College, and Phill has a position as a computer analyst at Household International which is based in one of Chicago's northwest suburbs.

At this point, I would like to include a few highlights about her husband, Phill. He was born in the Kivu Province of Zaire, Africa. His father is deceased; however, his mother, Kahambu Kisunzu, continues to reside in Central Africa. His American "parents," sponsors for his coming to the United States, are Mr. and Mrs. Kenneth Casper of Coquille, Oregon. His educational and professional experiences include the following: Bachelor's degree in Mathematics from Andrews University, Berrien Springs, Michigan; Master's degree in Mathematics from California Polytechnic University, Pomona, California; and Master's degree in Economics from Washington University, St. Louis, Missouri.

One of his fondest dreams was realized on July 16, 1992, when Phill became a naturalized American citizen. It was a long-awaited day, and he was most appreciative for the long-cherished freedom and rights bestowed upon him as an American citizen. For Phill and Cheryl, it was an unique experience to see people from varied countries eagerly waiting to become part of the American "melting pot." Phill's citizenship came just in time for the 1993 presidential election, and he was able to exercise one of his rights, the right to vote. Cheryl and Phill were excited about it, but were especially pleased that he had been chosen to share the meaning of citizenship with his colleagues. His company, Household International, selected him to be part of a "get-out-to-vote" video. It was during this taping that he shared what the right to vote meant to him. I am sure that they will treasure these experiences for as long as they live. I cannot help but be concerned about the many Americans who seem to just take these freedoms for granted.

Phill and Cheryl were blessed with a son, Conrad Stevon, on December 16, 1994. His birth brought joy, happiness and excitement to Phill, Cheryl, Jessica, and me. At this point, I now have seven grandchildren for which I am indeed thankful especially since they are all normal and healthy.

I am confident that Cheryl's mother would be very proud of her daughter for the accomplishments she has been able to make as an employee and particularly as a mother and homemaker.

"Goodness is the only investment that never fails"
—Thoreau

CHAPTER 16

WAYNE AND MARILYN

For some unexplained reason, Wayne seemed to have experienced more misfortunes growing up than Mike and Cheryl.

The first example worthy of note occurred during the summer of 1965. Herk and I had just completed our fourth summer school session at the University of Kentucky. With the exception of the first summer, the children had accompanied us. They took swimming lessons and other activities while we attended classes. We had living accommodations on campus in Shawneetown, and it was a lot of fun. Our mode of transportation at that time was a 1964 VW bug that we had ordered directly from the factory in Germany. It was shipped into the Port of Entry at Mobile, Alabama.

The last day of summer school was on a Friday; and as soon as our exams were finished, we were immediately on our way to Chicago. This was possible since our belongings were already packed in and on the car in the luggage carrier attached to the roof. Even though we had shipped a lot of our things home, we still had a lot of togetherness in that VW, but it was fun. It was well into the night when we arrived at Herk's brother Ben's house. We unloaded the car, since it was unsafe for the belongings to be left in it now that we were in the city. Much of the remainder of the night was spent having fun with our three children and Ben and Nancy's five.

The following morning, the Sabbath, we attended church and got some much needed rest.

The next day was Sunday. It was a rainy day, but Ben and Nancy convinced us that the fun thing to do that day was to take everybody to the baseball game that was being played that afternoon in Comiskey Park with the Chicago White Socks and the Houston Astros. For my family, it would be the first major league baseball game. After completing the preparation, we walked up to the EL station, a block or two from Ben and Nancy's house and boarded the "A" train. This was our first ride on an EL train so we had a lot of fun and excitement during our ride to the station just a block from the ball park.

Finally we were all in our seats in the bleachers enjoying the game, but the recurring showers made it necessary for the game to be called temporarily until the rain would stop, at which time, play would be resumed. After this happened two or three times, Nancy suggested that we move to another area. A few minutes later she suggested that we should check to see if everyone was present and accounted for. To our dismay and fright, we discovered that Wayne was missing. We reported it to the security police in the park, and they did not appear to have been too concerned. "It happens all the time," they said. They assured me that he would find us or we would find him at the end of the game. The game was finally "called" as a result of the rain, but still we could not find Wayne. At this point it became even more serious; so, the police requested a detailed description of him, including what he was wearing. Also, they requested that I ride with one of the policemen in his patrol car to see if I could assist in finding him. It was a traumatic experience for me when the bulletin came on our police "scanner"…"Missing, eight year old boy last seen in or near Comiskey Park, wearing short pants, blue shirt, etc." It is always a cause for concern when something like this happens, but when it's your own child, it really "hits home." This went on approximately two hours, even though it seemed like an eternity. Meanwhile, Nancy, her children, Herk, Mike, and Cheryl returned to Ben and Nancy's house where they found Wayne waiting on the steps. The police and I scouted the area and finally, the policeman gave up, and I boarded the EL train and returned to Ben and Nancy's house. When I arrived, everyone appeared sad, gloomy and disappointed that the policeman and I had not found Wayne. However, unbeknown to me, Wayne was already there and Ben was hiding him. When Ben sensed that I had had about all I could stand, Ben brought Wayne out of hiding; and I was finally put at ease. My first inclination after discovering that no harm had come to Wayne was to load up our stuff in that Volkswagen Bug and get out of the city and back to the safety of the country.

Wayne's explanation was that when we moved to a different area in the stands, he thought that we were going to Ben and Nancy's house; and somehow he got separated from us. When he discovered that he was lost, he walked back to the EL station; and a lady offered him fifty cents for his train fare, but he explained to her that he was only eight years old and did not have to pay to ride the EL train. As I recall, she insisted that he take it anyway. He remembered that we had ridden the

"A" train; consequently, he boarded it, and returned to the station where we had gotten on when we went to the park, got off, and walked the one or two blocks to Ben and Nancy's house. Our VW was parked on the street in front of their house, and this helped to convince him that he was at the right address.

I prayed fervently while looking for him that he would not be harmed because I was fully aware of the crime and abuse that lurked all around him. Praise the Lord! He gave His angels charge over him and no evil befell him.

Another experience that happened to him was that of falling off the rail out at the rear of the Washington High School building. This wing consisted of two stories; and Wayne was "skinning the cat" and lost his grip some way, causing him to fall and land on the hard clay below. In the process, he sustained a broken arm. This was on a Thursday afternoon, and our family doctor, Dr. Baxley, was off duty. Therefore, I rushed him to the emergency room at our local hospital, where they x-rayed his arm and confirmed that it was broken. Dr. James H. Crowdis was the doctor that set the arm in the emergency room.

Herk and I would constantly remind Wayne, Mike, and Cheryl to wait for us out front until we were ready to go; but it appeared that Wayne became bored and decided to go to the "off limits" area for a little fun and excitement, and that was the consequence.

A third thing that happened to him was a bout with pneumonia. It seems as if he ran his bath water, got in the tub, and fell asleep. When Herk and I got concerned and went to check on him, we discovered that he was asleep; and his bath water had gotten cold. Shortly thereafter, he came down with pneumonia and had to be hospitalized.

Finally, he and Mike were riding double on their Honda Motorcycle when the front tire blew out. They both sustained bruises but no broken bones. This experience more or less unnerved him and Mike so far as the Honda was concerned. Consequently, we sold it shortly after that life threatening experience.

Wayne was always very clever with words and wrote the following little note to me when at thirteen I cut his hair much shorter than he had desired:

"MY HAIR"

"My hair is very important to me. It gives me a sense of pride and it and I are good friends. I was happy to find that each week it had gotten a little longer and a little thicker than before.

"As it grew, it gave me a sense of dignity and built up my ego. It was a dignity that could hardly be explained. I was very attached to my hair.

"In the morning when I awake to see that patch of wool perching on top of my head, it gave me a challenge for the day. The challenge was to get that patch combed out and looking good. I was proud when I succeeded.

"My parents gave in to my brother so he always had more hair than me. This is why my little bit of hair and I were such good friends.

"Tonight, I lost my friend. My father (the 'barber') killed him. It is very hard for me to accept the fact that he is gone, but I console myself with the thought that some day he'll be back again."

Daddy
(A Thought)

"Love those who do you wrong; pray for those who despitefully use you.

Wayne
August 26, 1970"

Fortunately, things got better for Wayne after making it through his childhood. Following are some of his comments at the time that he was seeking admission to medical school:

"Perhaps a rural town in southwestern Georgia was not the most advantageous place for a Black child to be born in 1957, but it was in just such a setting that I came to be. The disciplined responsibility inherent in successful farm operations was an important factor in my early childhood experience. In spite of a strong commitment to agriculture, my parents played an active role in the education of the Black community of the area. My father was the principal of the local high school for Blacks and the supervising principal for educational facilities serving 75% of the Black community in the county. My mother served as guidance counselor for the same school system. Unfortu-

175

nately, though 60% of the local population was Black, economic disadvantage and racial polarity created a serious disparity in the quality of education found in black versus white educational systems.

"As a child, racial tensions were of incidental importance to me. It was not until the autumn of 1970 that I began the poignant experience of living in a pluralistic society. At this time massive desegregation programs were initiated after a sixteen-year delay. This transition period was quite smooth as I continued to do well in the more competitive integrated situation.

"The following year I traveled to Orlando, Florida, to study at Forest Lake Academy, a parochial entity of the Seventh-day Adventist church. Religious instruction had always been a vital component of my upbringing, and the years spent at this school were spiritually and morally edifying. Yet, even in a Christian school, racism was no abstract theory. With Blacks forming only 10% of the enrollment, I realized for the first time what it meant to be a minority.

"Curiously, acceptance came facilely for me; and I was very active in academic life. My extracurricular involvement included participation and leadership in various religious organizations, student politics, musical associations, and work with the school newspaper and yearbook staffs. At this time, the existence of a myriad of peoples and cultures became evident to me. Here also a growing relationship with the Latin community was established, and I eventually gained fluency in the Spanish language. As a member of a choral group from the academy, I spent the summer of 1973 aiding in church-oriented activities in England and several European countries. The following summer the group moved to Jacksonville, Florida, and tutored underprivileged Black children, spending the last three weeks touring the West African countries of Sierre Leone, Liberia, Ghana. I developed an intense interest in cultural diversity and an appreciation for the good in my own country. Nevertheless, recognition of the inequitable treatment received by fellow Blacks and other minorities was and has not been abated.

"The need for Black doctors is undisputed. Officials point out that of the 370,000 physicians in the United States in 1976, only 6,600 or 1.8% were Black. Nationally in 1976, there was one White doctor for every 538 White persons and one Black doctor for every 4,100 Blacks. This divergence was even greater that year in my native Georgia, where there was one White physician for every 926 Whites and only one Black physician for every 9,652 Blacks. Minorities have traditionally been neglected, and I hope to promote the reversal of this trend. I feel a moral responsibility to aid today's young people in finding direction in life and to serve community interests in a concerned manner.

"An affinity for the more quantitative aspects of medicine has developed from my choice of Chemistry as a major in college. Participation in collegiate extracurricular activities has been moderate, but by no means nonexistent. Community service concerns have convolved in research exploring the feasibility of employing crown ethers to dissolve polar reactants in inert solvents as a means of increasing yields.

"Early in college I was confronted with a personal dilemma. The aura with which many premedical students attempted to surround themselves was very disquieting to me. Self-gratification and overt efforts to fulfill only the minimum requirements for acceptance were their primary motivating factors. This, coupled with a seeming lack of intellectual curiosity among their ranks, strongly influenced me toward a career in the physical sciences. I do not mean to infer that all premedical students felt or behaved in this manner, but it was certainly no uncommon occurrence. This has led me to conclude that there exists a need for responsible leadership among physicians—the type of leadership I feel I can provide, with proper training. It is my desire to attend an institution which will equip me with the needed skills to become a qualified leader among physicians and scientists. I hopefully anticipate being found a suitable candidate for the entering class of 1979."

The Lord blessed Wayne to get accepted in medical school at Loma Linda University, Loma Linda, California, during which time he did the MD/PhD programs.

Upon graduating from the Loma Linda Medical School in 1988, he was accepted into a three-year residency program at Emory University School of Medicine, during which time he specialized in internal medicine. At the completion of his two-year residency, he fulfilled a two-year commitment with the Public Health Department in Chattanooga, Tennessee, after which he joined the Emory University faculty with duties at Grady Hospital. He has been accepted into a two-year fellowship program in oncology.

He was married to Marilyn Margaret Mahabee from the Bronx, New York, on September 6, 1981. She also attended Loma Linda University, where she received two Master's degrees, one in marriage counseling and the other in social work. While Wayne was in medical school, she earned her Ph.D. in clinical psychology from the California School of Professional Psychology in Los Angeles, California.

Before Wayne and Marilyn were married, Marilyn experienced a life-threatening accident that brought about a major change in her life; and she tells of this experience in the following:

"I have always been a Seventh-day Adventist. I grew up during the years when preachers gave sermons on a regular basis about the biblical admonishment for us to be 'in the world, but not of it.' We were admonished to be cautious about doing everything 'the world' was doing—particularly because many of those things were simply 'not good for us' and partially as a way for us to be 'different.' In other words, we were to be a peculiar people, so that we as Adventists could stand out in quiet and pure ways, thereby prompting others to develop an interest in finding out about our religion and to develop a desire to have Christ as their own personal friend and Savior, as well.

"Being a member of the 'peculiar people' group can be hard when you're a teenager and have to constantly refuse all kinds of enticing fun that other teens are enjoying. It can be especially hard when you go to a public school and are rather shy in the first place; so, it takes a lot of work to develop friendships and then have to miss out on most of the after-school activities the friends invite you to. I was sixteen years old when the assistant pastor of my church, Gaspar Colon, invited me to apply to be a member of a singing/witnessing team he was organizing for the summer of 1973. It sounded wonderful! The group was to be composed of about 20 high school and college youth, who would all live together in a large house in the town of Patchogue, Long Island, New York. The purpose of the group was to develop an interest in Seventh-day Adventists in this community so that the people would be inspired to take part in Bible studies, and then start a small Adventist church in this town. We proposed to do this by holding evangelistic meetings, as well as develop a large enough repertoire of songs so that we could sing in various malls, churches, and special events that would attract people to listen to us and want to find out more about our witnessing group.

There was just one problem. My parents had rarely let me spend the night at anyone else's house. How would they agree to let me live somewhere else for an entire summer? The Lord has His ways. It turned out that my mother had been a student at a Seventh-day Adventist high school in Cuba at the same time Pastor Colon's aunt went there. She trusted his family implicitly; so, with a little convincing of my father, permission was granted and I made my plans to join the group when school let out in June.

"I believe the Lord knows exactly where we are in our spiritual life, and He allows us to have experiences that jolt us closer to Him if we leave ourselves open to Him. The summer of 1973 was a major turning point in my life. As I said, I've always been a Seventh-day Adventist. I've never had any doubts as to whether or not I was a member of the 'right' religion; but when one has always been an Adventist, it's easy to do things out of habit but not feel like you have a deeply satisfying relationship with the Savior. That was the year when all the 'don'ts' involved in Adventism were getting tedious. 'Don't drink, don't smoke, don't dance, don't have sex before marriage, don't go to movies, don't drink coffee, don't do anything secular on Sabbath.' This list seemed endless at times and well, it was getting rather tiresome. I think the Lord talked my parents into letting their eldest daughter join the Greater New York Adventist Youth in Action (AYA) team that summer. He knew I needed to feel what it was like to have an intimate spiritual relationship with Him. He knew we all would need to witness to some other people in another community in New York that summer. He also knew that I would need to be prepared to be able to endure a far different experience that summer than I had planned and still maintain and strengthen my faith in Him.

"I loved being a member of a group of Adventist youth. Finally there was no need to explain anything at all about my lifestyle. It was great. Gaspar and his wife May-Ellen functioned as wonderful young parent substitutes as well. We were all supervised carefully, yet none of us felt intruded on as they respected and trusted each of us to conduct ourselves as model Christians for the surrounding community to observe. That was the summer I learned about prayer—about it's power and about how you really do develop a feeling of God's presence when you 'pray without ceasing' and include Him in all your decisions and activities. We started each day with individual prayer. Then we prepared breakfast, prayed for our food, and began morning devotions. We each were given a copy of Ellen White's *Christian Service*, which we took turns reading one or two paragraphs each (out loud) every morning. Then we had a circle prayer. After that we did basic chores and prepared for choir practice. We prayed for our practice sessions. We prayed for each other. We broke up in prayer bands at different times of the day when we had a special concern we needed the Lord to work out for us and before we engaged in any type of witnessing activity. We asked the Lord's guidance for everything. I was bewildered at first by all this prayer. What could I say that was different from what I'd said a half hour ago? Who wants to bore the Lord with the same old words and many others use fancy language better than I can? Those questions became unimportant after a while. I found that the Lord is accepting of any prayer a person has in his heart to give Him. I also found that this constant talking to God was really making me understand life and that God would take care of my needs in exactly the ways that were best for me if I would simply mold my will into obediently following His directions, rather than try and get Him to do what I thought was best.

"I became a committed Seventh-day Adventist Christian that summer. The fellowship and closeness we developed as a group was special. It is something I've never forgotten even as I write this now, almost 20 years later. I can hardly believe it's been that long already. We were actually together, all of us, for only about four weeks out of the twelve we had anticipated. It's funny how brief experiences in your life can change the course of the rest of it.

"After those four weeks I never cared about the 'don'ts' in being an Adventist anymore. I became convinced that the Lord had singled me out—as He does everyone—for some special purpose.

"That was the summer when the Lord allowed our little group to experience a terrible accident—tragic, yet terribly important in its effect on the spiritual lives of family members, friends, many strangers as a result of the ways in which we dealt with the event.

"The Lord works in mysterious ways. On July 14, 1973, our group sang at an Adventist campground in New York that was roughly 4 hours' distance from our residence in Patchogue. Many strange events combined, resulted in part of our group leaving for Patchogue at around 1:30 A.M., Gaspar and May-Ellen staying at Camp Berkshire, and the remaining 11 members leaving in a borrowed van about a half hour later. Our van never got to Patchogue that night. At approximately 3:30 A.M., while traveling on a rainy, slippery freeway that had numerous potholes, one of the wheels became lodged in a hole and the entire van spun around on the expressway. The vehicle slammed into a bridge abutment, wrapping itself around in a 'U' shape. I've been told by all who saw that they could not believe that anyone escaped there alive. The back doors flew open and two of our members were thrown down onto a freeway below us that ran under the bridge that we hit. A passing motorist got out and stopped the sparse oncoming traffic at that hour of the morning. Ana Marie Onori, age 15, died as a result of internal injuries. She was an only child. Raul Batista, who fell right next to her, had a concussion and suffered memory losses for many months, but he lived and he went to college that fall. There were other injuries—pulled muscles, a broken femur, a broken nose—all the rest lived.

"There were a lot of strange things about that night. Everyone had a parent who was inexplicably awake. The accident occurred in Yonkers, New York, which was within a half hour from my home. Everyone else's family lived much farther. When my parents arrived at the hospital, my mother looked in and noticed that I held my left hand strangely. The resident tried to get me to sit up; and when I struggled to do so, my mother asked him to just let me be there for the time being. He shrugged, admitted me for 'pulling of the muscles.' A few hours later it was determined that my injuries were much more serious. I had broken four of the seven cervical vertebrae of the neck (C4–7). Two of those were completely crushed. The physicians expected me to be a quadriplegic. If I had broken c-3, I would have needed to be on a respirator. As it was, my parents were told their 16 year old high school senior was not expected to walk out of the hospital if she lived.

"That event changed a lot of lives. I had no fear of death— I just worried about my parents. Proverbs 3:5–7 was an integral part of my life . I trusted the Lord implicitly and fully expected Him to keep me there as long as He saw fit and heal my spine as only He could. The entire medical staff was impressed by the group of young people who were patient, kind to other people, and who visited and sang for the staff and other patients each time they came to visit. Many of the nurses queried me about Seventh-day Adventists every day. Members of the Yonkers church came to visit, and people in that hospital were a witness to a 'different' group of Christians. I wonder sometimes if anyone gave his or her life to Christ as a result of our witness. We were, after all, a 'peculiar people,' yet we did not act as though we were better than they were—we just were following God's directive to be lights shining in the darkness so that people could identify us as Christians by our outward appearance and mannerisms and that others might be inspired to learn more about Jesus Christ. I know that the Lord worked a miracle in my life. Who can doubt that there is a God after being completely healed from a life-threatening injury? I needed to have the relationship with Christ before the accident. All I had to do was accept His leading in my life and maintain a daily connection with Him. Praise the Lord for experiences that make a difference."

I am eternally grateful to have been blessed with three God-fearing children who are dedicated to trying to make a difference in the lives of others. Not only am I thankful for them, but I am also extremely grateful that they found spouses that have Christian values. Further, I am thankful that they are striving to rear their children, my grandchildren, in the fear and admonition of the Lord.

"Let me live in my house by the side of the road
Where the races of men go by—
They are good, they are bad, they are weak,
they are strong,
Wise, foolish—so am I.
Then why should I sit in the scorner's seat
Or hurl the cynic's ban?—
Let me live in my house by the side of the road
And be a friend to man."
—Sam Walter Foss

CHAPTER 17

POLITICAL REFLECTIONS

It is difficult for me to accept the fact that I have lived to be a part of twelve presidential administrations. The first president was Calvin Coolidge, our thirtieth president, 1925–1929. I was born during his administration, November 29, 1927, and did not recognize the direct impact his administration might have had on me at such an early age; however, I do know that we were right on the threshold of the Great Depression.

Calvin Coolidge was vacationing on his father's farm in Vermont when President Warren G. Harding died in 1923. The elder Coolidge, a notary public, administered the oath of office in the dining room. Never before had this ceremony been performed by such a minor official or by a president's father

In 1924 Coolidge was elected to a full four year term. He enjoyed great popularity and probably could have been re-elected, but he decided to retire. His terse announcement became his most famous statement: "I do not choose to run for President in 1928."

Americans respected the views of the close-mouthed Coolidge, although he seldom said anything very original or profound. His reputation for wisdom was based on dry wit and robust common sense. He issued few unnecessary public statements and rarely wasted a word.

The solemn, frugal Coolidge seemed to be a misfit from another era; but people voted for him even if they did not imitate his conduct. They cherished him for having the virtues of their pioneer forefathers.

The second president during my lifetime was President Herbert Hoover, 1929–1933, our thirty-first U.S. president. I am sure that there must have been some noteworthy accomplishments during his administration; however, the one thing that I can more closely relate to was the Great Depression. Whether one takes the position that he inherited it or created it, it was the most serious and devastating on the nation as a whole. This was a very difficult time for my parents, my siblings, and me. My paternal grandmother did domestic work and earned very little; however, she sacrificed to help my parents to get through that most difficult time. Every two weeks she would have the "rolling store" man drop off a 24-pound sack of flour to help us survive. It was like manna from heaven, and there was much rejoicing when these deliveries were made. Sometimes she would have the rolling store man to include some salt fish, also, and that added even more joy and excitement. My parents did not own an automobile at that time; however, many who did were financially unable to operate them. Consequently, they converted them to carts that were horse, mule, or ox-drawn. The carts were generally referred to as Hoover carts. Even though I consider this period as being the most difficult for our family, I am thankful that the Lord sustained us and enabled us to survive it. To God be the glory!

President Hoover expected prosperity to continue. "Ours is a land rich in resources...," he said in his inaugural address. "In no nation are the fruits of accomplishments more secure."

The U.S. had been building up to a crash for a long time. Other groups besides farmers had not shared in the prosperity of the 1920's. In the coal mining and textile manufacturing industries, for example, working conditions were poor and wages were low. The economy was also weakened by widespread buying on credit. Thousands of persons had borrowed money to pay for stocks. Stock prices soared to record heights. Then, in October, 1929, the stock market crashed. The Great Depression had begun.

At first persons believed that the Depression would not affect the entire nation. Many thought the stock market would recover in a few weeks or months; but by the end of 1929, the crash had caused losses estimated at $40 billion. The value of stocks listed on the New York Stock Exchange had dropped 40 per cent. Fortunes had been wiped out. Thousands of workers had lost their jobs.

Hoover told the people that they had no reason to fear, but economic conditions grew worse. By 1932, more than 12,000,000 Americans were out of work. Factories closed and banks failed. Thousands of persons lost their homes because they could not keep up the mortgage payments. Many families lived in clumps of shacks that became known as Hoovervilles.

The Great Depression affected other nations, too. Germany could not pay the 1931 installment on its World War I reparations.

Other countries also had difficulty paying their war debts. At Hoover's suggestion, Congress postponed all of these payments.

Hoover was reluctant to interfere with the American economy. He called the Depression "a temporary crisis in the prosperity of a great people."

Hoover had believed that the states and local communities should provide relief for jobless workers, but it became clear that the unemployed needed much more help. Congress authorized the Reconstruction Finance Corporation (RFC) to lend up to $300,000 to the states for relief.

Hoover supported many public works and conservation programs. In part, they were designed to help provide jobs.

In the 1932 general election, the Democrats attacked Hoover's leadership in the Depression. Roosevelt, the Democratic nominee, called for a "New Deal" for the American people. He promised to balance the budget, bring relief to the unemployed, help the farmers, and end prohibition. In the election, Roosevelt carried 42 of the 48 states. He won by an electoral vote majority of 472–59.

Franklin Delano Roosevelt, our thirty-second president, provided the leadership for getting us out of the Great Depression and getting our economy on a sound footing. I tend to identify him primarily with World War II. He was the stabilizing influence that the nation needed to guide us through those perilous times. I can vividly remember how we would gather around the radio, which was the first one my parents owned, a Silvertone, sold by Sears, Roebuck and Company, and listen to him address the nation. One bit of admonition that still stands out in my mind is that "we have nothing to fear, but fear itself."

There were many sacrifices to be made during his twelve years as president. Noteworthy examples included the rationing of sugar, gasoline,and automobile tires during World War II. Nevertheless, he was able to inspire the nation to march on to victory.

It was, indeed, a sad day when the news came over the radio that our beloved F.D.R. had passed away while vacationing at the "Little White House" in Warm Springs, Georgia. He was the first president to die while in office during my lifetime.

Franklin Delano Roosevelt served as president for more than 12 years, longer than any other man. He was the only president elected four times. Roosevelt led the nation through the worst depression and through our worst war. He died just 83 days after becoming president for the fourth time.

A new era in American history began under Roosevelt. He called his program the New Deal. For the first time, the federal government took strong action to help make the United States prosperous. Roosevelt said he wanted to help the average American, whom he called the "forgotten man." He promised relief for unemployed workers. He said he would aid farmers. Under his leadership, the government put stronger controls on business companies than ever before. It spent billions of dollars on relief and public works to "prime the pump" of business activity. Dozens of new government agencies were set up. Many were known by their initials such as CCC, TVA, WPA, and NRA. Roosevelt himself became widely known by his initials, F.D.R.

Probably no other president since Abraham Lincoln has been so bitterly hated or so deeply loved. Critics charged that Roosevelt's policies gave the federal government too much power. They accused him of taking over many rights that belonged to the states under the Constitution. Many Americans thought that government controls over business might destroy the free enterprise system and lead to socialism, but millions believed that Roosevelt was the friend and protector of the common man. Their faith was the key to his success in politics.

About three weeks before Roosevelt took office, a banking panic began. It spread throughout the country as anxious depositors hurried to their banks to get cash and gold. The panic created "runs" that ruined many banks. On the day before Roosevelt's inauguration, more than 5,000 banks were out of business.

On March 6, 1933, Roosevelt declared a "bank holiday." He closed all banks in the United States until officials of the Department of the Treasury could examine every bank's books. Banks in good financial condition were allowed to reopen. Those found in doubtful condition were kept closed until they could be put on a sound basis. Many banks that had been badly operated never opened again.

The President's action restored confidence and ended the bank crisis. People knew that if a bank opened its doors, it was safe. Few wished to withdraw their money from a bank they knew was sound.

The New Deal, as Roosevelt called his reform program, included a wide range of activities. The President described it as a "use of the authority of government as on organized form of self-help for all classes and groups and sections of our country."

In the winter of 1933–1934, the government started a relief program called the Civil Works Administration, CWA. The CWA supplied funds to local authorities, such as mayors of cities and governors of states. These funds made possible such public projects as building streets, roads, bridges, and schoolhouses, cleaning up parks, or doing other useful tasks. A number of persons criticized the CWA. They said many CWA employees merely raked leaves or held other useless jobs.

Roosevelt ended CWA after a few months, but other employment relief programs were more permanent. The Civilian Conservation Corp, CCC, operated from 1933 until 1942. The CCC gave work and training to 500,000 young men. It achieved great success with its programs of flood control, forestry, and soil conservation. The Works Progress Administration, WPA, was established in 1935 to provide work for persons without jobs. It employed an average of 2,000,000 workers annually between 1935 and 1941.

On Sunday, December 7, 1941, Secretary of State Hull conferred with two Japanese diplomats. While they talked, Japanese planes attacked the U.S. Pacific Fleet, which lay at anchor in Pearl Harbor.

President Roosevelt addressed Congress the next day. He said December 7 was a "date that will live in infamy." The United States declared war on Japan. Four days later, on December 11, Germany and Italy declared war on the United States. America then declared war on these countries.

Most Americans realized that the nation faced a serious situation. The war extended across both the Atlantic and Pacific Oceans. The navy had been crippled by the attack on Pearl Harbor, but the draft had given the army more than a million men with at least a year's military training.

A great decision confronted the President after Pearl Harbor. He had to decide where to strike first. On the West Coast, many people felt that Japan was the chief foe. In the East, many wanted Germany defeated first.

Roosevelt conferred with Churchill in the White House in December, 1941, and January, 1942. The two leaders realized that the United States could not strike an effective blow against Japan until the Navy had recovered from its losses at Pearl Harbor. In addition,

German scientists were developing new weapons that could mean defeat for the Allies. Both the British and the Russians wanted to see Germany defeated as soon as possible. For these reasons, Roosevelt and Churchill decided that Germany, the most powerful enemy nation, must be defeated first.

Roosevelt suggested the name United Nations for the alliance that fought Germany, Italy and Japan. This alliance formed the basis for the peacetime United Nations Organization that later was established in 1945.

On November 7, 1942, the Allies invaded North Africa. It was the greatest landing operation in history up to that time. After the landings began, Roosevelt spoke by radio to the French people in their own language. He explained that the Allies had to drive the Germans out of French territory in North Africa. Roosevelt was the first president to give a radio address in a foreign language.

President Roosevelt left the United States many times during the war for conferences with Allied leaders. He was the first president to leave the country in wartime.

Early in the war, the Russians asked for a "second front" against the Germans in Western Europe. Churchill believed the Allies should first attack the Germans in Africa or in other places where they were relatively weak. He also feared that Russia would take control of eastern Europe at the war. In November, 1943, the Big Three met at Teheran, Iran. During and after the conference, Roosevelt worked to get Churchill and Stalin to agree on major war aims. At Teheran, he refused to have lunch with Churchill before meeting with Stalin. The President did not want Stalin to think he and Churchill had made a separate agreement.

Many changes in the White House routine were made after the United States entered World War II. The Roosevelts reduced their entertaining. Wartime security regulations went into effect. Machine guns were set up on the White House roof, and Secret Service agents took over a special office in the East Wing. Engineers built a bomb shelter in the White House basement. Prime Minister Churchill, a frequent wartime visitor, had his own nap room on the second floor.

On March 29, 1945, the President left for a rest at Warm Springs. He had prepared a speech for broadcast on April 13. Roosevelt had written: "The only limit to our realization of tomorrow will be our doubts of today. Let us move forward with strong and active faith."

April 12 began as usual. The President read newspapers and mail that had been flown from Washington. He planned to attend a barbecue in the afternoon. Before the barbecue, Roosevelt was working at his desk while an artist, Mrs. Elisabeth Schoumatoff, painted his portrait. Suddenly, he fell over in his chair. "I have a terrific headache," he whispered. These were Roosevelt's last words. He died a few hours later of a cerebral hemorrhage. As news of his death spread, a crowd gathered in front of the White House, silent with grief. Millions of people in all parts of the world mourned the dead president.

Harry S. Truman became President at one of the most critical moments in American history. He had been Vice-President for only 83 days when President F. D. R. died on April 12, 1945. World War II still had to be won. Plans to establish the United Nations organization had just been started. Prior to becoming Vice-President, Truman was known mainly for his work as chief of a wartime senate investigating committee that had saved millions of dollars in military contracts.

President Truman, our thirty-third president, proved himself to be a very capable successor to F. D. R. It was he who made the decision to drop the atomic bomb on Hiroshima and Nagasaki to end World War II. It was his responsibility to get the nation back on a peacetime basis and to rebuild Europe. His foreign policy, Truman Doctrine, was very successful. The Marshall Plan was very instrumental in helping Europe recover from the devastation of World War II.

The G.I. Bill for veterans was a significant accomplishment and tens of thousands of veterans took advantage of it by returning to school and earning college degrees or vocational skills. Personally, I consider the desegregation of the Armed Forces by executive order as one of the major accomplishments of President Truman. It was a very bold and courageous act on his part, and it has had far-reaching implications. Another unusual act on President Truman's part was the firing of General Douglas MacArthur as a result of differences over military strategy during the Korean conflict.

The Missouri Democrat met the challenges of his presidency with courage, determination, and imagination. During the first few weeks of his administration, the Allies won victory in Europe. Truman then made one of the most awesome decisions ever considered by one man—to use the powerful new atomic bomb against Japan to end World War II.

Truman faced other great problems throughout his years in the White House. The United States had to reorganize its economy from a wartime to a peacetime basis. Many war-torn countries needed large relief programs. To meet these challenges, Truman's administration created such far reaching programs as the Truman Doctrine, the Marshall Plan, the Point Four Program, and the North Atlantic Treaty Organization, NATO.

The Korean War began on June 25, 1950. Communist forces from North Korea invaded South Korea. The United Nations demanded that North Korea withdraw. Truman decided to intervene to save South Korea's independence. On June 27 he announced that he had sent U.S. planes and ships to help South Korea. Congress cheered the announcement. That same day, the UN approved sending troops of other nations to join South Korea and American units. Truman ordered ground forces to South Korea on June 30. He later said that sending U. S. troops to South Korea and thus taking the risk of starting World War III was the hardest decision of his political career.

General Douglas MacArthur commanded all UN forces in Korea. His troops brought most of Korea under UN control by October 1950, but later that month, Chinese Communist troops joined the North Koreans. Truman recognized the urgency of the situation and put the United States on a semi-war basis. MacArthur wanted to attack Chinese Communists bases in Manchuria, but Truman believed that fighting must be confined to Korea and not be allowed to spread into a possible global war. As I recall, President Truman's policy was to restrict our fighting to the 38th parallel line and not to cross it. General MacArthur felt that he should have been able to pursue the enemy across it. Consequently, as Commander-in-Chief, President Truman relieved him of his command. In April, 1951, Truman dismissed MacArthur, creating a nationwide furor. MacArthur accepted his dismissal with dignity by stating, "Old solders never die, they just slowly fade away."

On November 1, 1950, two Puerto Rican nationalists tried to invade Blair House and assassinate the President. They killed one Secret Service guard and wounded another. One of the gunmen was killed and the other captured. Truman commented that "A president has to expect those things." He kept all his appointments that day and took his usual walk the next morning.

While in the White House, early every morning, often as early as 5:30 A.M., Truman arose and went for a brisk walk, always accompanied by Secret Service agents and newsmen.

At the White House, Truman often played the piano for visitors and particularly enjoyed the music of Chopin and Mozart.

Another memory that I recall was the sign that he kept on his desk, "The buck stops here." The message that this sign conveyed was indicative of his style of leadership during his administration.

General Dwight David Eisenhower became our thirty-fourth president and the first Republican president in twenty years. He was a very popular war hero and was affectionately known as "Ike." Eisenhower became president eight years after serving as Supreme Allied Commander in Europe and leading the Allied armies to victory during World War II. As a General, he commanded the largest army in history. As President, he dedicated himself to fighting for peace.

Eisenhower was a two-term president, 1953–1961, and played a major role in the implementation of the 1954 U. S. Supreme Court desegregation decree outlawing segregation. The most drastic action in this connection was the use of the National Guard in Little Rock, Arkansas. It was not a popular move for him, but he took it so the safety of the Black students could be maintained. It required the presence of troops for a long period; but in the end, the mission was accomplished. In my opinion, this action sent a strong message to the states still resisting the desegregation of their public schools that it would be done either voluntarily or by force. These were, indeed, turbulent times because attitudes had to be changed; and that took time. Even today there still remain some who do not accept the change from a dual school system to a unitary school system as mandated by the U.S. Supreme Court decision on May 17, 1954. All kinds of efforts have been made to circumvent it; but, by and large, it has been implemented in spite of the strong opposition to it.

In September, 1957, Eisenhower sent federal troops to Little Rock, Arkansas, to enforce school integration. Governor Orval F. Faubus had defied a 1954 Supreme Court order to end segregation of Blacks and Whites in public schools. Faubus ordered the Arkansas National Guard to bar Black students from Central High School. He warned that rioting would break out if Blacks were admitted to the school. Eisenhower tried to persuade Faubus to enforce the law and prevent rioting. The President finally sent troops to protect the Black students.

Even though "Ike" had been Supreme Commander of Allied Forces during World War II, he was very reluctant to send troops to enforce school integration and only did it as a last resort. Even though it was another thirteen years before integration came to Early County, I admired his courage on making an unpopular decision.

Our thirty-fifth president, John F. Kennedy, was indeed an inspiration to me. I particularly liked his inaugural address in which he challenged his fellow Americans to "Ask not what your country can do for you; ask what you can do for your country." He continued by saying, "My fellow citizens of the world: ask not what America will do for you, but what together we can do for the freedom of man." He concluded by saying, "Whether you are a citizen of America or of the world, ask of us here the same high standards of strength and sacrifice that we ask of you. With a good conscience our only sure reward, with history the final judge of our deeds, let us go forth to lead the land we love, asking His blessing and His help, but knowing that here on earth God's work must truly be our own." In my opinion this challenge and the persuasive oratory in his delivery really motivated the nation and the world to unite in making America and the world a better place in which to live.

I also applauded the courageous stand that he took in demanding that Khrushchev take Russian missiles out of Cuba, even though it could have meant war. Fortunately, Mr. Khrushchev backed down, and the missiles were removed.

I believe that his most innovative idea was the creation of the Peace Corps in 1961. Its mission is to teach people in developing countries about America, to expose Americans to other cultures, and to work together for the common good. It now functions in 70 countries, with more than 6,000 trainees. It turns down two applicants for every one it accepts today. According to its former director, Paul Coverdell, a former Georgia state senator, "The Peace Corps is a vibrant, vital part of the U.S. foreign policy." He further stated that, "Today's Peace Corps is different. The average age is around 31, versus 24 in the 1960's. The skill level is up. It's equally balanced between male and female—in the 60's, it was mostly male. Recruiting and training are far more sophisticated, and throughout the world the

Peace Corps has earned the kind of support that emanates from real respect."

It has been observed that "it's a shame how much of the money provided in our foreign aid programs never gets to the people; it ends up in somebody's Swiss bank account. The Peace Corps gets more done on its individual, village-by-village level than most of these huge programs. It's too bad Washington doesn't realize one fact: The Peace Corps is the best foreign aid program we have."

There were numerous other noteworthy accomplishments during the Kennedy administration; however, it all came to a tragic and abrupt end on Friday afternoon, November 22, 1963 when an assassin, Lee Harvey Oswald, killed him while riding in a motorcade in Dallas, Texas, en route to a speaking engagement. I very vividly remember being in my office at Washington High School and one of my teachers, Mr. Clyde Mackey, came in and informed me that one of his home-room students, who had skipped school that day, was listening to his transistor radio and heard that President Kennedy had been shot. I sort of shrugged it off as not being true. Nevertheless, I turned on the radio on the intercom system; and very much to my dismay, it was indeed confirmed. By that time, all of the major networks were carrying an account of it. It was a most traumatic experience for our nation. My heart ached for his wife, Jackie, and children, Caroline and John, Jr., along with the entire Kennedy family. I was especially moved when I saw the T.V. picture of J.F.K.'s blood on Jackie's clothing.

Through all of the confusion and turmoil that followed, the wheels of government continued to turn. Shortly after the confirmation of President Kennedy's death, Vice President Lyndon Baines Johnson was sworn into office as the nation's thirty-sixth president. The ceremony took place aboard Air Force One while en route to Washington, D.C., with the slain president's body and his grieving widow on board.

I will never forget that tragic weekend. Herk, Michael, Cheryl, and Wayne, along with millions of other Americans were practically glued to the TV as the history-making events unfolded. To our surprise and amazement that following Sunday, Jack Ruby forced his way through the policemen and shot Lee Harvey Oswald to death, right before our eyes, as he was being transferred from one jail to another.

On Monday, November 25, 1963, the body of our beloved thirty-fifth president, John Fitzgerald Kennedy, was laid to rest. Prior to the burial it had lain in state in the Capital Rotunda as thousands paid their last respects. The procession to Arlington National Cemetery was indeed a moving experience, the heads of states from many countries taking part. The riderless horse, symbolizing the slain president, was a very solemn and sad experience as my family and I watched vicariously. This day was declared a national holiday; consequently, there was no school, which enabled us to observe every moment of the historical events.

As for Jack Ruby, he was tried in a court of law in 1964 and found guilty of murdering Lee Harvey Oswald; however, in 1966 the decision was reversed on the grounds that illegal testimony had been allowed. A new trial was scheduled for 1967, but Ruby died before the case could be tried.

There was much controversy about whether or not the assassin was Lee Harvey Oswald or a Russian spy who had used his identity; however, in 1981, a team of medical experts exhumed his body and in their opinion, confirmed that, in fact, Lee Harvey Oswald was the assassin.

John Fitzgerald Kennedy is the only U. S. president to be assassinated while in office during my lifetime. I hope and pray that there will never be another.

Our thirty-sixth president, Lyndon Baines Johnson, came into office under very difficult circumstances, as the nation was still mourning the loss of its young and energetic thirty-fifth president, John F. Kennedy; however, he was able to make a smooth transition, and the government continued without any significant disruption.

He faced unprecedented civil unrest during the civil rights struggle; however, he succeeded in getting Congress to pass the most comprehensive voting rights bill to date. He labeled his programs as "The Great Society." Education fared extremely well during his administration and the Entitlement programs were passed in Public Law 89-10. Included were "Head Start" for preschoolers and Title 1 funds for elementary and secondary students. As a former teacher, he was able to relate to the needs and problems of education. In my opinion, education was the centerpiece of his administration.

The Vietnam War proved to have been "a millstone around his neck," so to speak. After much agonizing, he decided not to seek re-election to a full term of office in 1969.

President Richard M. Nixon became our thirty-seventh president. He had served as Vice President in the Eisenhower administration. There were many positive accomplishments during his administration. The most noteworthy, in my opinion, was the improved relations with China. His efforts in this endeavor laid the foundation for the present diplomatic relations presently existing between the U. S. and China.

Unfortunately, the "Watergate" crisis cast a dark shadow over the second term of his administration. Several high ranking officials on his staff were prosecuted and convicted of crimes stemming from their involvement in that scandal. After much in-depth investigation, including televised hearings, President Nixon finally saw the "handwriting on the wall" and resigned so that he could avoid impeachment and the nation could return to normalcy. The resignation was submitted on August 8, 1974 and became effective at noon August 9, 1974. It was indeed a sad day for me as I watched him on TV as he bade farewell to the nation and he and his family boarded Air Force One for his last flight home. Thus far, he is the only U.S. president to be forced out of office in my life time.

Because of the circumstances surrounding his resignation, he has kept a very low profile as a former president, with the exception of authoring several books.

Vice President Gerald Ford became the nation's thirty-eighth president and served out the remainder of President Nixon's term. In my opinion, his major priority was to put "Watergate" behind us and thus allow the American people's political wounds to heal. I believe that he was rather successful in that endeavor. One of President Ford's first major actions after becoming President was to grant a presidential pardon to former President Nixon for his role in the Watergate scandal. This action was very controversial; and I personally did not agree with it. The Republican party nominated him to be its candidate in 1976; however, he was defeated by Jimmy Carter, the Democratic nominee. Although President Ford left the office with dignity, he chose a low profile for himself as one of our living U.S. presidents. President Ford served at a very crucial period in our nation's history as a result of the divisiveness and despair that gripped our nation as brought about by the Watergate scandal.

Jimmy Carter, a peanut farmer, from Plains, Georgia, became our thirty-ninth president. He had a degree from the U.S. Naval

Academy and had been a state senator and governor from our state of Georgia. He really put Plains and the state of Georgia on the map, so to speak.

At the beginning of his campaign, he faced a problem of name recognition, and people would frequently say "Jimmy who?" Even though he had not held a national office, he hit the ground running and took his campaign to practically every state in the nation. Herk, the children, and I visited Plains and the railroad station that he had used as his campaign headquarters. Tourists were there in droves, and the majority of their vehicles displayed out of state license plates. It was, indeed, an exciting time.

Not only did he go on to win the Democratic nomination in 1976, but also defeated President Gerald Ford, who was the Republican nominee. He was the perfect example of a small-town boy having made good.

His religious affiliation was Southern Baptist, and he was an excellent Sunday School teacher.

I also admired his mother, who was living at the time. She was affectionately known as "Miz Lillian" and worked in Blakely in the Blakely Convalescent Nursing Home. When most people were retiring and looking forward to taking it easy, she enlisted in the Peace Corps and served in India.

On President Carter's inauguration day, I was very much impressed when he and his wife Rosalyn ordered the chauffeur of the presidential limousine to stop, at which time they got out and walked with the people during the remainder of the parade route.

President Carter made a lot of enemies right up front when he got rid of all the hard liquor frequently served at many White House social functions. It was not a popular move for him, and many never forgave him; however, I personally appreciated his having the courage to take such an uncompromising position. Being a teetotaler himself, this enabled him to practice what he preached.

Black Americans were especially inspired by his commitment to human rights for all mankind. I appreciated his appointment of Andrew Young as our UN Ambassador.

In my opinion, the media was very unfair to President Carter in overplaying any event that could cast him in an unfavorable light. On the other hand, when his successor, President Ronald Reagan came along, it was just the opposite. I still feel that some of the negative attitudes stemmed from President Carter's stand on the liquor issue and his life style in general while in the White House.

Personally, I believe that history will confirm President Carter as one of our great U.S. presidents. There were major events during his administration over which he had no control, including the oil cartel and the major energy crisis. Also, the fall of the Shah of Iran was followed by the taking of American hostages. Inflation spiraled to double digit levels as a result of the energy situation.

He deserves much credit for his innovative measures implemented for energy conservation. In fact, they worked so well that the oil crisis was short lived. His uncompromising dedication to human rights worldwide endeared him to the hearts of many. His leadership also resulted in our giving back the Panama Canal to the Panamanian people.

In my opinion, one of his most noteworthy accomplishments while in office was the Camp David Accord worked out with the late Ansuar Sadat and M. Begin. It did not resolve all of the existing problems between these two leaders, but it was a giant step in that direction.

President Carter's brother Billy's intemperate life style was often potentially embarrassing to him. Nevertheless, he never publicly reprimanded him for the image that he portrayed by his intemperate life style. I thought that really spoke well for the president in that they were complete opposites. Although he did not condone what his brother did, he did not display a "holier than thou" attitude about it.

As an ex-president, Mr. Carter has remained totally committed to the same ideals he advocated during his campaign and while in office. He and his wife Rosalyn are very actively involved as Volunteers for Habitat for Humanity, a group that builds housing for the poor. The Carter Center supports agricultural and health programs in impoverished countries around the world.

In my opinion, President Carter is the most active and involved of all of our former presidents. Since he proved to be sincere in his commitment to human rights while president, leaders of undeveloped nations still trust him and respect him. This has enabled him to conduct diplomatic missions others found too daunting.

Although opinions may differ on Mr. Carter's contributions during his presidency from 1977 to 1981, several presidential scholars agree that his work at the Center is unprecedented.

He has not been content with going into retirement and just writing his memoirs. He could start a new chapter that could be titled: "The Legacy of the Carter Center."

"It's going to encourage future presidents to take more seriously their ongoing public service obligations," said Dr. Loch Johnson of the University of Georgia.

The Center's success has surprised even Mr. Carter. "I never dreamed that the Carter Center would be so expansive in its operations or successful in its projects," he said. "The Center is unique because it doesn't try to duplicate what others are doing, it maintains objectivity in politics, and its projects aren't done just for academic purposes."

Having an active former president at its helm also helps. Mr. Carter spends about 10 days a month there and uses his influence to undertake such projects as freeing political prisoners and fighting hunger and disease in developing countries.

The Center's accomplishments include:
1. Monitoring democratic elections in Panama, Nicaragua, Zambia, Haiti, Guyana and other countries.
2. Helping increase the immunization rate of the world's children from 20 to 80 percent over the past five years.
3. Helping 150,000 families in Ghana, Nigeria, Togo, Benin, and Tanzania increase food production by conducting agricultural training programs.
4. Helping prevent River Blindness, a disease caused by flies by distributing the drug Mectizan to 26 African nations.
5. Helping prevent Guinea Worm disease by distributing water filters and holding ongoing preventive programs. The debilitating disease, which affects 3 million people annually, is transmitted through water contaminated by worm larvae.

I am still very proud of our former president and admire him for his accomplishments in local, state, national and international levels of government. In many respects I can see a parallel in his life and mine in that he also "bucked the odds" and won in spite of the difficulties that he encountered.

Ronald Reagan became our fortieth president after defeating President Carter in the 1980 General Election. In my opinion, his defeat of former President Carter stemmed primarily from his failure to gain the release of the Iran hostages before the election. I believe that if the rescue mission had succeeded, former President Carter would have been re-elected. Nevertheless, that was not to be; and we will never know how different things might have been had he won a second term.

In the case of President Reagan, they were complete opposites, President Carter being a "hands-on" type of president, whereas President Reagan was more or less a "hands-off" president. In my opinion, many of his subordinates took advantage of his administrative style of handling the nation's business and did not always do what was in his best interest, as well as that of the country's. Consequently, his administration was plagued with corruption, including the Iran Contra fiasco. As of this writing, at least two of his most trusted senior staff members, namely, Lt. Col. Oliver North and Admiral John Poindexter, have been convicted in a court of law for their part in that very complicated operation.

It really bothers me to see our top governmental officials commit perjury, shred documents, and do other things that are not in the best interest of the American people. In my opinion, it is worthy of note that President Reagan called Lt. Col. North a hero.

President Reagan consistently stated that he could not remember what happened with regards to the weapons sold to Iran. This seems to me to have contradicted what his subordinates, Lt. Col North and Adm. John Poindexter said. I doubt that we will ever know the real truth about this very complicated affair. Nevertheless, I trust that we will learn from it and will be spared a repetition of anything like this in the future.

Another concern that I had about President Reagan's tenure in office was the extent that astrology might have influenced his decisions. This seemed to have been an ongoing activity handled by First Lady, Nancy Reagan; and I really wonder to what extent it was in the country's best interest.

In my opinion, Blacks did not fare very well during the Reagan years in that he did not seem to relate to our problems. Consequently, affirmative action programs were curtailed.

In spite of all the negative things that happened during the Reagan administration, he was very popular with the American people in general. Many referred to him as "the great communicator." His strength in this area was a very definite asset to him and enabled him to get away with things that he otherwise would have had to face.

Reagan first won public office in 1966 when he was elected Governor of California. He defeated Democratic Governor Edmond Pat Brown by a landslide.

In 1968 Reagan campaigned briefly for the Republican presidential nomination but did not win. In 1975 he tried again. He attracted much support among conservatives and won many delegates in the South and West, but Reagan lost the nomination to President Gerald R. Ford.

Reagan soon began to plan his campaign for the 1980 nomination. By November, 1979, when he announced his candidacy, he had a huge lead in the polls over his Republican rivals.

In July, 1980, Reagan easily won the nomination for president on the first ballot at the Republican National Convention in Detroit. At his request, George Bush was nominated for Vice President.

Reagan defeated Jimmy Carter in the General Election by a wide margin. Reagan carried 44 states for a total of 489 electoral votes, while President Carter carried only 6 states and the District of Columbia for 49 electoral votes.

It is interesting that after Ronald Reagan had tried for so long to get himself elected president of the United States, he was almost cut down by an assassin's bullet shortly after taking office. John Hinckley shot him with a Devastator bullet, which miraculously did not explode. It was finally found a quarter of an inch from his heart. His daughter Pati said in her book, "Without divine intervention, I don't know if he would have survived." I agree with her and I'm glad that the Lord did see fit to spare her father's life.

In 1982 and 1983 millions of Americans, especially Blacks, suffered from unemployment and reduction in social programs. Many people contended that Reagan's chief goal was to aid the rich, but a number of wealthy Americans criticized the President for supporting the tax increases. In addition, many business executives objected to the record deficits.

In October, 1983, explosives set off by a terrorist collapsed a four-story Marine headquarters building at the airport of Beirut, Lebanon's capital. A total of 241 U.S. troops died as a result of this explosion.

Also, in October, 1983, Reagan ordered the invasion of the Caribbean island of Grenada after Grenadian rebels overthrew the island's government. Reagan said the invasion was needed to protect the lives of Americans who were in Grenada, including almost 600 students at St. George's University School of Medicine. Reagan also said Cuba planned to use Grenada as a military base.

The one trait that President Reagan possessed that I consider to be extremely worthy of note was his stick-to-itiveness. He had sought the office of U.S. Presidency for several years before finally succeeding in 1980. By that time he had become an old man, but he did not let his age discourage him; thus, he succeeded in becoming our oldest president while in office. I believe that there is a lesson in this experience for all of us, and that is to never give up the pursuit of our goals when disappointments come along. Rather, we should persevere in spite of seemingly insurmountable odds. After all, we are admonished that the race is not to the swift nor to the strong but to him who holds out and endures to the end.

George Herbert Walker Bush came into office as the forty-first president of the United States with an impeccable record. Highlights include the following:

He volunteered for service in the U.S. Navy at age 18 and became a fighter pilot during World War II, during which time he was awarded the distinguished Flying Cross. He served as U. S representative to the United Nations, ambassador to China, congressman from Texas for two terms, Director of CIA for several years, Vice President of the U. S. for two terms during the Reagan administration, and became the Republican Party's presidential nominee in 1988. He waged a hard fought campaign and defeated Michael Dukakis, the Democratic party's nominee, by a landslide.

One noteworthy thing that he did that I especially appreciated was that he chose Louis Sullivan to be his Secretary of Health, Education, and Human Services. At the time of his appointment, Dr. Sullivan was serving as President of the Morehouse Medical School. He served President Bush with honor and brought much favorable publicity to Blakely, his home town. He had the opportunity to return to Blakely and address the 1991 graduating class of Early County High School. He recalled his own childhood in Blakely, Georgia, and the difficulties his parents encountered in rearing a family in the rural segregated South of the 1940's and 50's.

He went on to say that "Even though our family lacked many material goods, we did not consider ourselves poor. There was a richness which came from a caring community and two loving parents."

Dr. Sullivan who was the only Black member of President Bush's cabinet, said Black men have been " beaten down" by job discrimination, underemployment, and joblessness. They have been robbed of "hope for improving their condition and providing a better life for their children."

Sullivan also made a plea for less casual sex and violence on television and in the movies. "Today I call upon the media to turn down the volume on irresponsible sex and reckless violence," he said.

He called on parents to pay more attention to the messages their children were receiving from television, films and music, arguing that the media were giving young people twisted lessons about how to conduct their lives.

Again, I applaud President Bush for having the vision and courage to appoint Dr. Sullivan to his cabinet. His service in that capacity really put Early County and Blakely on the map. In my opinion, it will be a long time before Early County has another Cabinet member in Washington.

During President Bush's administration he only had the opportunity to make only one appointment to the U.S. Supreme Court, namely, Clarence Thomas. He became a very controversial nominee when Professor Anita Hill, a former colleague of his, accused him of sexual harassment. Nevertheless, his confirmation survived; and he became the successor to Justice Thurgood Marshall, the first Black to serve on the U. S. Supreme Court.

It was also during the administration of President Bush that the Berlin Wall came down on November 9, 1989. This set in motion the reunification of East and West Germany.

In my opinion, President Bush lost much of his credibility when he broke his "no new taxes" pledge. He was very emphatic about it and said in no uncertain terms "read my lips-no-new-taxes."

To his credit he received and deserved very high marks for his bold leadership in the conduct of the Persian Gulf war. As a result, his approval rating in the opinion polls was at an all-time high. At that point in his presidency, he appeared unbeatable for his election to a second term.

The Republicans chose him as their party's nominee, after which he ran a very negative campaign against the Democratic nominee, Bill Clinton. A major issue in the campaign was the economy. Many feel that it was a very significant factor in his defeat by Bill Clinton.

On Wednesday, January 20, shortly after President Clinton had taken the oath of office, George Bush returned to his adopted hometown of Houston, Texas, where he says he will go into the "grandchild business"; but he will also help set up his presidential library at Texas A & M University and will probably write his memoirs. Workers are remodeling an 11,000 square feet office that will be his official office. Sig Rogich, a media advisor, predicted that Mr. Bush would find a way to play a role as "a world statesman because he is still full of ideas and energy."

President Bill Clinton is the forty-second president to serve in that office.

I have observed him very closely from the time that he declared himself a candidate for the democratic nomination. Even though there were many attempts by the media to tarnish his character, he did not let them cause him to take his "eye off the prize," so to speak. Instead, he would shrug off the attempts and move on toward his goal.

He came from a very humble beginning in Hope, Arkansas, and is the product of a dysfunctional home. His accomplishments reaffirm my confidence in the "American Dream." Only in America could this happen.

After winning his party's nomination he chose Al Gore, Jr., as his vice-presidential running mate; and they conducted a very aggressive campaign. Throughout the campaign he was attacked for not having served in the military. Nevertheless, he did not allow these attacks to cause him to falter. That was a character trait that I especially liked.

The following are excerpts from President Clinton's inaugural address:

"My fellow citizens: Today, we celebrate the mystery of American renewal....

"On behalf of our nation, I salute my predecessor, President Bush, for his half century of service to America, and I thank the millions of men and women whose steadfastness and sacrifice triumphed over depression, fascism, and communism.

"Today, a generation raised in the shadows of the Cold War assumes new responsibilities in a world warmed by the sunshine of freedom but threatened still by ancient hatreds and new plagues....

"When George Washington first took the oath I have just sworn to uphold, news traveled slowly across the land by horseback and across the ocean by boat. Now, the sights and sounds of this ceremony are broadcast instantaneously to billions around the world....

"We know we have to face hard truths and take strong steps. But we have not done so. Instead, we have drifted, and that drifting has eroded our resources, fractured our economy and shaken our confidence.

"Though our challenges are fearsome, so are our strengths. Americans have ever been a restless, questing, hopeful people. And we must bring to our task today the vision and will of those who came before us....

"We must do what no generation has had to do before. We must invest more in our own people, in their jobs and in their future, and at the same time cut our massive debt. And we must do so in a world in which we must compete for every opportunity.

"It will not be easy; it will require sacrifice. But it can be done, and done fairly, not choosing sacrifice for its own sake, but for our own sake. We must provide for our nation the way a family provides for its children....

"We must do what America does best: offer more opportunity to all and demand more responsibility from all.

"It is time to break the bad habit of expecting something for nothing, from our government or from each other. Let us all take more responsibility not only for ourselves and our families but for our communities and our country....

"Today, as an old order passes, the new world is more free but less stable. Communism's collapse has called forth old animosities and new dangers. Clearly, America must continue to lead the world we did so much to make....

"Our hopes, our hearts, our hands are with those on every continent who are building democracy and freedom. Their cause is America's cause....

"Today, we do more than celebrate America; we rededicate ourselves to the very idea of America:

"An idea born in revolution and renewed through two centuries of challenge;

"An idea tempered by the knowledge that, but for fate, we—the fortunate and the unfortunate—might have been each other;

"An idea ennobled by the faith that our nation can summon from its myriad diversities the deepest measure of unity;

"An idea infused with the conviction that America's long heroic journey must go forever upward.

"And so my fellow Americans, as we stand at the edge of the 21st century, let us begin with energy and hope with faith and discipline, and let us work until our work is done. The Scripture says, 'And let us not be weary in well-doing for in due season we shall reap, if we faint not.'

"From this joyful mountain top of celebration, we hear a call to service in the valley.

"We have heard the trumpets. We have changed the guard. And now—each in our own way, and with God's help—we must answer the call."

In my opinion, President Clinton hit the ground running and did not waste any time before beginning to address some of the many problems facing him. Many of these problems are very controversial; the most notable thus far appears to be his proposal to lift the ban on gays, homosexuals, serving in the military. Other major problems being addressed by the new president are national health reform and the economy.

Even though not everyone shares my view, I appreciate the way the President and the First Lady, Hillary, work together as a team. I think this is especially germane in times like these when our traditional family values are eroding at an alarming degree. President Clinton's appointment of the First Lady to chair the Task Force on National Health Reform is indicative of his confidence in her ability to get the job done. I wish her well as she supports the efforts of the President.

Realistically, I believe we have come to a point in history where many of the problems faced by our President and other world leaders are simply beyond man's ability to solve. Nevertheless, I applaud our President for "giving it his best shot" as he struggles to find solutions for unprecedented problems.

I believe President Clinton's choice of Mike Espy, from Yazoo City, Mississippi, as Secretary of Agriculture was a good one. In my opinion, he is sensitive to problems of our farmers and is off to a good beginning. I wish him well in his challenging job.

The Lord has blessed me to experience and witness a lot of historical events during my lifetime, for which I am indeed thankful. In my opinion, we must be living in the time of the end when the Bible says..."Many shall run to and fro, and knowledge shall be increased."

Daniel 12:4. I believe that in spite of man's best efforts, there will be no lasting peace until Christ, the Prince of Peace, intervenes.

President Clinton commissioned the Black poet, Maya Angelou, to write a special poem for his inauguration. The following are excerpts:

> "History, despite its wrenching pain,
> Cannot be unlived, and if faced
> With courage, need not be lived again.
> Lift up your eyes upon
> The day breaking for you.
> Give birth again
> To the dream.
> Women, children, men,
> Take it into the palms of your hands.
> Mold it into the shape of your most
> Private need. Sculpt it into
> The image of your most public self.
> Lift up your hearts.
> Each new hour holds new chances
> For new beginnings.
> Do not be wedded forever
> To fear, yoked eternally
> To brutishness.
> The horizon leans forward,
> Offering you space to place new steps of change.
> Here, on the pulse of this fine day,
> You may have the courage
> To look up and out upon me, the
> Rock, the River, the Tree, your country.
> No less to Midas than the mendicant.
> No less to you now than the mastodon then.
> Here on the pulse of this new day,
> You may have the grace to look up and out
> And into your sister's eyes into
> Your brother's face, your country,
> And say simply,
> Very simply,
> With hope,
> Good morning."
> —Maya Angelou

CHAPTER 18

AGRIRAMA

One of the highest honors bestowed upon me thus far was my appointment to the Georgia Agrirama Development Authority by former Governor Joe Frank Harris on January 25, 1985. The swearing-in ceremony was held in the Governor's office and was witnessed by Representative Ralph Balkcom and Senator Jimmy Hodge Timmons, both from Blakely. I was informed that I had been recommended by them and that Governor Harris accepted this recommendation. I have really enjoyed my service as a member of the Authority and have had the opportunity to meet and interact with a lot of prominent individuals that I would not have met otherwise.

Former Governor Harris appointed me to a second four year term, which expired January 25, 1993. I am the only member of the Authority who happens to be Black. I was cordially received by my peers and trust that I have been an asset to the Authority.

Before becoming a member of this body, I did not know very much about the Agrirama. Presently, as a result of the insight gained during the past eight years, I can highly recommend it to anyone who would like to experience what life was like in rural Georgia during the period of 1870–1910. I have visited the museum many times, and I have never become bored. Even though I do not consider myself to be a very old person, I find that I am able to relate to many of the things that make up the Living History Museum.

The Georgia Agrirama Development Authority consists of fifteen members, including Tommy Irvin, Georgia Secretary of Agriculture; Max Cleland, Georgia Secretary of State; and Bobby Rowan, member of the Georgia Public Service Commission.

In the Georgia Agrirama's annual report of 1989, this was said about the Agrirama:

"Long before Georgia created its museum in Tifton, private interests and public officials were realizing the need to preserve the state's agricultural heritage. Thus began a joint effort to preserve,

Former Governor Joe Frank Harris of Georgia administering the oath of office to Charles A. Harris and John R. Harris for a four-year term on the Georgia Agrirama Board of Directors, January 25, 1985

exhibit and demonstrate the history of one of the nation's leading agricultural states.

"Late in the 1960's, plans for the Georgia Agrirama began to take shape. The Georgia General Assembly, with support from the Governor, provided public funds for a development plan, site preparation, utilities, basic buildings and general operations. While these funds were used to build a drainage system, lay water lines, and shape a landscape for small farmsteads and a rural town, private citizens contributed regional artifacts to create a distinguished living history museum.

"Around the State, primitive farm machinery was rusting away. Tools and furnishings of frontier generations—butter churns, iron stoves, rope beds, quilts, and other valuable household items—were hidden away in dark attics or being damaged by the hot Georgia sun. Here and there stood abandoned railroad passenger stations, Victorian-style houses, and log homes often covered by rough-sawn board and batten lumber. Unpainted, muleless barns and wooden fence rails dotted the rural South Georgia landscape waiting for those who saw the need to rescue these agricultural artifacts of 18th and 19th century Georgia.

"The long-outdated machinery of the cotton era and the sawmilling and turpentining industries, all of which transformed the 'Wiregrass' region of Georgia after the Civil War, rested under rusting, tin-covered structures.

"Cotton gins, steam boilers, large circular saws and the log carriages which fed them, huge iron kettles for making syrup or turpentine, and unused farm equipment of every size and shape seemed to invite acquisition by history-minded people.

"Because people were willing to donate the family-owned treasures of their ancestors, the Georgia Agrirama has developed one of the nation's largest collections of agricultural artifacts from the 19th and 20th centuries.

"The monumental task of acquiring, disassembling, moving and restoring hundreds of artifacts, buildings and pieces of antiquated machinery resulted in the partnership venture of private citizens and public officials to create Georgia's Living History Museum.

"However, this exciting endeavor includes more than the donation of artifacts, buildings, land, and money. Volunteers assist the museum in its interpretive programs and operations.

"In any given year, 200 to 300 volunteers join with the personnel of the Georgia Agrirama to provide educational services, produce exhibits, and demonstrate crafts.

"While this partnership has resulted in substantial achievements, the venture is not yet complete. The State and its citizens are challenged to continue these cooperative efforts.

"The Georgia Agrirama appreciates the many people and companies who have given unselfishly of their time, energy, and money to further the preservation of Georgia's agricultural heritage."

There are a variety of classes offered at the Agrirama. Some of those classes are as follows:

"1. *The Living History Workshop* is an intensive, all-day program that provides a 'hands-on' experience for your students. Dressed in costumes of the era, students may work and eat as South Georgians did a century ago. Designed for a maximum of 25 students in grades 5 through 12, Living History Workshops are held year-round. Lunch is cooked over the open hearth and on the wood-burning stove. The teacher and one adult per 10 students are admitted free. The teacher, however does not participate in this workshop. Audio-visual and printed curriculum materials will be sent in advance; with adequate preparation time, some classes larger than 25 may be accommodated.

"2. *A Day In A One-Room School* provides a unique combination of 1890's teaching techniques with current objectives called for in Georgia's Quality Basic Education Act. Headquartered in the one-room Sand Hill School on Georgia Agrirama's historic site, the workshop offers lessons in reading, writing, arithmetic, and more. The teacher does participate by instructing the students, and curriculum packets to assist in lesson planning will be sent in advance. The program is open to all grades and Agrirama education personnel will be at the school to aid with the classroom portion of the workshops. Both teacher and students will be costumed to participate in the workshop experience. Classes are also encouraged to tour the historic site for an overview of life in the 19th century.

"3. *A Visit To The Past Group Tour* offers a general school tour of some two hours. Historic site interpreters in costume will share their skills as they discuss the history of life in the 1890's with your students. Included on the tour will be the 19th century Georgia Agrirama drug store, the printing office, cotton gin, sawmill, turpentine still, farms and gardens, farmhouses, one-room school, country church, and more.

"4. *Special Classes To Meet Your Needs.* Georgia Agrirama will work with you in any way possible to design educational programming experiences which are best suited to the unique needs of your class or school system.

"5. *The Cluster Workshop* is designed to instruct a large assemblage of students that the other workshops could not adequately address. The program utilizes components of the site tour, Living History Workshops, and A Day In A One Room School. The classes will be divided into three groups with each segment having a limited experience in each of the three respective modules. Audio-visual and printed curriculum materials will be sent out in advance of your tour date. Agrirama educational personnel will direct the Living History portion and aid with the classroom portion, while each teacher will be responsible for leading the site tour. The program is open to all grades but no costuming is available for this particular program."

The Georgia Agrirama Development Authority has set forth its purpose in the 1991 and 1992 Annual Report as follows:

"The Georgia Agrirama Development Authority was created by an act of the General Assembly to provide the mechanism for the preservation and demonstration of Georgia's rural, agrarian society in a museum complex. Specifically, the museum is committed to acquire and collect the material culture of rural Georgia and its inhabitants; to preserve those objects for the future; to study them to derive information about the past; and to use the resultant body of knowledge from such study to interpret to the public the rural history and culture of Georgia through any and all effective means of communication."

In 1980 the General Assembly passed a resolution naming Georgia Agrirama the State Museum of Agriculture. As a museum dedicated to the State's rural traditions, Georgia Agrirama shall:

"Systematically acquire and collect the material culture of Georgia as it pertains to its rural history. The needs of the museum's interpretive programs will be met by selectively collecting objects which best exemplify the State's rural history.

"Exercise responsibility in the care and preservation of objects collected. The preservation of the collection for present and future generations shall be accomplished through a program of care and maintenance of physical structures that house them within the constraints of available resources.

"Provide for research which forms the primary source of information for all museum programs. Research is necessary to authenticate the collections as well as increase the body of knowledge in the field of rural history.

"Disseminate the information gained through research to the general public in order to expand their knowledge and understanding of the past. Interpretation of this information through exhibit production and public programs shall be a major and continuing activity of the museum within the constraints of available resources. The museum shall provide research facilities and time to serious scholars of material culture and rural history.

"By the preservation of material culture, solid historical research, and the presentation of historical topics in a strong interpretive program, Georgia Agrirama shall accomplish its purpose of the preservation of the state's rural history for both present and future generations."

The Agrirama has made many significant accomplishments during my tenure as a member of the Georgia Agrirama Development Authority. One noteworthy example is the sponsoring of a series of special events in connection with the observance of Black History month. Even though it is still in the developmental stage, it has generated a lot of interest and enthusiasm.

The Agrirama is located in Tifton, Georgia, right off Interstate 75, Exit 20. If you have not already visited the Agrirama, I urge you to do so at your earliest convenience.

"THE THINKER

"Back of the beating hammer
By which the steel is wrought,
Back of the workshop's clamor
The seeker may find the thought;
The thought that is ever master
Of iron and steam and steel,
That rises above disaster
And tramples it under heel!
Might of the roaring boiler,
Force of the engine's thrust,
Strength of the sweating toiler,
Greatly in these we trust.
But back of them stands the schemer,
The thinker who drives things through;
Back of the job—the dreamer,
Who's making the dream come true!"
—Benton Braley

CHAPTER 19

FAMILY VALUES

The passing along of family values to our posterity is of vital importance if we are going to continue to make progress. The traditional family that I grew up in has undergone many changes, including an alarming rate of single parent families

For those of us who are fortunate, the word "family" evokes feelings of warm human relations and emotions of love, peace and joy. Visions of happy gatherings such as Thanksgiving and Christmas were especially meaningful. We did not have very much in terms of material possessions, but we were happy. There was a bonding that held us together that is missing in a large number of our families today.

Not all of us are fortunate enough to have the benefit of a loving, caring, and concerned family. Families are changing. For too many children growing up in America today, family is no longer a place of security and counsel and a place to learn values. The family is going through a long and perilous crisis; and with that crisis, the basic institution for transferring values in our society is threatened as never before.

It has been said that as the family goes, so goes the nation. In my opinion, this is really cause for concern; and we cannot continue to go along, business as usual, and expect the problem to correct itself.

In the tumultuous age of the nineties, not only is the family disintegrating; but the Black family is in a crisis situation. The importance of each family member to work and do all we can to hold our family together cannot be overestimated. Our family is the most precious thing we have on this earth. When we all get to heaven, we are going to be just one big family. I am so glad we belong to the family of God. Until then, however, we must work together, press together, hold together, and pursue a common goal. The same old-fashioned values our parents sought to instill in us as children, we must continue to teach to our offspring and future generations.

I had an opportunity to hear Marian Wright Edelman when she addressed the 1992 graduating class of Tuskegee University, at which time she placed great emphasis on family values. She had just published her new book entitled *The Measure of Our Success, A Letter to My Children and Yours*. The following are several excerpts from her book: "You can get all A's and still flunk life.

"Life was not easy back in the 1940's and 1950's in rural South Carolina for many parents and grandparents. We buried children who died from poverty (and I can't stand it that we still do). Little Johnny Harrington, three houses down from my church parsonage, stepped on and died from a nail because his grandmother had no doctor to advise her nor the money to pay for health care. (Half of all low-income urban children under two are still not fully immunized against preventable childhood diseases like tetanus and polio and measles.) My classmate, Henry Munnerlyn, broke his neck when he jumped off the bridge into the town creek because only White children were allowed in the public swimming pool. I later heard that the creek where Blacks swam and fished was the hospital sewage outlet. (Today thousands of Black children in our cities and rural areas are losing their lives to cocaine and heroin and alcohol and gang violence because they don't have enough constructive outlets.) The migrant family who collided with a truck on the highway near my home and the ambulance driver who refused to take them to the hospital because they were Black still live in my mind every time I hear about babies who die or are handicapped from birth when they are turned away from hospitals in emergencies or their mothers are turned away in labor because they have no health insurance and cannot pay preadmission deposits to enter a hospital. I and my brothers and sister might have lost hope—as so many young people today have lost hope—except for the stable, caring attentive adults in our family, school, congregation, civic and political life who struggled with and for us against the obstacles we faced and provided us positive alternatives and the sense of possibility we needed....

"There's nothing wrong with wanting a BMW or nice clothes. But a BMW is not an advanced degree, and a designer coat or jacket is not a life goal or worth a life. I was watching one of President Johnson's inaugural balls on television with a Black college president's wife in Mississippi when Mrs. Hamer, that great lady of the Mississippi civil rights movement who lacked a college degree, but certainly not intelligence or clear purpose, came onto the screen. The college president's wife moaned: 'Oh my, there's Miz Hamer at the

President's ball and she doesn't even have on a long dress.' My response was: 'That's all right. Mrs. Hamer with no long gown is there, and you and I with our long gowns are not....'

"*Never give up.* Never think life is not worth living. I don't care how hard it gets. An old proverb reminds: 'When you get to your wit's end, remember that God lives there.' Harriet Beecher Stowe wrote that when you get into a 'tight place and everything goes against you, till it seems as though you could not hang on a minute longer, never give up then, for that is just the place and time that the tide will turn.' Hang in with life. Hang in for what you believe is right even if every other soul is going a different way....

"Sissela Bok, in her *Alva Myrdal: A Life*, quotes the Nobel Peace laureate: 'I know only two things for certain. One is that we gain nothing by walking around the difficulties and merely indulging in wishful thinking. The other is that there is always something one can do oneself. The greatness of being human...lies in not giving up, in not accepting one's own limitations.'...

"And do not think that you have to make big waves in order to contribute. My role model, Sojourner Truth, slave woman, could neither read nor write but could not stand slavery and second-class treatment of women. One day during an anti-slavery speech she was heckled by an old man. 'Old woman, do you think that your talk about slavery does any good? Why I don't care any more for your talk than I do for the bite of a flea.' 'Perhaps not, but the Lord willing, I'll keep you scratching,' she replied.

"A lot of people think they have to be big dogs to make a difference. That's not true. You just need to be a flea for justice, bent on building a more decent home life, neighborhood, work place, and America. Enough committed fleas biting strategically can make even the biggest dog uncomfortable and transform even the biggest nation, as we will and must transform America in the 1990's.

"Be a flea for justice wherever you are and in whatever career you choose in life and help transform America by biting political and business leaders until they respond....

"*Don't be afraid of hard work or of teaching your children to work.* For all her great accomplishments, Mary McLeod Bethune never forgot the importance of practical work. When asked by a train conductor, 'Auntie, do you know how to cook good biscuits?' she responded, 'Sir, I am an advisor to presidents, the founder of an accredited four-year college, a nationally known leader of women, and founder of the National Council of Negro Women. And yes, I also cook good biscuits.'...

"*Remember your roots, your history, and the forebears' shoulders on which you stand.* And pass those roots on to your children and to other children. Young people who do not know where they come from and the struggle it took to get them where they are now will not know where they are going or what to do for anyone besides themselves if and when they finally get somewhere. All Black children need to feel the rightful pride of a great people that produced Harriet Tubman and Sojourner Truth and Frederick Douglass from slavery, and Benjamin Mays and Martin Luther King and Mrs. Fannie Lou Hamer from segregation—people second to none in helping transform America from a theoretical to a more living democracy....

"If we do not act immediately to protect America's children and change the misguided national choices that leave too many of them unhealthy, unhoused, ill-fed, and undereducated, during the next four years

1,080,000	American babies will be born at low birth-weight, multiplying their risk of death or disability.
143,619	babies will die before their first birthday.
4,400,000	babies will be born to unmarried women.
2,000,000	babies will be born to teen mothers.
15,856	children 19 or younger will die by firearms.
2,784	children younger than 5 will die by homicide.
9,208	children 19 or younger will commit suicide.
1,620,000	young people ages 16 to 24 will fail to complete high school.
3,780,000	young people will finish high school but not enroll in college.
599,076	children younger than 18 will be arrested for alcohol-related offenses, 359,600 for drug offenses, and 338,292 for violent crimes.
7,911,532	public school students will be suspended.
3,600,000	infants will be born into poverty...

"Every day, 135,000 children bring a gun to school. In 1987, 415,000 violent crimes occurred in and around schools. Some inner-city children are exposed to violence so routinely that they exhibit post traumatic stress symptoms similar to those that plague many Vietnam combat veterans. Still, our country is unwilling to take semiautomatic machine guns out of the hands of its citizens. Every day twenty-three teens and young adults are killed by firearms in America...."

If you have not had an opportunity to read Marian Edelman's book, I highly recommend it, as I find it very stimulating and inspiring. I can relate to many of the situations that she described.

I really believe that we gain much when we take time out from our busy schedules as a family, when everyone is happy and excited about being together again. In far too many instances, if we are not careful, we will find ourselves staying away year after year until someone passes or some other crisis occurs in the family. It seems to me that the best way to avoid this is to make family gatherings or reunions a top priority. I am pleased with the progress that the Lord has enabled our family to make with this endeavor. These gatherings present the family an opportunity to function as a unit in planning and coordinating an array of activities. Everyone's input is solicited as we try to make each event better than the previous ones.

Following the death of our brother, Charles Reefus, in 1968, we became keenly aware of how fleeting and uncertain life is and just how quickly death can become a reality. This tragedy prompted us to focus on the family unit and the importance of making the time to come together as family to share happy times together. We began to meet informally as often as we could arrange to do so.

As time moved on, we lost our youngest brother, William Arnold, in 1974. Subsequently, our parents' declining health made it impossible for them to be cared for adequately in their home. Consequently, our sister Nellie moved them to Thomasville, Georgia, where they resided in her home until their deaths. During their stay in Thomasville, the family remained close, united, and committed to ensuring the comfort of our parents and making certain that they knew how much they were loved by all of us. Thomasville became the family gathering place, and we continued to come together to share happy times.

On Daddy's death bed, he asked my sisters Annette and Mary, who were at his bedside, to join hands with him. His last words were "Walk together, children." From that day, keeping the family together has become a shared commitment. It takes a special effort to keep a family close after both parents have passed away. Nevertheless, this is the challenge we've accepted, and we feel very strongly that God will enable us to carry out Daddy's wish for the family.

Often during Daddy's lifetime, he was heard to quote Psalms 133. The first verse of this Psalm has become the focal point of our family reunions. It says, "Behold, how good and pleasant it is for brethren to dwell together in unity." It is this spirit of unity that Harris Family Reunions seek to perpetuate.

We began to communicate with all of the descendants of Rufus and Charlie Mae Harris. A questionnaire was circulated to gather input for scheduling a formal family reunion. Important information regarding family members was submitted to our sister Mary who kept the entire Harris clan aware of family happenings, accomplishments, births, illnesses, graduations, weddings, etc. through memorandums.

The Harris Family has committed itself to coming together biannually to celebrate our heritage. We feel strongly about our Early County roots. We want our children, their children, and future generations to know from whence we've come. By coming back to our roots, simulating activities of the past, and visiting the resting places of our ancestors, the heritage becomes real. Each family member can catch a personal glimpse of the inspiration that propelled our forefathers and mothers to bypass the highway of mediocrity and trudge the less traveled road of faith and perseverance. They paved the way with their blood, sweat, tears, and hard work. Because they envisioned that one day life would be better for their children and future generations, we are where we are today. The same noble qualities that enhanced their lives are the qualities that Harris Family Reunions seek to keep alive. Not only will they enable us to make a positive difference in society, but they will most definitely hold us close as a family unit.

Our first family reunion was held in Blakely, Georgia, in August, 1983. It was a glorious occasion when all of the surviving children, grandchildren, and great grandchildren shared this event. Little did we realize at this happy occasion that it would be Herk's last reunion. Since then, we have met for family reunions in Thomasville, Georgia; Ozark, Alabama; and back to Blakely, Georgia, for the last two reunions.

Because we're family, there is a closeness that binds us together no matter how many miles are between us. We share a wealth of memories to keep us company when we are apart. We have many years of happy family celebrations and traditions about which to reminisce.

We have a treasured legacy to perpetuate—a legacy that is Christ-centered; a legacy that embodies vision, determination, strength, bravery, courage, love and devotion, and honesty; and a legacy that compels us to share these noble qualities of our heritage that have made us what we are today with our offspring. Family reunions will enable them to keep the heritage alive as they perpetuate the legacy to each generation that follows.

One strong tenet that the Harris clan claims is the belief that with the Lord, all things are possible. Even though there may have been or will be times when our plans, goals, or aspirations meet with disappointment or discouragement, we believe that if we continue to let the Lord be the center of all our activities, plans, efforts, and endeavors, He will enable us to make our goals realities. Our expectations must be realistic. So long as we make the Lord first, last, and always in all the endeavors we undertake, we are assured of His blessings right up front.

The Lord has richly blessed our family through the family reunions. The family has been strengthened. Family reunions are the glue that holds us together. The Lord established the family back at the very beginning of time. He knew that the family unit was an extremely important facet of society. Therefore, He did not delegate its establishment to anyone else. He set up the family structure Himself. He admonished parents in the book of Proverbs, Chapter 22 and verse 6, to "train up a child in the way he should go and when he is old, he will not depart from it." To further strengthen the family unit, God instructed the children in Exodus 20:12 to "Honor thy father and thy mother that thy days may be long upon the land which the Lord thy God giveth thee" and in Ephesians 6:1, "Children, obey your parents in the Lord, for this is right."

I have been especially inspired at each family reunion that the Lord has blessed us to sponsor. Even though I considered each facet of the celebration to have been a "mountain-top experience," I believe the singing is the most rewarding. In 1990 the group gathered at our house on Friday evening and my nephew, Stevie, played the piano, while the others blended their voices in praise and adoration to the Lord. This event lasted for several hours and it really blessed my soul. At the 1992 reunion we met in the fellowship hall at our church, had vespers and another old fashioned singspiration. As I reflected on how the Lord had blessed us as a family, I could not help but shed tears of joy, for He indeed has brought us a mighty long way.

On each Sabbath during the reunion, members of the Harris family take charge of the services for the entire day. This includes early morning prayer service at 9:00 a.m., Sabbath School at 9:30 a.m., Divine Worship Service at 11:00 a.m. and AYS, Adventist Youth Society, at 7:00 p.m. I am always overjoyed when I see different family members leading with such rewarding and fulfilling activities.

Another thrilling facet of the 1992 reunion was a guided tour that was scheduled between the fellowship dinner and the AYS program. The tour started at the Greene Cemetery where the majority of our deceased family members are buried. Many of their graves were pointed out and a brief commentary of their life works given. The next stop on the tour was our old home where ten of my parents children were born. This was a thrilling and exciting experience for the younger set, many of whom had never seen the house where we had grown up. The third stop on the tour was what my siblings and I affectionately call the "new ground" which was the second tract of land that my parents were able to acquire. Our final stop on the tour was the Good Hope Cemetery. This is the burial place of my father's mother, Mary Perry Harris. By the end of the tour, it was time for our AYS program and Vespers Service.

Since the beginning of time God has given human beings a longing to be connected to relatives, to a place, to a past. Children need something that will always be there for them: a heritage, a sense of belonging.

Children aren't the only ones who need this connectedness. Adults, too, need a sense of family. Isolation, the feeling that no one knows or cares, is a devastating factor in our present day society.

I think we should seriously consider what makes a family strong. It doesn't just happen by chance. Our family has achieved whatever measure of success we have experienced as a result of family unity, of years of living and loving, prayer and sacrifice, misunderstanding and forgiveness. Birth, education, marriage, death, success, and failure—all this and more make up our years together.

It has taken years to recognize that building these relationships is a lifelong endeavor. Our roots connect to the past, continue in the present, and stretch to the future. But the precious memories that we have shared at each reunion have been both rewarding and fulfilling.

As family, we must remember that whenever we are inclined to become discouraged, we must remind ourselves that through Christ we are able to be victorious in our endeavors. There are going to be times when we may become discouraged and feel like we are outnumbered and that we are as grasshoppers in terms of the possibilities or our capabilities; but, may I remind you (as Mike concluded in his sermon August 15, 1992) that those "lions" are out there. They come in many forms. They come in different situations. Nevertheless, we are told that if we stand up to the Devil and resist him, he will flee from us. This faith will continue to keep the family ties strong. It will enable us to continue to celebrate each other's joys and share each other's sorrows. Because we ARE a family, we will continue to be there for each other, always willing to lend a helping hand or a shoulder to cry on.

> "I would rather plant a single acorn that will
> make an oak of a century and a forest of a
> thousand years than sow a thousand morning
> glories that give joy for a day and are gone
> tomorrow. For the same reason, I would rather
> plant one living truth in the heart of a child
> that will multiply through the ages than scatter
> a thousand brilliant conceits before a great
> audience that will flash like sparks for
> an instant and like sparks disappear forever."
> —Edward Leigh Pell

CHAPTER 20

LYNCHING IN EARLY COUNTY

The term *lynching* is best defined as legal evidence of a person's illegal death and group participation in a killing under the pretext of service to justice, race, or tradition.

It is not known how many Blacks were lynched in the U.S., but it would be well into the tens of thousands. In many cases only the people in an immediate area would have any knowledge about it. In other cases, no dead body was ever found; so the family never knew what actually had happened to a person. However, in most cases, the lynching was meant to "send a message" to the living not to do what the deceased had done or the same fate awaited them.

In my opinion, race relations in Early County during my lifetime were quite similar to those in the South in general. The "separate but equal" doctrine was practiced without any significant overt resistance.

When I was growing up, my parents shared with me one note-worthy racial crisis that happened in Early County. They referred to it as the Grandison Goolsby Scrape. As my parents understood it, in 1915 or 1916 one of Mr. Grandison Goolsby's sons was coming home from a wedding with his girlfriend in the buggy on a muddy road; and a White man who had been drinking failed to pull his buggy to the side far enough, and the buggy wheels interlocked. The White man hit the Goolsby lad with a whip several times, and they got the wheels untangled and went home.

Mr. Grandison Goolsby was eating a late Sunday dinner or early supper when his son got home and told him what happened. Grandison and his sons got their guns and went to see the White man, Mr. Henry J. Villipigue.

Grandison went to the front door rather than the back and hailed for him, "Mr. Henry, I hear you done hit my boy; and I done come to get some satisfaction about it."

Mr. Villipigue asked if that was the same boy he had beaten earlier in the day. When told that it was, he grabbed his pistol and

222

started shooting; and Mr. Grandison, in returning the fire, hit and fatally wounded Mr. Villipigue.

Mr. Grandison left the scene and preceded to a nearby Black church in the New Hope area where he holed up with his Winchester rifles and much ammunition.

The deceased Mr. Villipigue's relatives that lived in the northern part of Early County could not or would not wait for the posse to get together early on Monday morning. There were apparently four or five wagon loads of men with their guns seeking revenge.

As the wagons got in shooting range of Mr. Grandison, he began to fire on the wagons. From his vantage point, high in the church steeple, he one by one picked off the men in the wagons.

At some point, a posse or lynch mob was able to rush the building from all sides and set fire to the church; and Mr. Grandison was burned to death. Those men that were in the rushing of the building on the line of fire side paid a heavy price. Many sustained injuries that resulted in the amputation of legs and arms while many were killed outright. In the Black community it was believed that Mr. Grandison killed in excess of 50 White men in Early County. They based this on men that they knew by name or sight and never saw or heard anything of again. There were several dozen amputees around; and you could hear one Black say to another softly, "There goes one of old Grandison Goolsby's right there."

The aftermath of this incident was horrific. Every Black Masonic hall in Early County was burned. Many of the Black churches suffered the same fate. They attempted to wipe out the entire Goolsby family. My Dad said that for over a year, a Black person could not walk the Columbia highway, or he was subject to be shot down by men loyal to Mr. Villipigue. Blacks also could not buy high-powered rifles or ammunition in Early County for years after this incident.

I can still recall 15 years after the incident of being warned to not claim kin to any of the Goolsbys. In spite of the fear for their lives at this time, some of the Masonic brothers and Eastern Star sisters apparently gave safe haven to the family members; therefore, some members of the Goolsby family were spared. Fifteen to twenty years later it still caused much excitement when Grandison Goolsby's granddaughters came to spend the weekend with my sisters, Nellie and Mary. For weeks before their visit, they were the topic of apprehensive conversation.

Throughout my developmental years my parents would peri-odically make reference to this tragedy and it would always trigger a feeling of fear and sadness within me. As previously stated, this happened more than ten years prior to my birth. Even though I do not know of any other documented cases of lynching, my parents and several of the older folk in the community felt that there were other isolated cases.

"Which Are You?
An attender or an absenter?
A pillar or a sleeper?
A wing or a weight?
A power or a problem?
A promoter or a provoker?
A giver or a getter?
A goer or a gadder?
A doer or a deadhead?
A booter or a bucker?
A supporter or a sponger?"
A soldier or a sorehead?
A worker or a worrier?
A friend or a fault-finder?
A helper or a hinderer?
A campaigner or a camper?
—The Baptist

CHAPTER 21

CIVIL RIGHTS MOVEMENT

The Civil Rights Movement of the decade of the 1960's had a great and lasting impact on my life. While I never actively participated in any of the sit-ins, marches, or other forms of protest, I was sympathetic to the cause and felt that there were many wrongs that needed to be changed.

The greatest influence on my life was, outside of my parents, that exerted by Dr. Martin Luther King, Jr. One of the reasons that I felt so inspired by him was the sacrifice that he was willing to make to bring about change. I was approximately two years older than he, and our children were about the same ages. I loved my family and was devoted to them as he must have been to his. Nevertheless, he was willing to sacrifice the time and companionship that he could have otherwise spent with his family so that the movement might succeed. In my opinion, this reflected a genuine commitment and dedication on his part.

Another reason for my admiration for Dr. King was his concern for his fellowmen. With his fame and fortune, he could have very easily chosen to "pass by on the other side," so to speak. Nevertheless, he allowed himself to be abused and humiliated so that those who were oppressed could be liberated. He had a rare ability to inspire and motivate people, many of whom joined him in his nonviolent movement for change. The movement was not just of Black problems but encompassed many ethnic groups who wanted to see the injustices abolished.

In my opinion, Dr. King was divinely inspired and called by God to lead out in the most far-reaching movement for nonviolent change in my lifetime.

On October 31, 1954, he became the pastor of the Dexter Avenue Baptist Church, Montgomery, Alabama. While serving in that capacity he continued to gain even more name recognition.

On December 1, 1955, Mrs. Rosa Parks, a forty-two year old Montgomery seamstress, refused to relinquish her bus seat to a white man and was arrested. This event proved to be the catalyst that gave rise to the Montgomery Bus Boycott. At first, the Montgomery Bus Company refused to negotiate; and on December 10, 1955, suspended service in Black neighborhoods. The boycott lasted for more than a year; but on December 21, 1956, the Montgomery buses were integrated The economic impact on the bus company and the city of Montgomery was significant. Throughout the Civil Rights Movement, the boycott, in my opinion, was used as a most effective weapon in combating the forces of segregation and discrimination.

Even though Dr. King preached and practiced nonviolence, he was arrested many times for refusing to obey unjust laws. Frequently, he was the victim of police brutality when they arrested him; but he was so committed to the philosophy of nonviolence that he just turned the other cheek, so to speak. His being in jail did not stop him from focusing on the problems of injustice. In my opinion, his "Letter from a Birmingham Jail" was a classic example of his determination to focus on man's inhumanity to man, even when it had to be done under adverse circumstances. In his letter he responded to some of his critics who proclaimed among other things that he did not spend enough time in jail and that he urged others to do things that he did not do. He rarely took time to defend himself from his opponents, but eight prominent "liberal" Alabama clergymen published an open letter earlier in January that called on Dr. King to allow the battle for integration to continue in the local and federal courts. They further warned that King's nonviolent resistance would have the effect of inciting civil disturbances. Dr. King wanted Christian ministers to see that the meaning of Christian discipleship was the heart of the African American struggle for freedom, justice and equality.

In his letter he warned his fellow clergymen that he "could not sit idly by in Atlanta and not be concerned about what happens in Birmingham. Injustice anywhere is a threat to justice everywhere."

He reminded his critics, "We know through painful experience that freedom is never voluntarily given by the oppressor; it must be demanded by the oppressed."

I respected the way that Dr. King responded to his fellow ministers. While he did not change his position, he defended it in a Christlike manner. "If I have said anything in this letter that is an overstatement of the truth and is indicative of an unreasonable impatience, I beg you to forgive me. If I have said anything in this letter that is an understatement of the truth and is indicative of my having a patience that makes me patient with anything less than brotherhood, I beg God to forgive me." This, in my opinion, was indeed the attitude of a true Christian.

On August 28, 1963, the march on Washington, the first large integrated protest march, was held in Washington, D.C. Dr. King and other civil rights leaders met with President John F. Kennedy in the White House, and afterwards Dr. King delivered his "I have a Dream" speech on the steps of the Lincoln Memorial. It is estimated that at least two hundred thousand people attended that event. I always considered Dr. King to have been an eloquent speaker; and, in my opinion, he was always dynamic and challenging. However, I believe his "I Have a Dream" speech is my favorite. For that reason I have included parts of it in this chapter.

"I am happy to join with you today in what will go down in history as the greatest demonstration for freedom in the history of our nation.

"Fivescore years ago, a great American, in whose symbolic shadow we stand today, signed the Emancipation Proclamation. This momentous decree came as a great beacon light of hope to millions of Negro slaves who had been seared in the flames of withering injustice. It came as a joyous daybreak to end the long night of their captivity.

"And as we walk, we must make the pledge that we shall always march ahead. We cannot turn back. There are those who are asking the devotees of civil rights, 'When will you be satisfied?' We can never be satisfied as long as the Negro is the victim of the unspeakable horrors of police brutality.

"We can never be satisfied as long as our bodies, heavy with fatigue of travel, cannot gain lodging in the motels of the highways and the hotels of the cities. We cannot be satisfied as long as the Negro's basic mobility is from a smaller ghetto to a larger one.

"We can never be satisfied as long as a Negro in Mississippi cannot vote and a Negro in New York believes he has nothing for which to vote. No, we are not satisfied, and we will not be satisfied until justice rolls down like waters and righteousness like a mighty stream.

"I am not unmindful that some of you come here out of excessive trials and tribulation. Some of you have come fresh from narrow jail cells. Some of you have come from areas where your quest for freedom left you battered by the storms of persecution and staggered by the winds of police brutality. You have been the veterans of creative suffering. Continue to work with the faith that unearned suffering is redemptive.

"Go back to Mississippi; go back to Alabama; go back to South Carolina; go back to Georgia; go back to Louisiana; go back to the slums and ghettos of the northern cities, knowing that somehow this situation can, and will be changed. Let us not wallow in the valley of despair.

"So I say to you, my friends, that even though we must face the difficulties of today and tomorrow, I still have a dream. It is a dream deeply rooted in the American dream that one day this nation will rise up and live out the true meaning of its creed—we hold these truths to be self-evident, that all men are created equal.

"I have a dream that one day on the red hills of Georgia, sons of former slaves and sons of former slave-owners will be able to sit down together at the table of brotherhood.

"I have a dream that one day, even the state of Mississippi, a state sweltering with the heat of injustice, sweltering with the heat of oppression, will be transformed into an oasis of freedom and justice.

"I have a dream that my four little children will one day live in a nation where they will not be judged by the color of their skin but by the content of their character. I have a dream today!

"I have a dream that one day, down in Alabama, with its vicious racists, with its governor having his lips dripping with the words of interposition and nullification, that one day, right there in Alabama, little Black boys and Black girls will be able to join hands with little White boys and White girls as sisters and brothers. I have a dream today!

"With this faith we will be able to hew out of the mountain of despair a stone of hope. With this faith we will be able to transform the jangling discords of our nation into a beautiful symphony of brotherhood.

"With this faith we will be able to work together, to pray together, to struggle together, to go to jail together, to stand up for freedom together, knowing that we will be free one day. This will be the day when all of God's children will be able to sing with new meaning—'My country 'tis of thee; sweet land of liberty; of thee I sing; land where my fathers died, land of the pilgrims' pride; from every mountain side, let freedom ring'—and if America is to be a great nation, this must become true.

"So let freedom ring from the prodigious hilltops of New Hampshire.

"Let freedom ring from the mighty mountains of New York.

"Let freedom ring for the heightening Alleghenies of Pennsylvania!

"Let freedom ring from the snowcapped Rockies of Colorado!

"Let freedom ring from the curvaceous peaks of California!

"But not only that.

"Let freedom ring from Stone Mountain of Georgia!

"Let freedom ring from Lookout Mountain of Tennessee!

"Let freedom ring from every hill and molehill of Mississippi. From every mountainside, let freedom ring.

"When we let freedom ring, when we let it ring from every village and every hamlet, from every state and every city, we will be able to speed up that day when all of God's children—Black men and White men, Jews and Gentiles, Protestants and Catholics—will be able to join hands and to sing in the words of the old Negro spiritual, 'Free at last! Free at last! Thank God Almighty, we are free at last!'"

There is so much more that could be said about Dr. King, including the fact that he won the Nobel Peace Prize, December 10, 1964. However, I feel that I must limit myself. Nevertheless, he characterized himself as a "Drum Major for Justice." I honestly feel that it was a very appropriate description of his life's work.

Dr. King surrounded himself with a very supportive and capable staff which included Dr. Ralph David Abernathy, Sr., who became his successor; Andrew Young, former congressman, U.N. Ambassador and mayor of Atlanta; Hosea Williams, former member of the Georgia State Legislature and the Atlanta City Council; Jesse Jackson, presidential candidate for the Democratic party in 1988 and founder of Operation PUSH; and John Lewis, U. S. Congressman from Atlanta. There were many more who gave their loyal and dedicated service. Some even gave their lives, including James Reeb, a Unitarian minister, who was beaten so severely by four White segregationists in Selma, Alabama, that he died two days later. There was also Mrs. Viola Liuzzo, wife of a Teamsters Union business agent, who was shot and killed while driving a carload of marchers back to Selma. Both of these individuals could have made excuses, because as nonBlacks they already enjoyed the freedom their Black brothers and sisters were still struggling to achieve. To me, they went beyond the call of duty by giving their lives for their fellowmen who were less fortunate.

One of the saddest and most inhumane events that I can recall during the civil rights struggle was the brutal attacks on the marchers/protesters by police dogs. In addition to the attacks by the police dogs, high-pressure fire hoses were turned on the marchers with such force that they were knocked to the ground or sidewalk. All of this brutality was inflicted on the demonstrators by orders of Eugene "Bull" Connor, Director of Public Safety for the City of Birmingham. In retrospect, it seems completely unrealistic that one human being would inflict so much pain and suffering on another human being. Nevertheless, it did happen; and I feel that a day of reckoning will come for Mr. Connor and others who were responsible for such cruel treatment of fellow human beings.

I was impressed by the way that Dr. King characterized himself as a drum major for justice, peace, and righteousness. The following are several excerpts from him:

"Every now and then I guess we all think realistically about that day when we will be victimized with what is life's final common denominator—that something we call death. We all think about it. And every now and then I think about my own death, and I think about my own funeral. And I don't think of it in a morbid sense. Every now and then I ask myself, 'What is it that I would want said?' and I leave the word to you this morning.

"If any of you are around when I have to meet my day, I don't want a long funeral. And if you get somebody to deliver the eulogy, tell them not to talk too long. Every now and then I wonder what I want them to say. Tell them not to mention that I have a Nobel Peace Prize, that isn't important. Tell them not to mention that I have three or four hundred other awards, that's not important. Tell them not to mention where I went to school.

"I'd like somebody to mention that day that Martin Luther King, Jr. tried to give his life serving others. I'd like for somebody to say that day that Martin Luther King, Jr., tried to love somebody. I want you to say that day that I tried to be right on the war question. I want you to be able to say that day that I did try to feed the hungry. And I want you to be able to say that day that I did try, in my life, to clothe those who were naked. I want you to say on that day that I did try, in my life, to visit those who were in prison. I want you to say that I tried to love and serve humanity.

"Yes, if you want to say that I was a drum major, say that I was a drum major for justice; say that I was a drum major for peace; I was a drum major for righteousness. And all of the other shallow things will not matter. I won't have any money to leave behind. I won't have the fine and luxurious things of life to leave behind. But I just want to leave a committed life behind.

"And that's all I want to say...if I can help somebody as I pass along, if I can cheer somebody with a word or song, if I can show somebody he's traveling wrong, then my living will not be in vain. If I can do my duty as a Christian ought, if I can bring salvation to a world once wrought, if I can spread the message as the master taught, then my living will not be in vain.

"Yes, Jesus, I want to be on your right side or your left side, not for any selfish reason. I want to be on your right or your best side, not in terms of some political kingdom or ambition, but I just want to be there in love and in justice and in truth and in commitment to others, so that we can make of this old world a new world."

Another very impressive event in Dr. King's life was his "I See the Promised Land" speech. It seems as if he had a premonition that his life on this earth was going to end shortly. Nevertheless, he faced the future with courage and fortitude. The following are a few excepts from that speech:

"You know, several years ago, I was in New York City auto-graphing the first book that I had written. And while sitting there autographing books, a demented Black woman came up. The only question I heard from her was, 'Are you Martin Luther King?'

"And I was looking down writing, and I said 'yes.' And the next minute I felt something beating on my chest. Before I knew it, I had been stabbed by this demented woman. I was rushed to Harlem Hospital. It was a dark Saturday afternoon. And that blade had gone through, and the X-rays revealed that the tip of the blade was on the edge of my aorta, the main artery. And once that's punctured, you drown in your own blood—that's the end of you.

"It came out in the New York Times the next morning, that if I had sneezed, I would have died. Well, about four days later, they allowed me, after the operation, after my chest had been opened, and the blade had been taken out, to move around in the wheel chair in the hospital. They allowed me to read some of the mail that came in; and from all over the states and the world, kind letters came in. I read a few, but one of them I will never forget. I had received one from the President and the Vice President. I've forgotten what those telegrams said. I'd received a visit and a letter from the Governor of New York, but I've forgotten what the letter said. But there was another letter that came from a little girl, a young girl who was a student at the White Plains High School. And I looked at that letter, and I'll never forget it. It said simply, 'Dear Dr. King: I am a ninth-grade student at the White Plains High School.' She said, 'While it should not matter, I would like to mention that I am a White girl. I read in the paper of your misfortune and of your suffering. And I read that if you had sneezed, you would have died. And I'm simply writing you to say that I'm so happy that you didn't sneeze.'

"And I want to say tonight, I want to say that I am happy that I didn't sneeze. Because if I had sneezed, I wouldn't have been around here in 1960 when students all over the South started sitting-in at lunch counters. And I knew that as they were sitting in, they were really standing up for the best in the American dream. And taking the whole nation back to those great wells of democracy which were dug deep by the Founding Fathers in the Declaration of Independence and the Constitution. If I had sneezed, I wouldn't have been around in 1962, when Negroes in Albany, Georgia, decided to straighten their backs up. And whenever men and women straighten their backs up, they are going somewhere, because a man can't ride your back unless it is bent. If I had sneezed, I wouldn't have been here in 1963, when the Black people of Birmingham, Alabama, aroused the conscience of this nation, and brought into being the Civil Rights Bill. If I had sneezed, I wouldn't have had a chance later that year, in August, to try to tell America about a dream that I had. If I had sneezed, I wouldn't have been down in Selma, Alabama, to see the great movement there. If I had sneezed, I wouldn't have been in Memphis to see the community rally around those brothers and sisters who are suffering. I'm so happy that I didn't sneeze.

"And they were telling me now that it doesn't matter now. It really doesn't matter what happens now. I left Atlanta this morning, and as we got started on the plane, there were six of us, the pilot said over the public address system, 'We are sorry for the delay, but we have Dr. Martin Luther King on the plane, we had to check out everything carefully. And we've had the plane protected and guarded all night.'

"And then I got into Memphis. And some began to say the threats, or talk about the threats that were out. What would happen to me from some of our sick White brothers?

"Well, I don't know what will happen now. We've got some difficult days ahead. But it doesn't matter with me now. Because I've been to the mountaintop. And I don't mind. Like anybody, I would like to live a long life. Longevity has its place. But I'm not concerned about that now. I just want to do God's will. And He's allowed me to go up to the mountain. And I've looked over. And I've seen the promised land. I may not get there with you. But I want you to know tonight, that we, as a people, will get to the promised land. And I'm happy, tonight. I'm not worried about anything. I'm not fearing any man. Mine eyes have seen the glory of the coming of the Lord."

Even though Dr. King knew he was a "marked man," so to speak, he kept on with his work. He delivered his last speech entitled "I've Been to the Mountain Top" on April 3, 1968, in Memphis, Tennessee. The following day Dr. King was assassinated by a sniper as he stood talking on the balcony of his second floor room at the Lorraine Motel in Memphis. He died in St. Joseph's Hospital from a gunshot wound to the neck. James Earl Ray was captured, tried and convicted of the murder.

The death of Dr. King was a very sad experience for my family and me. I consider my grief for him, his wife, children, parents and extended family to have been as great or greater than what I had experienced for President John F. Kennedy when he was assassinated in 1963. I could only imagine what it must have been like for Dr. King's aged parents. However, through it all the Lord sustained them. It must have been devastating for his widow, Coretta Scott King, and their four children. However, the Lord has blessed them; and, in my opinion, they have been very successful in "Keeping the dream alive."

In my opinion, it was ironic that even though Dr. King had given his life for the philosophy of nonviolence, at his death, many of the same "brothers'" for which he had died to help, took to the streets and engaged in widespread looting and rioting. I am sure he would not have approved of such conduct, even though some attempted to justify it on the basis that the participants were giving vent to their frustrations. I personally think that there must have been a better way.

On Saturday, August 28, 1993, thirty years later, an assertive new generation of thousands marched on Washington, D. C., pressing fresh demands for jobs and justice and to honor the dream.

The marchers retraced 1963's "Emancipation March on Washington" but this time they argued that legal equality is empty without economic opportunity.

"We want more than just fair treatment," said Dr. Benjamin Chavis, the new president of the NAACP. "We want a fair share of the economy."

And from the steps where Dr. King spoke, an old King ally, the Rev. Joseph Lowery, president of the Southern Christian Leadership Conference, pleaded with minorities to lock arms in friendship.

"Let's turn to each other and not on each other," he said. "When we have justice, we'll have peace in the 'hood and peace in the 'burbs."

At noon, Dr. King's widow, Coretta Scott King, and his children and sister started the parade to the monument.

Behind them came Attorney General Janet Reno, arm in arm with the Rev. Jesse Jackson.

Flanking them was Carol Moseley-Braun, the first Black woman to sit in the U. S. Senate.

The Rev. Jesse Jackson in his speech said that in many ways America's poor are worse off now than they were 30 years ago. "Jobs have gone," he said. "Guns and drugs have spread. Hope is down, violence is up."

He sounded his familiar "keep hope alive" theme. "Don't let them break your spirit, though the tide of fascist, racist behavior is on the rise," he said.

Among the participants were veterans of battles old and new: Rosa Parks, whose refusal to yield her bus seat to a White man inspired a successful Black boycott of the bus system in Montgomery, Ala. and Lani Guinier, who was recently nominated by President Clinton to be the nation's chief civil rights attorney but then withdrew her name from consideration.

Also on hand: Mayor David Dinkins of New York, wearing an African print baseball cap; Andrew Young, one of Dr. King's lieutenants and a former mayor of Atlanta; Sharon Pratt Kelly, the mayor of Washington, who seized the chance to make a plea for statehood for the District of Columbia; Henry Cisneros, secretary of Housing and Urban Development and one of the nation's Hispanic leaders; Rep

John Lewis (D-Ga.), who spoke as a student at the 1963 march, and Gov. Douglas Wilder of Virginia.

One of them, Barbara Wiggins, president of the Greater Hartford, Connecticut, NAACP, said, "We hope to accomplish what we didn't accomplish 30 years ago—justice and peace and equality for everyone."

While marchers sang the old civil rights anthems, they marched for a variety of new causes not on the nation's mind 30 years ago—for sexual equality; against abortion restrictions; for gun control, disarmament, and the environment, for the aged and the victims of AIDS; and for statehood for Puerto Rico.

From his vacation at Martha's Vineyard on the New England coast, Mr. Clinton sent a message of support:

"As a son of the South, I have seen in my own lifetime how racism held all of us down and how the Civil Rights Movement set all of us free. We must never forget the hard-earned lesson that America can only move forward when we move forward together."

Dr. King had more or less hand picked Dr. Ralph David Abernathy to be his successor, and upon his death, Dr. Abernathy took over the reins of leadership. In my opinion, he did a good job. However, Dr. King had "left some big shoes to fill," and he was no Dr. King, by any stretch of the imagination. Before Dr. Abernathy's death he wrote his autobiography titled *And the Walls Come Tumbling Down*. The book generated a nationwide furor over Dr. King's sexual indiscretions the night before he died. As a result, he was repudiated by civil rights leaders who felt that he had broken the code of Dr. King's inner circle. I do not know whether or not Dr. King was guilty of the allegations; but even if he were, I feel that there are some things better left unsaid. In my opinion, this was a classic example. I do not see that anything positive could have been gained by exposing him.

On Tuesday, April 17, 1990, Ralph David Abernathy died of cardiac arrest at age 64. His funeral was almost a carbon copy of Dr. King's. At the funeral Mrs. Christine King Farris, elder sister of Dr. King, spoke on behalf of her family. She said that the Rev. Abernathy and Dr. King "were like brothers." She went on to say, "The Ralph I remember was adopted by my parents. They adopted him like another son."

In his autobiography, the Rev. Abernathy recalled his return from Memphis in April, 1968, with Dr. King's body: "Now he (Dr.

King) was unworried and at peace. For just an instant," he wrote, "staring at the greening woods below and thinking of what was to come, I almost envied him."

" 'When a twin dies, the other suffers from protracted loneliness,' stated Jesse Jackson at the funeral. He further stated that it was clear Dr. Abernathy never adjusted; and he said on more than one occasion, 'Why couldn't we go together?' "

Unfortunately, in 1968, the nation was dealt what may be called a double whammy with the assassination of Sen. Robert Kennedy.

I liked the description of the tragic evens that took place as told by Roosevelt (Rosey) Grier, a Black man from Cuthbert, Georgia, in his autobiography, *Rosey, The Gentle Giant.* Rosey is a very close friend of the Kennedy family in general and Bobby Kennedy in particular. His narrative is chronicled in the chapter entitled "The Shattered Dream," which I have included in its' entirety:

"With Ethel beside me, I could see over the crowd that Bobby was not far ahead of us. I was trying to catch up. Then he turned a corner. That's when the shots rang out. They didn't sound very loud, but they were such sad sounds.

"Either I pushed Ethel down or she dropped. I have never been able to reconstruct in my mind exactly what happened. She had a habit of crumpling up whenever she heard the sound of anything like gunfire. However she got to the floor, I fell over her and covered her with my body.

"The next thing I remember was taking off and running. I hit the corner opposite the curve in the hall, then I went around the curve and saw a little man with a gun. Bill Barry was struggling with him and shouted, 'Take him, Rosey, take him!'

"People were grabbing at him, and I flew forward. As I reached to grab hold of the man, someone knocked the gun out of his hand. For a second, it was laying on the table. Then it was back in his hand. I grabbed his leg and pulled him back up onto a big serving table. Some of the newspaper reports said I 'threw him up' onto the steel table.

"He was trying frantically to get loose. I don't know what he was saying, but he seemed to have superhuman strength. I gave up any thought of being gentle and locked his legs. Jesse Unruh, the powerful California Democratic politician, was grasping at the man also. George Plimpton got hold of his gun hand, but the gun was pointing right into George's face. That gun pointing at my sister's face years before this in New Jersey came vividly to mind at that moment. That flash of memory made this scene in California in 1968 seem even more nightmarish and unreal. I reached up and covered the young man's gun hand, and locked my thumb behind the trigger so it couldn't fire anymore—just as I had with my sister that time in New Jersey. Then I held on and looked around.

"I wanted to see who had been shot. I still didn't realize for sure that Bobby had been hit. I could see Paul Schrade lying on the floor, down with a head wound. But I saw none of the five other people who were also wounded that night. I know I saw Bobby lying there, but my mind refused to accept it.

"I finally wrenched the gun from the young man's hand. It took all my strength, as big as I was, to pull the gun away from him. People started coming at him and trying to hurt him. They were furious, nearly out of their minds with rage. One man tried to break his leg. I kicked that guy, and Rafer Johnson got up on the table trying to question the suspect. Other people were still trying to hit him from my side, and I had to fight them off. I put the gun in my pocket and began to weep.

"Someone said to me that Bobby had only been shot in the side and that he was going to be all right. But I looked at him and saw his right leg up like the man who died next to me when I was a child in Georgia. The similarity between those two scenes haunted me. And I knew something awful had happened, something unthinkable that didn't seem real. One of the young kitchen workers had a rosary and someone had handed it to Bobby. Ethel was putting ice in a towel on his head.

"Someone else shouted, 'Pray!' That stood out clearly in the middle of all the cursing and screaming. I saw Bobby close his hand over the rosary. He was lying on the concrete floor in the middle of kitchen litter, cigarette butts, and trash—with Ethel beside him. After a while, the police came and took away the man I had been holding, and an ambulance took Bobby to Central Receiving and later to Good Samaritan Hospital for surgery. I sat down on the floor—I didn't know what else to do—and cried.

"Rafer came back a little later and asked about the pistol. When I told him it was in my pocket, he asked me to give it to him. I reached in, took it out, and placed it in his hand. George and Freddy Plimpton knew how much I cared personally about Bobby. They were concerned for me and walked with me to a little room where I could be alone for a bit.

"Later, I went down to police headquarters and made a statement about what I recalled. But I couldn't stop crying. The shooting happened shortly after midnight on June 5. I went home for a while, then Wednesday morning I got a call from the hospital. So I went down there and found a lot of people sitting around outside who had been there since Bobby was admitted. Some were crying, and some were praying. I went inside and stood around. No one seemed to know what was happening.

"I stood in the hallway and hurt when people said they didn't think Bobby was going to make it. Ethel and Jackie—Jackie had just flown in from New York—came through, and Ethel came over and hugged me. She murmured sadly, 'My hero.'

"It amazed me to see her strength and hope. Later that day, when they let me go up to Bobby's room, Ethel was lying on the bed beside him. She looked up, 'Hello, Rosey, thank you for coming.'

"I nodded silently. Bobby lay very still, although he was breathing. Teddy was there, too, along with Jackie, Stephen and Jean Smith, and Pat Lawford. I shook their hands and left very shortly.

"A few minutes before two o'clock in the morning on Thursday, just about twenty-six hours after the shooting, Frank Mankiewicz, Bobby's press secretary, came to the room where his friends were and told us that Bobby's heart had just stopped beating—he was gone. Then he went to the press room across the street from the hospital where he reported, with faltering voice, 'I have a short announcement to read which I will read at this time. Senator Robert Francis Kennedy died at 1:44 A.M. today, June 6, 1968. With Senator Kennedy at the time of his death were his wife, Ethel; his sisters, Mrs. Stephen Smith and Patricia Lawford; his brother-in-law, Stephen Smith; and Mrs. John F. Kennedy. He was forty-two years old.' Frank omitted to mention that Senator Edward Moore Kennedy was there only because he forgot and was himself so upset (Robert Blair Kaiser, *'R.F.K. Must Die!'*, New York: Dutton, 1970, p. 106).

"I went back home with an empty, dark, hopeless hole in me. So much enthusiasm, so much hope and so much drive, all gone for nothing. Just like that, like snapping your fingers, everything I'd ever hoped to see in our nation was changed. It seemed as if it all died with Bobby.

"Thursday morning, I watched on television as Ethel, the family, and some of Bobby's friends got on a plane to take the body home to New York. I couldn't stop crying when I saw that plane take off. Somewhere in that same time frame I first heard the name of the alleged assassin: Sirhan.

"I went to the studio that afternoon to do my television show, and couldn't do it. I walked off the set crying again. Later that afternoon, I got a call that Ethel wanted me to join the family at their New York apartment. There was a ticket at the airport for me, and someone would meet me in New York with a limousine to take me to Ethel's. All I had to do was come. I went. At the apartment, there were people everywhere, but I let Ethel know I was there, and she thanked me for coming!

"Friday night, we sat up and watched over the body at St. Patrick's Cathedral. People came, and they came, and they came. And they cried. On Saturday morning, the mass was said. Teddy Kennedy spoke movingly and we sang 'The Battle Hymn of the Republic.' It was hard for me to sing, though.

"Then the casket was placed aboard a special funeral train that would travel slowly to Washington for Bobby's burial. At Grand Central Station the line seemed to last forever, all of those people getting on the train. I was told not to stray too far away in case Ethel needed me for anything, so I stayed close by. As the train moved slowly along, people stood along the tracks on either side—up on the banks. Some wept and waved, some stood silently, others stood to attention and saluted.

"Near Philadelphia, a train approaching us plowed through some people standing on the track watching for us. Some of them were killed. It was horrible beyond words—grief was added to grief. How much could we take?

"As the train neared Washington, Ethel announced, 'I want to go through the train and thank everyone.' A lot of the people with her thought it would be too much for her, but she really wanted to do it.

"So I said, 'Let's do it.'

"I went ahead into each of the cars to tell them she was coming. 'Mrs. Kennedy will be arriving here in a few minutes,' I would say. 'I want all of you to stand up, and I want you to put any beer or anything else like that out of sight. She wants to thank you.'

"So we went throughout the train, and it was a long one. I don't know how many cars there were, but she went through all of them, thanking each person, one at a time. It was touching to watch.

"When we arrived in Washington, I began to help with the logistics, making sure everyone was in the right car and things like that. I was glad to have something to do. At last, all the people were in the cars on the way to the cemetery. Everybody but me. Then someone stopped to pick me up. Once there, we had to make a long trek up to the grave site. I walked with Frank Gifford part of the way. It was something to see all the people I knew and all those I had read about. President Johnson and Lady Bird were there, and Averell Harriman, cabinet officers and justices of the Supreme Court, and more senators and congressmen than I could count.

"After the burial, many of Bobby's friends went back to Hickory Hill. I hadn't known him as long as some of the others, but I loved him as much. I slept that night with Bobby, Jr., in his room. Bobby's dog shared the bed with us.

"I'm not one for sharing my bed with a dog, and then it got cold (the Kennedys are fresh-air fiends). Consequently, I rose early and went downstairs. I was standing outside and one of the eleven kids, four year old Max, was already out there.

'Hi, Rosey,' he greeted me.

'Morning, Max,' I returned, astonished that he knew my name.

'Rosey, you were there, weren't you?'

'Yes, I was.'

'Why did that man kill my dad?'

'Maxwell,' I said (his full name was Matthew Maxwell Taylor Kennedy), 'some people are full of hate. The man who killed your daddy was one of them. We don't know why he was full of hate, though.' I picked him up, put him on my shoulder and started walking. 'I don't think we'll ever understand,' I continued, 'why he did what he did.'

"Maxwell showed me all the animals on the place, and there were quite a few. Hickory Hill was noted for its 'menagerie.' He and I became good friends that day. During the rest of my stay at Hickory Hill, he stayed near me. As the day went on, we were able to laugh.

"It seemed to me all of us were trying to break through our grief by laughing, all these loving people who cared about Ethel and the family. We stood around and sat around and talked. I tried to get off in a room somewhere by myself where I could give way to sadness, but Ethel wouldn't let me.

"She came in and sat down beside me and said, 'You can't sit here like this. We've got to go outside and do something. Come on out of here.'

"I obeyed and, after a while I joined in a game of touch football. It was a hot day, and, after the game, we jumped in the pool to cool off. I don't swim, but I delighted everyone with a bigger-than-usual splash when I cannon-balled into the pool.

"Ethel didn't let anyone get downhearted or depressed or sit around and mope. She kept some kind of activity going on all the time to keep our spirits up. The whole time I was with Ethel or any of the family that week, I never remember any of them giving way to grief. The only time I thought Ethel came close to weeping was much later. I called her, and she told me someone's comments about the upcoming trial of Bobby's assassin. The person she named had said a lot of nasty things about Sirhan, displaying a great deal of hostility and anger.

"I said, 'I don't know why he had to call you up and tell you all of that. Why rake all that up in your memory? We've all got to appear at the trial, and that's time enough to think about what happened.'

"It seemed as if she broke down for a few minutes and couldn't say anything. I waited and didn't say anything either. In a few minutes, she was composed and back on the phone, and we talked a little longer, then said goodbye.

"Bobby Kennedy's abrupt death wrenched me more deeply and catastrophically than I can express. I grieved for him a long time. For years, I agonized about what I could have done differently. 'What,' I asked myself, 'can anyone do to prevent an act of violence against a human being?'

"Bobby, quoting Aeschylus, had called us to dedicate ourselves to the task of taming the savageness of man and to make gentle the life of the world. I had to answer that call. I resolved that the rest of my life would be given to that goal as never before. The Rams might have heard me talk about love and comradeship before, but they hadn't heard anything yet.

"I had sat too long on the sidelines of life, refusing to do more than be grieved by the suffering that came to my attention. 'Someone ought to do something about that,' I would say.

'Someone?' Who is that? Usually no one.

"Martin Luther King, Jr. showed me that change by nonviolent means was possible. Bobby Kennedy had invited me to pay the price of becoming personally involved in that process of change.

'People Make the World What It Is,' a song written by a friend of mine, Bobby Womack, says it best.

"Before I met Bobby Kennedy, I only knew how to play football and to sing. Granted, the seeds of gentleness were planted mysteriously in my heart during my childhood—perhaps even before my birth. And I had moved as a man with a gentle heart in the violent world of the NFL. It was a contradiction for which I had no resolution. But football had given me a life I would never have enjoyed otherwise. I owed a lot to football, and, yet, I needed more because it had given me little opportunity to express my heart. After I met Bobby, I found all the opportunity I needed.

"I loved all Americans—Black, White, and otherwise—and I wanted us all to live in freedom, equality and harmony. But I was learning this wasn't possible unless I was willing to make myself part of the struggle.

"When I returned to California after the funeral, it was the middle of June. I had to make a decision about my football career. I hated making decisions. I liked it better when they were made for me. That way I didn't have to take the blame for them if they turned out badly. (I know this was immature, but, for what it's worth, a study has shown that people who refuse to take responsibility in this way live longer and healthier lives.)

"My habit at this time each year was to work out in preparation for training camp. So, in the name of habit and not making a decision, I was working out in Pasadena with Deacon Jones, Merlin Olsen, and Merlin's little girl, Kelly, who was about six years old. As we ran around the track, Merlin and Deacon steadily pulled out in front. But, then, a little later, I found that Kelly was setting a pace with which I also could not keep up.

"Pretty soon I was trailing well behind them all. So I started to walk—and think. My career as an entertainer had developed slowly and unspectacularly, but steadily, since I had come back from the army with that guitar in 1958. Now, ten years hence, it could probably sustain me if I gave it my full-time attention. And it would allow me even greater freedom to pursue the vision that my friendship with Bobby Kennedy had given me.

"Training camp was scheduled to begin, as usual, on July 14. Putting off the final decision as long as possible, I waited until the 14th to call George Allen. 'Coach,' I said, 'this is Rosey Grier. I've made up my mind to retire.'

'But, Rose, your tendon's okay, right?'

'Yeah.'

'Why don't you come on down here to camp and at least give it a try? What could it hurt?'

'No,' I replied after a moment's hesitation. 'I don't understand it all, but I know the time has come for me to hang up my cleats once and for all.' "

Had Bobby Kennedy lived, it is quite possible that he would have also become President of the United States. At the time of his death he was U.S. Senator from the state of New York and was actively seeking the nomination of the Democratic party for President of the United States.

As I recall, I was in Hawthorne, Florida, attending our annual church camp meeting when I heard the sad news of Bobby Kennedy's assassination. I grieved much for the Kennedy family because of the grief and pain that had been inflicted upon them for a second time during the decade of the sixties. I was especially grieved for the matriarch of the family, Mrs. Rose Kennedy, for the loss of three sons. The first was the death of son Joseph during World War II, the second President John F. Kennedy on November 25, 1963, and now a third son, Bobby, was killed. The Lord sustained her and blessed her with longevity for which I am grateful.

While the social and economic status of African-Americans and other minorities have improved since the 1963 March on Washington, the position of Blacks and others relative to White Americans continues to lag in many areas. However, the struggle continues; and, in my opinion, will continue throughout the foreseeable future. Nevertheless, we should strive to do our best to love and treat our fellowmen with respect and dignity. In my opinion, we do not have to enact more civil rights laws to do that, because you can't legislate love; it comes from the heart. May the Lord help each of us to go the extra mile in helping to make Bobby Kennedy's dream become a reality.

I have always felt that our churches should have been out front in combating the evils and injustices that were so prevalent during the Civil Rights Movement. Even today the church, in my opinion, could

243

still be a catalyst for change when it involves man's inhumanity to man.

Dr. William G. Johnson, Editor of the *Advent Review*, made the following comments in an editorial dated February 8, 1990:

"In 1943 a light-skinned woman, Lucy Byard, was admitted to a hospital in the Washington, D. C., area. Soon it was discovered that she was Black, however, and although she was seriously ill, she was sent to another hospital. She died shortly afterward of pneumonia.

"Mrs. Byard was a Seventh-day Adventist, and the hospital that refused to treat her was the Washington Sanitarium.

"Today we can hardly believe that it could have happened. Yet we need to remember that the Review and Herald cafeteria, which served the publishing house and General Conference staff just one mile away from the sanitarium, also operated on a Whites-only basis.

"Our people at the Washington Sanitarium, like those who ran the Review and Herald cafeteria, were no worse than others in the society of that time. They simply reflected prevailing attitudes toward Blacks. But while they were not behind their contemporaries, unfortunately they were not ahead of them.

"The social situation in North America has changed enormously during the past 50 years. Blacks, after prolonged struggle, have won civil rights that guarantee by law their equality.

"And the Seventh-day Adventist Church has changed also. None of our institutions in North America are segregated today. We have Black churches and White churches, but these arise out of cultural differences, preferred alternatives in worship style. No Adventist church may turn away from worship or membership any person on the basis of race or color.

"However, integration among Adventists also came with struggle. We moved only because society moved. In some cases it took the threat of legal action to goad us to reformation of behavior in civil rights. What a tragedy!

"I grew up in Australia. For many years I remained ignorant of the struggles of American Blacks, and American Black Adventists, for treatment as equals. If anyone had suggested I was racist, I would have laughed—one of my best friends at Avondale College was an Ethiopian.

"Yet I was racist without knowing it. Not racist in terms of all non-Whites, but toward the Aborigines of Australia. I grew up thinking of them as less than second-class citizens. I was an Adventist for many years before I realized how evil, how Antithetical to the gospel, is that attitude.

"My reflection on my own background and attitudes suggests three factors, significant to all Adventists, as we seek by the grace of God to build the just community:

"1. The root of racist pride is belief in our inherent superiority.

"We think we are superior because we are *born* superior. We are born superior because we have this color of skin or that ethnic origin, and so on.

"Such thinking contradicts the doctrines of creation and redemption. God made humanity in His image, the Bible tells us (Gen. 1:26, 27)—not a particular race of mankind. He who prides himself above another because of the accidence of birth impugns the Creator, who is Father of us all.

"And Jesus died for *every* person. If we belong to Christ, 'there is neither Jew nor Greek, slave nor free, male nor female' (Gal. 3:28, NIV). 'In Christ we are one. As we come in sight of Calvary, and view the royal Sufferer who in man's nature bore the curse of the law in his behalf, all national distinctions, all sectarian differences, are obliterated; all honor of rank, all pride of caste, is lost' (*Selected Messages*, book 1, p. 258).

"2. Belief in our superiority leads to injustice.

"If people of another race are inferior to us—inferior because they were so born—why should we deal with them as equals? To take an extreme example: we believe that animals' rights are important, but we would not argue that those rights should equal human rights.

"Humanity's history demonstrates the terrible correlation between attitudes of racial superiority and injustice. In the church, we will never free ourselves from this weight of evil until we step out into the light of the equality for all that the gospel brings.

"3. Being a Christian doesn't automatically solve the problem.

"Racist attitudes, feelings, and behaviors are learned early. We may live for many years—perhaps our whole lifetime—without realizing the filth of racism that has stuck to us.

"So we need education. The church needs to help its members examine their attitudes and prejudices in the light of the Scriptures.

That will be painful. But then we must go beyond the past, beyond society, into the growth the gospel calls us to.

"Some concerns of Adventism we teach well—vegetarianism, for instance—and I am glad we do. But the Adventist who is a vegetarian but racist displays a shocking reversal of moral values. Hitler also was a vegetarian!

"Our church is growing fast. The prophecy of Revelation 14:6,7 finds fulfillment in our day. But I am troubled. How well are we doing in helping our people cope with that vision of Revelation 14—*one* people out of a host of ethnic backgrounds? Incidents of racism, casteism, and blatant inequality that at times raise their heads in our midst today lead me to fear we have largely neglected this vital area."

Dr. Johnson's counsel is strong medicine, and I admire him for speaking out on these issues that even today can be very sensitive. I was very reluctant to include the examples that he gave of the extreme measures taken to preserve and maintain segregation. In my opinion, we have come a long way; but we still have a long way to go. However, I firmly believe that we will not resolve many of our racial problems until Christ comes back and takes us to heaven. It is really serious business because if we can't get along down here on this earth, we certainly would not get along in heaven.

We did not have civil rights marches in Blakely; however, a few of our students from Washington High School did participate in some sit-ins at the lunch counters in the drug stores and other eating establishments.

Albany, Georgia, was the closest city to Blakely where Dr. King led marches, conducted sit-ins, bus boycotts, and voter-registration drives. Even though Blakely was never targeted as a city for active demonstrations, I believe that they did have an impact for change.

Blakely and Early County have made significant progress since those turbulent days of the Civil Rights Movement. Specific examples include the following: an Afro-American postmaster, Walter Davis; a rural mail carrier, Charles Slaton and a part time mail carrier. All three of the banks have Black cashiers, and the Bank of Early has a Black loan officer. Most of our stores have Black cashiers. Our law enforcement departments (sheriff and police) are well integrated. The City Council has two Black members, Peter Harris and Andrew Wynds; and the Early County Board of Education has two Black members, Bishop Hunter and Gwen Harris. It is worthy of note that

Bishop is the chairperson for that body. I think that represents tremendous progress when one considers how far we have come. However, I am concerned that the central office staff remains unintegrated, unless the Chapter 1 Coordinator, Mr. Fred Daniels, Jr., is considered to be on that staff. Even if that is the case, I believe that there should be more. However, it is commendable that in other areas such as the maintenance staff for the buildings and grounds and the shop foreman for the system school buses are black. I am encouraged by this and feel that progress is being made to promote equality for all.

"Some men see things as they are and say, 'Why?' I dream things that never were and say, 'why not?' "

—George Bernard Shaw

CHAPTER 22

BLACK AMERICANS WITH ROOTS IN EARLY COUNTY

There are a very significant number of Black people of Early County who have made outstanding contributions to the progress of our society. I shall cite only a sampling of these individuals.

The first individual to be cited is Professor B. R. Holmes. "Mr. B. R. Holmes was born in the Pleasant Grove Community, about ten miles from Blakely. He received his early training in the public school in the Pleasant Grove Community. According to autobiographic information compiled about himself in 'A Struggling Student,' his first teacher was Professor A. Speight. The school term was only three months. His father, Mr. Jacob Holmes, desired a better opportunity to educate his children; so, he bought a farm of two hundred and fifty acres from Col. R. H. Powell. At that time, it was located approximately one mile from Blakely.

"Mr. Holmes matriculated in the Blakely Academy, during which time Professor J. W. F. Webb was the principal. It is interesting to note that Professor Webb was my grandfather. Mr. Holmes graduated in May, 1897, after which he was elected Assistant Principal of the same school and taught one term. After being elected Assistant Principal he was given an examination by the Superintendent of Schools, Mr. T. F. Jones. Mr. Holmes passed the examination and was given license to teach in the public schools of Georgia.

"In June Mr. Holmes was elected Principal of the Oak Grove Public School. The enrollment of the school was seventy-two students. The term was three months, with a paid salary of fifty dollars for the term. Mr. Holmes observed that the salary he was receiving would not help him to continue his training. He opened a night school and succeeded in enrolling forty students, paying one dollar per month.

"On September 7, 1897, Mr. Holmes, having an ambition to complete his training ever since he was a little boy, packed his trunk and left on the morning train for Atlanta via Central of Georgia Railroad at 7 A.M. Many friends had assembled at the station to bid

Mr. Holmes goodbye and a successful term in college. As the train pulled out from the station, Mr. Holmes stood on the rear of the train and waved his handkerchief until the train was out of sight. Mr. Holmes returned to his seat and sat beside the window all day as the train passed through Albany, Thomasville, Americus, and Macon, arriving in Atlanta at 7 p.m. Mr. Holmes was met at the station by his first cousin, Rev C. G. Gray. Mr. Holmes came out of the station, and saw his first electric car. He thought the people on the cars were joyriding. He and Rev. Gray walked home to give him an opportunity to see some of the city.

"It was the custom of the boy students to initiate the new students the first morning they went from the dormitory to the dining room in the next building. There was a space of about fifty feet between the two buildings. The girls would come to the windows to see the initiation program. Mr. Blocker, Mr. Holmes' roommate, had informed him of the initiation. The morning that Mr. Holmes made his first trip, the other boys belonging to the committee had preceded him and were standing together, waiting for him to come out. When he began the trip to the dining room, the boys who were to initiate him became quiet as mice when the old cat was around. Rev. W. B. Lawrence, who was president of the initiation committee, would give orders when to begin the work. Rev. Lawrence observed the flash of Mr. Holmes' eyes as he passed him. He advised the boys not to attempt to initiate Mr. Holmes because some of them may get seriously hurt. The girls who were looking out the window yelled, 'You have met your match,' when they failed to give Mr. Holmes his first lesson in college.

"Mr. Holmes reported to his classes the first morning. Mrs. Landrum gave him a cordial welcome to the class.

"Mr. Holmes did not have money to pay his expenses in college for the remainder of the term. He notified the President of his intention. Mr. Holmes returned home and was elected principal of the St. Maryland Public School January 1, 1899. The term of school was four months; the salary for the term was $60.

"During the ten years Mr. Holmes was in college, he supported himself. The ten years of struggle to receive an education will always be remembered. In order to support himself in college, he continued to publish the *Blakely Messenger*. Most of the subscribers lived in Blakely, Georgia. To get better support in Atlanta, the name of the paper was changed to the *Atlanta Justice*, which was continued. Mr.

Holmes merged the *Atlanta Justice* with the *Atlanta Independent* and became Business Manager of the same.

"Mr. Holmes was suspended from class recitations many times by the President for nonpayment of tuition. Mr. Holmes did not give up but continued to stand the embarrassment. He would go in the city and solicit funds among his friends. In a few hours he would return with the money. The President would send a notice to the teachers to permit his to continue his recitations.

"Came many times when Mr. Holmes had no money, but no one had a knowledge of it. Several students whose parents were in good financial condition sent twenty-five dollars to their children to spend during the holidays. Mr. Holmes kept a good spirit of being jolly because he believed this condition would not last always. One Christmas morning when Mr. Holmes was found as usual with no money, he had promised one of his classmates (a girl) a present. In order to make his promise good, he went to Mr. C. C. Cater, who was conducting a grocery store on the corner of Bell and Auburn Avenue, to secure a loan of fifty cents after explaining to Mr. Cater how he would pay it back. After careful consideration of Mr. Holmes' statement, Mr. Cater told him he would give him the fifty cents. Mr. Holmes hastened to the city and bought a present for fifty cents and put it on the Christmas tree, which was held in Morris Brown Chapel. The girl received the present. This was all the money Mr. Holmes had during the holidays.

"Mr. Holmes and other students boarded with a lady who was very strict about collecting board money the exact date it was due. Many times Mr. Holmes would not have the money to pay on the date it was due. Mr. Holmes would leave on the morning the board was due early and would not return until he had the money. The lesson taught Mr. Holmes about being punctual in paying bills and helped to make him more exact in meeting obligations.

"During the last year Dr. Henderson was President, Mr. Holmes was suspended from classes for nonpayment of tuition. It was the week that the teachers were giving their final examinations for the term. Students were not permitted to take the examination who were behind with their bills. On entering college the morning of the examination, Mr. Holmes had studied all night until five o'clock in the morning. He was informed by the teachers that he could not take the final examination until the bill was paid.

"Mr. Holmes immediately left the chapel. Many students made fun of him. Mr. Holmes hastened to the home of Bishop H. M. Turner and explained the situation. Bishop Turner called President Henderson over the phone and advised the President to send the bill to him, whatever Mr. Holmes owed for tuition, and he would pay same. This was the end of the embarrassment. President Henderson never did send the bill to Bishop Turner. Mr. Holmes returned to college and took the examinations. Bishop Turner was Presiding Bishop of Georgia and President of the Trustee Board of the college.

"Mr. Holmes wrote his father to visit the commencement of his first graduation. His father was present and saw his son who had spent eleven years of sacrifice, receive the certificate of graduation.

"Mr. Jacob Holmes, the father of Rev. B. R. Holmes, was born a slave in Blakely, Georgia, in 1845. He was owned by Dr. Holmes, one of the leading doctors of that community. He was married to Miss Amanda Wade, who was owned by Mr. John W. Wade. The law was that if a colored man married and his wife was owned by another, the name of the wife remained in the name of her owner; and the children would belong to the wife's owner.

"The rule was that a man could not visit his wife but once a week when they did not have the same owner. The custom was that you would have to get a pass from your owner before you could visit your wife. If your wife's owner lived fifty miles, you had to report in time to be on the job the next morning, which was sun up. If you were caught without a pass, you would be punished.

To the union was born twelve children, eight boys and four girls. After the emancipation, Dr. Holmes made Mr. Jacob Holmes Agent to look after his farms in Early County near Pleasant Grove, Georgia. He gave Mr. Holmes a house and a farm as long as Dr. Holmes lived. The contract was kept. All the children of Mr. and Mrs. Holmes were born on the farm. Dr. Holmes moved to Rome, Georgia, after emancipation. He would visit Blakely once or twice a year. One visit would be just before Christmas, when he would give all his old ex-slaves presents and also collect his rent, which was turned over by his Agent. One cold day, when we were picking cotton near the Chattahoochee River, the news came that Dr. Holmes had passed in Rome, Georgia. Mr. Holmes and the tenants of Dr. Holmes' farms were much grieved. Mr. Holmes did not attend his funeral, because the news came too late.

"Dr. Holmes observed that Mr. Jacob Holmes was worried because he could not see his new wife but once a week. In order to give relief to the situation, Dr. Holmes, after a long-drawn-out conversation with Mr. Wade, the owner of Mr. Holmes' wife, he agreed to sell her to Dr. Holmes. Mr. Jacob Holmes was the house boy of Dr. Holmes, and his wife was made the house girl. This ended the unfortunate condition that existed between Mr. Holmes and his wife as to living together.

"Mr. Holmes never attended school a day. He was taught his A. B. C.'s by Dr. Holmes' wife, his owner. He received his learning from self-help. He would come from the farm many times after a hard day's work and bring pine wood knots; sometimes he would dig up old pine wood stumps in order that he may have light to see how to study at night. There were a few lamps in the community and kerosene oil, which was used by the rich people. He did not have the money to buy because he had a family of twelve children, and most of them were small and too young to work on the farm...."The Holmes Institute was organized by Rev. B. R. Holmes, in 1917, on the corner of Fort and Clifton Streets, (Atlanta) in a dilapidated tabernacle with no floor, with an enrollment of sixteen students, who were turned away from the city public schools because of the crowded conditions and inability to buy books.

"In the same year, a lot was purchased on the same site; and a three-room frame building was erected. In 1918 a lot was purchased adjoining the same lot, and a three-story frame building was erected with ten rooms. This site being too small for the increasing attendance, a new site was purchased on the corner of Hillard and Currier Streets in 1920. In 1923 a five-story modern brick building was erected at a cost of $50,000.00

"In March, 1934, a fire destroyed the building and its contents between the hours of one and two o'clock in the morning. The trustees purchased a new site with three buildings on Bedford Place, N.E., near Forrest Avenue. In 1938 a three-story brick building was erected and furnished, which houses the chapel, classrooms, Domestic Science, Laundering, girls' dormitory; Barber, Tailoring and Shoe Shops; and Dressmaking Department. The late Bishop Henry McNeal Turner, of the African Methodist Episcopal Church, was elected the first President of the Trustee Board.

"The Holmes Institute was organized for the training of the colored youth religiously, intellectually, and industrially. Imparting knowledge is a very small part of the work of the Institute. Emphasis is placed upon the development of character and self-reliance."

Mr. Holmes did have a difficult struggle, but he did not give up. I admire him for the courage that he displayed when he would find himself "between a rock and a hard place." It was his courage and perseverance that finally enabled him to establish The Holmes Institute.

I was especially saddened as I read about the struggle his slave parents endured as they tried to hold their family together and provide a quality education for them. I was further saddened when I learned that the 250 acre farm that Mr. Jacob Holmes, Mr. B. R. Holmes' father, bought is no longer in the family. This seems to be part of a trend that many Blacks experienced in that they allowed land that was bought with the sweat and tears of their ancestors to get away from them. In many instances, it stemmed from failure to pay the taxes; or it was used for collateral and lost for a fraction of its worth when the loan was not paid on time. This factor has had a negative influence on Black landowners.

The next individual that I would like to highlight is Mr. James Alexander Slaton. He finished Albany State College in 1930 and went to Edison, Georgia, as principal of the colored elementary school in the fall of that year. This was his first job. The highest grade at that time was the sixth. His first objective was to get more children in school. Mr. Slaton made a public announcement for all children who had finished the sixth grade or dropped out of school to come back and enroll. Children all over the county came because there were ten or twelve feeder schools in the county. The enrollment grew rapidly to approximately one hundred ninety students. There were three teachers employed.

Mr. Slaton explained to the public that the eleventh grade would be added to the curriculum. This gave students and parents something to look forward to.

The first eleventh grade graduating class was in 1936. The last eleventh grade graduating class was in 1951. In 1952 there was no graduating class because the twelfth grade was added to the curriculum. Many of the eleventh graders came back and enrolled in the twelfth grade, making a very large number. By this time the people in the community were full of enthusiasm and greatly impressed with Mr. Slaton's work—both Black and White. The first graduating class from the twelfth grade was in 1953, with a packed auditorium. Out of the class, sixty-seven percent went to college. After 1953 the percentage of children attending college became greater.

In 1957 the Henry Tucker Singleton High School was completed in Morgan, Georgia, the county seat of Calhoun County. The school moved from Edison to Morgan after the first semester, January 28th. By that time the enrollment was approximately seven hundred fifty students and a staff of more than twenty-five. New courses were added to the curriculum.

During his thirty-eight years in the county, his successes were many, including his marriage to his childhood sweetheart, Ms. Lila Mae Bable.

His students made outstanding achievements in such areas as doctors, lawyers, teachers, nurses, counselors, farmers, accountants, preachers, etc.

He was a man of character and never satisfied unless he knew that you had done your very best. He was never too tired to listen to students and their problems. He was also dedicated to helping all humanity. Edison is a better place by his having been there.

Another outstanding person from Early County is Dr. Louis W. Sullivan. Dr. Louis Sullivan and his brother, Dr. Walter Sullivan, did not attend school in Early County but spent many of their summers in Blakely. I decided to let Dr. Louis Sullivan tell of those experiences in his own words.

"Thomas Wolfe said, 'You can't go home again.' That is true. I had the pleasure of returning to Blakely, Ga., recently to address the students at Early County High School. Home was never so different.

"I told them what Blakely was like in the 1940s and '50s, well over 40 years ago. I lived in an environment of overt racism, made all the more harrowing because my father began the first chapter of the NAACP in Blakely.

"I told them that my parents sent me and my brother, Walter, to public schools in Atlanta, rather than to segregated, academically second-rate schools in southwest Georgia. When the White schools in Early County received new books, the old ones were passed to the Black schools.

"Opportunities for my race were few. Segregation was the rule of the day. And so, I'm glad I can't go home again to the Blakely of the 1940s and '50s.

"Instead, I returned to a new Blakely—to a hometown that welcomed me. I was welcomed by Blacks and Whites who are wiser and more tolerant of each other. As I looked out on the gathering of young people at this special time in their lives, I reflected on my own opportunities.

"Despite the racial climate of a former time, I made it through— and so did a respectable handful of other Blacks.

"Those who had gone before me encouraged me. My father and mother sought to instill in me high standards and a strong character to strive for. If my compatriots and I could succeed, during an especially dark and discouraging period in our nation's history, think of the opportunities these young people have in 1991.

"I felt triumphant upon my return—and also a little saddened, reminded once again of the struggles my family had to endure.

"But things change. Blakely has changed. It has set a modest example for the rest of the country, which also must change. People must look at things differently—their attitudes and their values must shift.

"In too many areas of the country, there is a soul sickness, a bankruptcy of values. People are drifting. Families are abandoned or never formed; and our young people turn to drugs and violence, instead of to the time-honored institutions that used to sustain us all—our churches, social organizations, schools and families. We had strong vibrant communities some 40 years ago.

"When I grew up in Blakely, my neighborhood functioned like one big family. Everyone looked out for the children of the neighborhood. And people took personal responsibility for the consequences of their actions. We were all part of a bigger whole.

"The glue that held us together was love, faith, hope, selflessness, integrity, and a sense of responsibility toward our fellow man. There seems to be a dearth of those values today.

"We must heal our communities. Individuals must commit to serve their neighborhoods and be active. They must become participants.

"The country must follow the example of Blakely. We must renew our culture of character, and strengthen our values and institutions. It is in a culture of character that our young people can reap the advantages of their opportunities today—just as we did 40 to 55 years ago."

Mr. W. W. Sullivan, Sr., was the father of Dr. Louis Sullivan and Dr. Walter W. Sullivan, Jr. He lived in Blakely for many years and was the owner of Sullivan Funeral Home. In addition to being a successful businessman, he was very much involved in civic/community affairs. In that connection, he served as President of the local chapter of the NAACP. I admired him for being a man who was not afraid to stand up for what he believed, including equal justice for everyone.

Dr. Ralph W. Turner is from my community and grew up on the farm as I did. His father kept him out of school to assist him with farm chores, thus causing him to miss many days from school. Finally, Mrs. Kate Slaton made a visit to Ralph's home and had a one-on-one discussion with his father, and he promised her that he would find a way to keep Ralph in school. His father kept his word, and Ralph was able to finish high school with honors.

Mr. Curtis Stanley was his principal and was instrumental in getting him admitted to his Alma Mater, Johnson C. Smith, in Charlotte, North Carolina.

From there he went on to the University of Pittsburgh, which was also Mr. Stanley's Alma Mater, where Ralph earned his Master's Degree and Ph.D in chemistry.

His professional experiences have been at Florida A. & M. University, Tallahassee, Florida, where he presently serves as chairperson for the Science Department.

I trust that Dr. Turner's accomplishments will serve as an inspiration and encouragement to young people in their endeavors to be all that they can be.

Attorney Jesse L. Echols is another successful man with roots in my community. We attended the same one-room school at Allen Chapel during the time that my mother was the teacher, after which, he transferred to Washington High School and graduated in 1951.

He did his undergraduate work at Fort Valley State College, Fort Valley, Georgia, and received his B. S. Degree in Health and Physical Education in 1955. Further study was done at Atlanta University, Atlanta, Georgia, on a part-time basis.

He became interested in becoming an attorney and studied law at the Woodrow Wilson College of Law from 1970–1973 at which time he received his Juris Doctorate Degree.

He was admitted to the State Bar of Georgia in 1974.

His legal background includes an array of experiences which I shall not list. Presently, Jesse is Associate City Attorney for the City of Atlanta. He and his family reside in Lithonia, Georgia.

I am proud of the accomplishments of James L. Toson, Jr. James L. Toson, a 1964 graduate of Washington High School, Blakely, Georgia, and the son of Melba and Lowell Daniels of Jakin, is presently Editor of the U. S. Postal Service's *Central Region Bulletin* and Assistant Regional Communications Administrator. The *Central Region*, with Headquarters in Chicago, employs 174,007 postal workers and covers 15 Midwestern states.

As editor of the *Bulletin*, Mr. Toson publishes a monthly newspaper of 20,000 containing information for middle and upper postal management. As Assistant Communications Administrator, he is part of the team responsible for managing the flow of information and media interaction (print, radio, and television) within the Region.

A three-time graduate of the Department of Defense Information School, Mr. Toson began his journalism career as an Information Specialist in the U. S. Marine Corps in 1969 after attending Tennessee State University. During the Vietnam war, he was managing editor of a weekly newspaper based in the Far East and a contributor to *Stars and Stripes*, the world-known military newspaper. After serving for three years as Public Affairs Chief at Headquarters, 6th Marine Corps District, in Atlanta, his last year in the Marines was spent in the Advertising Department at Headquarters, U. S. Marine Corps. During his ten-year career, Mr. Toson was cited many times (including commendations by the Commandant of the Marine Corps and the Joint Chiefs of Staff) for outstanding performance.

After leaving the Marines, Mr. Toson worked on Madison Avenue in New York with a national and international news-gathering organization before rejoining the government as a writer with the National Endowment for the Humanities. In 1982 Mr. Toson became self-employed and worked as a management consultant until he joined the Postal Service in 1988.

Dr. Shirley Hodge Hardin is from Jakin, Georgia, and is a graduate of Early County High School. Her parents are Mr. and Mrs.

Freddie Hodge, Sr. Shirley received her Ph.D in English from Florida State University, Tallahassee, Florida.

She is married to Dr. Moses Hardin, who holds a Ph.D in Modern Foreign Languages from Florida State University, Tallahassee, Florida. In fact, they both received their Ph.D.'s at the same time. Presently, they are employed as assistant professors at Valdosta State University, Valdosta, Georgia. They have two children, Keltrice and Eric.

Annette Hubbard is another Black Early Countian that has done exceptionally well in the nursing profession. It is interesting to note that when she finished Washington High School in 1951, it was unaccredited; but she didn't become discouraged. Her parents arranged for Mr. and Mrs. John Slaton (Mrs. Slaton had been her high school science teacher) to take them to the Grady Memorial Hospital School of Nursing , Atlanta, Georgia, to see what could be done. Since she had such a good high school record, the admission officer allowed her to take the entrance examination; and she passed it with flying colors. Her parents accompanied her and they were told by the admission officer, that on the basis of her excellent performance on the entrance exam, they would admit her to the Grady Nursing program. However, there was one problem; namely, all the slots were filled; but if anyone dropped out, she would be given that slot. Apparently, the Lord heard her prayer; and someone did drop out, thus enabling her to get into the Grady Hospital Nursing Program.

The Lord blessed Annette while she was at Grady, and she completed the program without any difficulty and received her nursing diploma in 1955.

She continued to upgrade her professional skills and received her B.S. Nursing Degree from Seton Hall University, South Orange, New Jersey, in 1965.

She continued to study and received her M.A. Degree in Guidance and Counseling from Jersey City State College, Jersey City, New Jersey, in 1977. In 1981 she received her professional diploma state certification in school psychology from the same institution.

She has had a wide array of professional experiences that I will not list. Also she has received numerous honors and awards.

I salute her for such outstanding accomplishments. I know that it has not been easy, but she hung tough and beat the odds.

Also from the Hubbard family is Annette's older brother, James, who also graduated from Washington High School, did his undergraduate work at Dillard University in New Orleans, Louisiana, and received his Doctor's Degree in medicine from Meharry Medical College, Nashville, Tennessee. He served a tour of duty in the U. S. Navy before moving to Albany, Georgia. His specialties are Gynecology and Obstetrics. He has a very lucrative practice in Albany and is very highly respected by his peers. I am proud of Dr. Hubbard and especially when I realize it all started right here in Blakely and Early County.

Specifically, I appreciate what he and his siblings are doing in awarding scholarships for deserving high school graduates from the Early County School System. The scholarships are given in the memory of their mother, Mrs. Senella Hubbard, who was an exceptionally good nurse.

She assisted with the birth of our three children and I am eternally grateful for the tender loving care that she provided.

Another young man of whom I am justly proud and consider to be a very good role model is Walter Davis.

After finishing Washington High School, he was drafted into the U. S. Army and served in Vietnam. While there he lost a foot as a result of being hit by a hand grenade. This made it necessary for him to spend approximately eighteen months recovering from his wound and getting adjusted to his prosthesis. His recovery was very successful—so successful, in fact, that today he plays basketball as if the injury never occurred; and he does not allow it to slow him down.

When Walter got out of the army, he continued his education and earned his Bachelor's Degree from Albany State College, Albany, Georgia.

He has been employed by the U. S. Postal Service for twenty five years and is presently our local Postmaster, a position he has held since November 3, 1990.

Walter faced many odds in pursuit of his goal, but he kept his eyes on the prize and he won.

He has a very supportive wife, Annette, who was his high school sweetheart. She is an educator in the Dougherty County School System where she serves as Principal of the Isabella Elementary School.

In the field of dentistry we have Dr. Marvin Benjamin Pittman, who has an exemplary academic and professional record. He graduated from Washington High School in 1949 and Savannah State

College, Savannah, Georgia, in 1953. He received his Master's Degree from the University of Michigan in 1957 and his Doctor of Dental Surgery from Howard University, Washington, D. C., in 1966.

He has had an outstanding professional career, including Veterans Administration Center, Los Angeles, California, as a research biochemist from 1957–62. He has served as president and chief executive officer for the J. W. Ross Medical Center, Los Angeles, California, and also works as a self-employed dentist.

Presently, he is employed at the 349th General Hospital, Los Angeles, California, as Deputy Chief of Professional Services and Chief of Dental Services.

Dr. Pittman also has an outstanding military record, having served a total of 27 years and 7 months (6 years of active duty and 21 years and 7 months of reserve duty.) He presently holds the rank of Colonel in the U. S. Army Reserves.

He is the son of Mr. Johnnie Will Pittman and Mrs. Lucile Brewster Pittman. He is the nephew of Mr. Watson Brewster of Blakely, Georgia.

In the field of education, Fountain Wims has a very outstanding success story, which I will begin with his graduation from Washington High School in 1956.

He received his Bachelor's Degree from Albany State College, Albany, Georgia, in 1960.

His graduate work included the Master's Degree from Tuskegee University, Tuskegee, Alabama, and his Specialist Degree from Georgia State University, Atlanta, Georgia.

With the exception of two years spent in the military and two years in Seattle, Washington, he has worked in the Stewart County and Quitman County School Systems. His teaching experience has run the gamut from classroom teacher, to assistant principal, to high school principal of the Stewart-Quitman County High School, to his present position, Superintendent of the Stewart County School System.

I am especially proud of Fountain's accomplishments because when our schools were desegregated in 1970–71, Black high school principals became an endangered species. Not only did he beat the odds in that respect, but even more so in getting himself elected Superintendent of the school system. It's not easy, but he is living proof that it can be done.

In my opinion, Johnnie Mae Graham has achieved outstanding success in the legal profession; highlights include the following:

She received her high school diploma in 1973 from Early County High School.

In 1976 she graduated summa cum laude from Savannah State College in Savannah with a Bachelor of Arts Degree in history and political science.

She received her Juris Doctorate in 1981 from the University of Georgia, Athens, Georgia; and in the same year she was also admitted to the Georgia Bar.

Her professional affiliations, in addition to the usual affiliations of lawyers, also include the Georgia Association of Black Women Attorneys, C. B. King (a famous civil rights attorney) Bar Association, and President of Dougherty Circuit Bar Association.

In addition to a busy professional life, she has also been very active in civic affairs, serving as a Board Member of Liberty House, Dougherty County Commission on Children and Youth, and member of the 1990–91 Class of Leadership Albany.

She has served as a U.S. Senate Aide to Senator Sam Nunn.

Her parents are Mr. Verdell Graham, Sr., and Mrs. Vera Graham of Blakely.

Johnnie Mae is just another example of one who has beat the odds, and I am especially proud of her.

So far in this chapter, I have tried to focus on the individual accomplishments of several personalities. In this instance, I am going to recognize a particular family; namely, the Herbert Hunter, Sr. family. Herbert and his wife, Lillie, are the proud parents of six children, all of whom have college degrees; three have Master's Degrees.

Three of their children are commissioned officers in the U. S. Air Force.

The following is a brief biographical sketch of each of the six children:

Patricia Hunter Devine has a Bachelor of Science in Psychology and a Master's in Public Administration from Albany State College. She resides in Albany, Georgia.

Herbert Hunter, Jr. has a Bachelor of Science in Business Administration and a Master's in Business Administration from Tuskegee University. He has been in the Air Force for 12 years and has reached the rank of major. He is presently stationed at Hanscon Air Force Base.

Janice Hunter received her Bachelor of Science in computers and a Master's Degree in Business Administration from Tuskegee University. She served in the U. S. Air Force for eight years and had the rank of Captain before becoming employed by General Electric in Alexandria, Virginia.

Terry Hunter received his Bachelor of Science Degree in Accounting from Tuskegee University. Captain Hunter is a pilot and has served in the U. S. Air Force for nine years. He has been stationed at Howard Air Force Base and the Panama Canal.

Thaddeus Hunter received a Bachelor of Science in Accounting at Tuskegee University and is employed at Southern Nuclear Plant at Farley . He resides in Dothan, Alabama.

Melissa Hunter received her Bachelor of Science Degree in Computer Science from Tuskegee University and is employed by IBM in Lexington, Kentucky,

It is interesting to note, that five out of six of the children received undergraduate degrees from Tuskegee University, Tuskegee, Alabama.

I am fully aware that we may have other Black families in Early County whose accomplishments are just as great; nevertheless, since I could not present all of them, I chose this family as my sample. I trust that everyone will understand.

Rosa Reddick Burroughs graduated number three out of a class of 100 in 1970. Her class was the last to graduate before Washington High School was phased out as a part of the desegregation program.

She continued her education at Fisk University, Nashville, Tennessee, and received her Bachelor of Arts Degree in Chemistry in 1974.

Her dental training was received at the Medical College of Georgia, Augusta, Georgia; and she received her Doctor of Medical Dentistry in 1980.

She worked a year in Chattanooga, Tennessee, and a year in Macon, Georgia, before moving to Americus, Georgia, in 1983.

Presently, she has a very successful dental practice in Americus.

Her husband is a physician with a specialty in Internal Medicine and has a very successful practice in Americus.

They are the proud parents of two children. I just thank the Lord for the way He has blessed Rosa thus far and extend to her and her family my heartfelt congratulations.

It is interesting to note that Rosa's father died when she was in the eleventh grade. Even though her mother did not have any salable skills, she kept Rosa in school in spite of the sacrifice.

In my interview with Rose she was highly appreciative for the assistance and one-on-one counseling on financial assistance that my wife, Herk, obtained for her.

This has been a very rewarding and exciting chapter to write because I have discovered so many success stories on the part of those with whom I worked throughout my professional career.

Dr. Larry Lewis is another hometown young man who has made good. He is a product of the Early County School System and a 1961 graduate of Washington High School.

His additional academic training included the B. S. Degree in Mathematics from Alabama State University in 1965, the M. A. T. Degree from Purdue University in Mathematics in 1969, and his doctorate (Ed. D.) in Mathematics was received from Utah State University in 1976.

He has had an array of professional experiences, including his present position as Assistant Professor of Mathematics at Fort Valley State College, a position he has held since 1985. His duties include teaching developmental mathematics and coordinating Developmental Studies mathematics.

Dr. Lewis holds membership in several professional organizations and is the recipient of many honors and awards, including the Martin Luther King Fellowship for his doctorate at Utah State University.

It is also worthy of note that he was elected to *Who's Who in American Education* for the 1992–93 school year.

When I think from whence Dr. Lewis has come, I feel like saying, "Praise the Lord!" for He has brought him from a mighty long way. His parents are Mr. and Mrs. Julius Lewis of Blakely.

I trust some of our youngsters who are still in high school will try to emulate what he has accomplished.

Mrs. Betty Orange is another young lady who has been very successful as an educator.

She is a 1971 graduate of Early County High School and continued her education at Albany State College, Albany, Georgia, where she received her B. S. Degree in Elementary Education in 1976. Her Master's Degree in Early Childhood Education was received from Georgia Southwestern College, Americus, Georgia, in 1987. In 1989 she received her Master's Degree in Administration and Supervision from Troy State University, Troy, Alabama. Her Educational Specialist Degree was received from Nova University, Tallahassee, Florida.

She is the recipient of many awards and special recognition, including the following: graduated from college cum laude and was on the Dean's List during her Master's Degree program at Georgia Southwestern College, Americus, Georgia.

Her professional experiences include the following:

Data Collector for the assessment of beginning teachers from 1978 through 1991, conducted Staff Development Workshops for professional personnel for the Early County School System 1978 through 1990, tutored At-Risk children, trained teachers for the Writing to Win program, trained teachers for the IBM Writing to Read program, evaluated beginning and veteran teachers, and assessed counselors and media specialists.

I have observed Betty throughout her years as a student, teacher, and administrator; and I congratulate her for her outstanding accomplishments.

Presently, she is serving as principal of Early County Middle School, a position she has held since 1990. I appreciate her contributions to the community and pray the Lord's richest blessings upon her.

Attorney William Snipes has made outstanding accomplishments in the legal profession.

He was born in Chicago; however, his parents felt that they needed a more favorable environment for him and his siblings. This desire resulted in the family moving to Early County, which is his mother's home.

His parents sacrificed and sent him and her other children to church school; but when they moved to Early County, Jerry and his brother Lynn enrolled in the Early County High School, where they both graduated.

He continued his education by attending Oakwood College in Huntsville, Alabama, and subsequently transferred to Albany State College, Albany, Georgia, where he received his Bachelor of Arts

Degree in Biology in 1980. By this time he had decided that he wanted to become a lawyer; so, he entered Howard University Law School, where he earned his Juris Doctorate Degree cum laude in May, 1983.

After graduating from Howard University, he was admitted to Harvard University Law School, where he received his Master's in Letters of Law.

Jerry's academic record is impeccable. It is interesting to note that his professional record is equally impressive and includes the following: Judicial Law Clerk for Judge Paul A. Simmons. He was a summer associate with Howrey & Simon in Washington, D. C. in the summer of 1983. He was a fall associate with Arnold & Porter in Washington, D. C. in the fall of 1982. He worked as a summer associate with Aetna Life & Casualty in Hartford, Connecticut, in 1982 and was a research assistant with Goler T. Butcher at Howard University School of Law in Washington, D. C., in 1981.

He was admitted to the bar with Pennsylvania Supreme Court, U. S. District Court, the Western District of Pennsylvania.

He has worked with Sullivan & Cromwell, becoming a partner in January 1992.

I admire Jerry for what the Lord has enabled him to accomplish thus far. I am especially proud of him for the special interest that he has shown in his mother, who is a widow. Specifically, I congratulate him for the nice house he bought for her on North Main Street in Blakely. I know that the Lord will bless him for such love and concern for his dear mother.

Harvet Roberts, a 1970 Washington High School graduate, has had a very successful professional career. It is interesting to note that he was born in Early County and was reared by his uncle and aunt (Charlie Roberts and Maeetta Roberts), both of whom are deceased. He received his B. S. Degree in Agricultural Education from Fort Valley State College, Fort Valley, Georgia in June, 1974.

He taught vocational agriculture at Bainbridge High School, Bainbridge, Georgia from July 1, 1974–June 30, 1978.

After leaving Bainbridge High School in 1978 he was employed by the Dooly County School System for approximately eight months before being appointed Director of Camp John Hope, State F.F.A.-F.H.A. Camp, in March 1989. He continues to serve in that capacity and is doing an outstanding job.

In May of 1981 he received his Masters Degree in Agricultural Education from Tuskegee University, Tuskegee, Alabama.He is married to Mrs. Mayala Brown Roberts from our community, and they are parents of two boys.

He is a member of all his professional organizations and has received numerous honors and awards.

James Walter Ford is another Washington High School graduate who has had an outstanding professional success in the field of vocational agriculture. James is from the Carver, Jakin, community.

He received his B. S. Degree in Agricultural Education from Fort Valley State College, Fort Valley, Georgia. His Master's Degree was received from the University of Georgia, Athens, Georgia.

His work experience includes the following:

Soil conservation agent in Clarke County, Georgia, and in Baldwin County, Georgia.; District Director for the Flint River Soil Conservation District, Albany, Georgia; and Associate State Soil Conservation Director, Athens, Georgia.

I am very proud of James' outstanding accomplishments and pray the Lord's richest blessings upon him.

The last example of a local Black person who has beat the odds, that I shall focus on in this chapter is Dr. Earlie Mae Biddings Steel. She is a 1958 graduate of Washington High School and went on to earn her Doctorate Degree from Peabody University, Nashville, Tennessee.

Even though I do not have the benefit of her resume, I know that she has had a very successful educational career in Nashville. Presently, she is an assistant principal of one of the senior high schools in Nashville, Tennessee. In my opinion, this is an outstanding accomplishment and I am happy to salute her for being such a good role model.

I have enjoyed writing this chapter, primarily because of the many discoveries that I have made pursuant to the accomplishments made by so many of those whose roots are here in Blakely and Early County. The Lord has really blessed and I pray that our youth who are coming on the scene will be challenged to do even better.

> "I have learned that success is to be measured
> not so much by the position that one has
> reached in life as by the obstacles which he
> has overcome while trying to succeed."
> —Booker T. Washington

CHAPTER 23

VISIT TO SOUTH AFRICA

For the past three or four years my son Mike and his wife Enid periodically tried to persuade me to visit them before their tour of mission service at Bethel College ended December 31, 1993. I always declined and never seriously considered it; however, I did get my passport just in case. They continued to try to get me to promise that I would give it serious consideration. Finally, in September of 1993, I decided to "go for it."

My son Wayne assisted me in getting travel options and other pertinent information from the travel agency. After approximately thirty days I received my tickets; and from that time forward I tried to do my homework so that, in so far as possible, everything would go well.

At first, the idea seemed somewhat far fetched; but then around the first of November, it started to dawn on me that I was only days away from my scheduled departure date, set for Sunday, November 28, 1993.

I left home on Wednesday, November 24, 1993, and arrived at Wayne and Marilyn's residence in Stone Mountain, Georgia, about 4:15 P. M. My cousin, Kathy Hailey, accompanied me on the trip from Blakely to Stone Mountain.

I celebrated Thanksgiving with Wayne, Marilyn, and their three children. It was a very special Thanksgiving in that it was our first Thanksgiving with their youngest child, little David Gabriel, born October 6, 1993. He is healthy and normal, which I consider cause for special thanks. Wayne and Marilyn's pastor and his family also joined us for dinner, and the fellowship was very special.

As the time approached for my departure I found myself somewhat apprehensive; but I consoled myself with the thought that the same God who is here is also in South Africa and that there is no completely safe place on this earth. Therefore, I prayed that the Lord would give his angels charge over me so that I might be able to go and return safely.

Friday, the day after Thanksgiving was somewhat uneventful. Wayne and Marilyn had the day off, and we enjoyed each others'

Bethel College Library, Butterworth, South Africa
(Mike and Enid's offices are located in this building.)

company, which culminated with an appetizing dinner. Even though the dinner consisted mainly of leftovers from our Thanksgiving dinner, it seemed even better than when served the first time.

After dinner was finished we drove across town to visit Herk's mother, who was spending the Thanksgiving holidays with her son, Earle and his family. She was eighty-four and in reasonably good health for her age. I was glad to visit with her before leaving for my trip to South Africa.

On Sabbath, after Thanksgiving, we attended church at the Central Spanish Seventh-day Adventist Church. Wayne and Marilyn translated the services for me. After the Sabbath worship services were over, we met at my cousin Jeanne's house in Lithonia, Georgia, and celebrated my Uncle Melva's eighty-fourth birthday and my 66th birthday, even though his was early November and mine was not until the 29th of the month. It was a very happy and festive occasion.

Marilyn had baked a birthday cake for me, which was very delicious and very much appreciated. I did not eat any of it on the Sabbath, but I took a slice with me when I left for the airport on Sunday.

On Sunday I found myself a little apprehensive about the trip, but I felt that I had reached the point of no return. So, I finished packing what I thought I could get along with while away. Wayne, Marilyn, the children and I climbed into their Dodge Caravan, and Wayne drove me to Hartsfield International Airport in Atlanta. The departure was scheduled for 2:45 P.M.; so, they called for the passengers to start boarding the plane around 2:05 P.M. We formed a circle, said a little prayer for traveling mercies, kissed each other goodbye, and I boarded the TWA Flight Number 587 for the trip to Miami's International Airport. We arrived around 4:30 in the afternoon. This allowed adequate time to make connection with South African Airways for the nonstop flight to Capetown, South Africa. The plane was a Boeing 747 with an upstairs section. My seat was Number 54-C; and the Lord blessed me with two wonderful seatmates, Doug Bailey and his wife Lenore, from West Palm Beach, Florida. They are South African Whites and gave me the impression that they were really genuine Christian people; and I enjoyed their company throughout the thirteen-and-one-half hours nonstop flight from Miami to Capetown, South Africa. Doug was celebrating his birthday that Sunday, and I celebrated mine the following Monday. It is interesting to note that the plane carried approximately 600 passengers, their luggage, and fuel for the flight, which was almost 6,000 miles. Doug stated that he and his wife Lenore left South Africa seventeen years ago, and this was their first return visit. They were looking forward to a lot of fun with family and friends before returning to West Palm Beach in mid-January. Their flight continued on to Johannesburg and I bade them goodbye as I deplaned in Capetown. I had some concerns about getting through customs, but the Lord prepared the way; and the officials did not look in any of my bags.

As prearranged, Enid's brother-in-law, Colin Trotter, his wife Naomi, Enid's mother, her oldest daughter Marie, her husband, Percy, and Enid's brother John all met me at the Capetown Airport and visited with me until it was time for my flight to East London. I was met at the East London Airport by Mike, Enid, Matt and Joel, their two boys. The scenery from the airport in East London to Mike and Enid's home was very beautiful.

I was aware of the fact that in South Africa motor vehicles were driven on the left of the highway instead of the right as in the United States; but had never had first-hand experience with this. I was fascinated with this "different" way of driving and all of the controls being on the right side of the vehicle.

After the drive home I presented gifts to Matt and Joel that Wayne and Marilyn had sent them. I had several items for Enid that she had requested me to bring her. Also, I had a couple of the "Week of Prayer" VCR tapes for Mike; so there was something for everyone.

Even though the day was filled with excitement and gratitude, the most noteworthy event was my 66 birthday that was spent in transit to South Africa. It was also special because it was the tenth anniversary of Herk's death; so it was a time of reflection over the memories of the wife she had been to me and the mother that she had been to our children. It was a time that we tried to focus not so much on her death, but the very fulfilling and productive life that she lived.

Tuesday, November 30th was my first full day in South Africa and was very "low key." After a delightful breakfast, I visited with Mike in his office, which is located in the college library, and made phone calls back to Wayne, Cheryl, Eric, and my sister Annette to assure them that the Lord had indeed blessed me with a safe arrival and for them to pass the word along to certain others who might have been concerned that all was well with me. I was also able to take in a few other campus scenes. It was a very beautiful campus.

I suppose the highlight of the day was a dinner served at Mike and Enid's home at which time they hosted Dr. Solomon Lebese, the Rector of the college and his wife Helen. The Lebeses are very down to earth and are American-educated. I had met them at Mike and Enid's wedding in 1980. There were several other staff members and friends of Mike and Enid who stopped by briefly during the day.

Wednesday, December 1, was a delightful day; and my first noteworthy experience was a ride into Butterworth, the closest town to Bethel College. I estimated the distance to be approximately five miles and the population seemed to have been about 99 percent Black. It was quite a contrast to what I had seen in Capetown and East London. Poverty was very much evident, but the people seemed happy; and if we can be happy, even in adverse circumstances, I think that means a lot. As I thought of that situation I found myself saying, "If not for the grace of God, there go I."

Another highlight of the day was a brief visit by Dr. Rosa Taylor Banks, from the General Conference of Seventh-day Adventists, Silver Springs, Maryland. She was accompanied by Pastor Jonathan Julie, one of the area pastors. Dr. Banks had visited Bethel College in 1983 while on the Oakwood College professional staff and wanted to see first-hand the progress that had been made during the interim. She was in the area until December 12, 1993, participating in a couple of women's retreats.

Mike had to go out of town to Durban, South Africa, on a business trip on Thursday, December 2, 1993. It was approximately 7½ hours one way so he stayed overnight and returned the next day. The major portion of that day, was spent reading a book that Enid shared with me.

The title was *Against all Odds*, by Art Miller. It was a very interesting and fascinating book about Dr. Helen Morton, who succeeded in defeating overwhelming odds and became a teacher, a nurse, and a physician. Following retirement from the health services of a California College at age 65, she volunteered as a medical missionary to the mountain people of Thailand. In spite of the life-threatening diseases of encephalitis and malaria and in the face of bigotry, poverty, and ignorance, she strove diligently to bring Thailand into the 20th century. Unfortunately, she was murdered by those that she served.

It pleased the local people greatly that Dr. Helen's body was not sent back to her native country, America. They claimed that her heart belonged to Thailand and that she should be buried close to her beloved clinic. On the hilltop near the clinic, only a few steps from where excavation had started on Helen's new home, her resting place, a simple grave, was chosen as the site for this courageous, dedicated Christian doctor. It is situated exactly where she would have chosen in the mountain country of northern Thailand.

Friday, December 3rd, it was almost sunset when Mike returned from Durban. The purpose of his trip was to close the transaction on a 1985 Toyota Venturebus. Matt and Joel were filled with glee and excitement when they heard him drive up. Even though it was raining, they did not let it dampen their joy. I was happy for them. This vehicle was the fourth that Mike and Enid have had since being in South Africa. The first was a Toyota Corolla, the second a 1978 240 D Mercedes Benz; and the third was a 1982 Mercedes 230. This was the car that Mike drove to East London to meet me on my arrival from Capetown. I enjoyed the ride and was very much impressed with it. The only other ride that I had in it was from the campus to the nearby town of Butterworth. I did not know that Mike was considering getting rid of it until after I had arrived. However, it seems as if he had been wanting a camper for quite sometime and the opportunity finally came. In my opinion, it was very nice and they had a lot of fun with it. Some of the features included: a pop-up top, a stove, refrigerator, sleeping accommodations for four people, and a tent for additional camping space. It had been well maintained and gave Mike and his family a lot of dependable service. The boys were still on "cloud nine," so to speak.

The Sabbath, December 4th, was a rainy day including the previous night, but we did manage to get to church, which was located just a short walk from Mike and Enid's residence. I enjoyed the services, which included the lesson study taught by Mike, the title was "Spiritual Rehabilitation," and the sermon title was "Stand Still and See the Salvation of the Lord." The main focus of the sermon was the crossing of the Red Sea by the children of Israel and the drowning of Pharaoh's army as it pursued the Israelites. In spite of the wet chilly weather, we experienced a very spiritual feast.

In the afternoon several families came over to Mike and Enid's home for a very delicious "potluck" dinner. There was an abundance of food and it was very delicious.

Sunday, December 5th, the rain had ceased; and I was able to get my walk in. Mike, Enid, Matt and Joel cleaned the Venturebus because it was muddy from the rainy, long drive from Durban on Friday. As usual, a number of their friends stopped by to meet and greet me. That day also marked the end of my first week since leaving the United States. How fast the first week passed! If the remaining three weeks were like the first, it would be time for my return to the U. S. much sooner than I had thought.

Monday, December 6th was a beautiful and exciting day, the skies were blue and there was an abundance of sunshine. Highlights of the day included a drive into Butterworth, where Mike and Enid took care of several business transactions. Enid needed to cash a check before our upcoming trip of 1½ hours to East London; so Mike dropped her off at the bank and we went to a nearby service station to fuel the Venturebus and do one or two other errands. When we finished, Mike checked to see whether or not Enid had finished her transaction at the bank and discovered that she was still in line with several others ahead of her. It took her almost an hour to get her check cashed. On a previous occasion Mike had stood in line for almost two hours before he was able to cash his check. Most of the passenger buses I saw in the Butterworth area were filled to capacity and the roof was stacked high with luggage. It was really a sight to behold.

This was the first trip that Mike's family and I had made in their Venturebus since Mike had driven it home from Durban on the previous Friday. Shortly after leaving Butterworth, the pop-up roof popped up, and Mike had to pull over as soon as he came to a safe place. His investigation revealed that when he had the top up on Sunday, he failed to lock it back securely into place. Once that was taken care of the remainder of our trip to East London was uneventful. East London is a beautiful modern city, about the size of Albany,

Georgia. While in East London I had an opportunity to visit the shopping mall where Mike and Enid did most of their shopping. I was really impressed with its modernization. In my opinion, it was equal to anything I have seen in the United States.

Before returning to the campus where Mike and his family reside, they took me by the home of Roland and Shirley Esau. They are very close friends of theirs and Mike did not want me to fail to meet them. By this time, it was almost sunset; but we enjoyed a very cordial visit with them and their two girls. I was glad that they made it possible for me to meet the Esaus. It was a long day, but we arrived home around 9:45 P.M.

On Tuesday, December 7th, I spent the major portion of the day accompanying Mike as he tried to get their Venturebus inspected and registered with the Motor Vehicle Division for the Transkei area. He was somewhat disappointed when he discovered that this procedure was only being done on Wednesdays. Nevertheless, he was able to take care of some preliminary matters that would hopefully expedite the process on Wednesday.

It was interesting to note that while we were waiting for the installation of the tires on the Venturebus, I heard what sounded like music coming from someone's car radio; however, we discovered that it was coming from a group of demonstrators on the opposite side of the street. It was exactly like what I had seen on TV but peaceful; and as soon as they finished, they disbanded and went their separate ways. I could hardly believe that I had been within a few feet of what I had seen on the evening news back in the U. S.

I spent Wednesday, December 8th, accompanying Mike to and from East London as he checked on last minute details before getting on the road for some of the traveling that we hoped to do during the latter half of my stay. On the return trip Mike drove by the residence of the Wright family—Vigil, his wife Zelna, and their two children. They resided in the small town of Komga, South Africa, and were former students of Mike and Enid. They lived approximately 30 Kilometers from Butterworth. We missed Vigil but had a lovely visit with Zelna and the children.

Mike and I arrived home about 8:10 P.M. It had been a long day; so, after eating a good meal that Enid had prepared, we had family worship and retired for the night.

Thursday, December 9, was spent more or less assisting Mike, Enid, and the boys with organizing and packing the Venturebus with what we thought would be needed for the first leg of our trip, which was Barberton. It was approximately fourteen-hours' drive from Butterworth, and it was where Enid's sister Dephnee and her family lived. Our plans called for spending three or four days with them. Mike had intended leaving during the afternoon but decided to wait until early the next morning. A major reason for the delay was the problem of what to do with their dog, "Flash." Anyway, he finally decided to leave her with one of the neighbors that he felt could be trusted to look after her.

Earlier in the day we toured the campus and took some pictures that I hoped to share with my immediate family, my extended family, and my church family.

On Friday, December 10, the day's activities started very early, around 3:00 A.M. to be exact. By that time the Venturebus had been packed and was ready for the long trip to Barberton, South Africa. By 5:10 A.M. the fuel tank on the Venturebus was filled with "petrol" and checked to make sure that nothing had been overlooked.

On the way out, Mike gave a ride to an attendant at the service station where he bought petrol before getting started on the trip. It seemed as if the attendant lived approximately 10–15 kilometers away from Butterworth, but it was on our route. He said that he had hitched a ride to work the day before, worked all night at the service station, and then needed to hitch a ride home. It seems that this practice is not that uncommon in the areas that I traveled while there.

Our trip through the Transkei, an independent homeland, was long and interesting. There were thatched-roofed buildings, some of which were very elaborate and attractive, while others were primitive and in disrepair. It was interesting to note that oxen were still being used in some of the fields that we passed on our route. In some instances, the oxen were worked in a single pair, while in other instances they were worked in pairs of two or three all hitched to the same implement. Two men were required for the job, one to guide and hold the implement being used and another to lead the oxen. I really felt that this type of work was a thing of the past, but I am convinced that I was wrong. We also saw donkeys being used in the same way as the oxen but not to the same extent as the oxen.

Tractors were very rare in the areas that we traveled. Bethel College had one tractor, a Massey Ferguson; and I also saw a few Fords and John Deeres in some of the areas visited.

Another surprise that I experienced was that there were toll roads in some places in South Africa. The toll roads traveled to this point were comparable to what we have in the U. S.

Our route from Butterworth to Barberton was very mountainous, but extremely beautiful. I was somewhat concerned about the Venturebus' ability to take the challenge of the steep mountain roads, but I was pleased with its performance. It had a 2.2 liter engine that, to this point, proved adequate for the job.

At times we encountered very dense fog that made driving rather hazardous; however, the Lord blessed us with a safe arrival at the residence of Enid's sister Dephnee, her husband Shaddy, and their two children, Lyndyll and Joshua, at or about 9:15 P.M. It had been a long day for all of us but especially for Mike since he had driven the entire distance. I wanted to assist him, but I did not feel comfortable with the left hand driving and the controls being on the right side of the vehicle.

The day culminated with a very delicious meal that Enid's sister had prepared for us, followed by a restful night's sleep.

On Sabbath, December 11, we were all up by 8:00 A.M. and enjoyed a very delightful breakfast, prepared and served by Enid's sister and her husband Shaddy.

In addition to the delectable cooked food, there was also a variety of fresh fruits, some of which they had grown themselves. The mangoes were one example.

We worshiped at Enid's sister and her husband Shaddy's church. Sabbath School was very interesting and featured an inspiring presentation given by Enid's sister entitled "Keys to Happiness." In that connection, she pointed out that some have tried fame, escape, work, rebellion, conformity, and wealth; but the key to true happiness was Jesus Christ.

During the divine worship service, Mike preached a very thought-provoking and inspirational sermon entitled "A Command That Saved Lives." His text was Matthew 28:18–20. At the conclusion of the service, I had an opportunity to meet a number of the members along with some of Dephnee and Shaddy's friends and relatives. After feasting on our spiritual food at church, we returned to the home of Dephnee and Shaddy, at which time a very delicious meal was served.

Not only was the food delicious, but it also included a variety of dishes. We thoroughly enjoyed every morsel of it.

Around midafternoon Mike took us on a very scenic sightseeing tour of the nearby mountains, after which we traveled about 60 km. from Barberton where we spent the weekend. Sunset came before we arrived at the resort area; so, Mike pulled over at a roadside park, and we had Vespers before continuing on our way to the resort area.

The Swazis called it "talking mountain." President Paul Kruger proclaimed it a "healing spring for the perpetual use of the nation." Presently, Aventura Badplaas is one of the most popular family destinations in the South Eastern Transvaal—and no wonder!

Badplaas offered everything you would expect to find at a modern, well-run resort: 12 different types of accommodations to suit every lifestyle, a beautiful natural setting, a vast choice of indoor and outdoor activities, and, of course, the famous mineral water that gave the resort its name.

You can float away your cares in the large open-air hot mineral pool, the cool swimming pools, or the modern Hydro Spa, and indulge in soothing treatments in the bubble-jet baths. Children have their own hot and cold outdoor pools.

There was a lot more: from mini-golf to a game reserve. The main complex offered everything from a cafeteria, bottle store, and a brand new Spur Steak Ranch to conference facilities.

Enid's sister had made all of the arrangements for our accommodations. I was very much surprised to see such an elaborate and beautiful facility in South Africa. It was very much like the mineral springs in Hot Springs, Arkansas, in the United States.

Sunday, December 12—Matthew and Joel were so excited that they could hardly wait for daybreak so that they could rejoin their cousin Josh, Enid's sister's son, for the beginning of a day of fun and excitement. Joel was up the first time around 5:30. Mike and Enid had to insist that he go back to bed. However, he and Matt were up again within the hour. They got in a full day of fun-filled joy and excitement.

I got up around 8:00 A.M. after a very restful night, after which I enjoyed a very delicious breakfast. After breakfast, Mike accompanied me on a tour of the many beautiful attractions in the resort area. I am not sure that I have ever seen so much natural beauty in any one place.

Enid and her sister prepared and served a very delicious picnic lunch that we very much enjoyed.

Mike, Enid, and Dephnee finally convinced me to go into the hydro spa, even though I was somewhat reluctant, one reason being that I had not included any shorts in the items of clothing that I had brought on the trip. However, Dephnee had brought along several pairs that were my exact size. At that point, I felt that I really had no choice without being rude. Mike, Enid, Dephnee, and the children all ended up in the pool with me. I must say that I thoroughly enjoyed it. The mineral springs have therapeutic value, and I spent at least two hours enjoying the soothing and invigorating water. Dephnee persuaded me to go down to the opposite end of the pool where jet streams of water were directed on my body with a strong and soothing force. There were three separate pools ranging from very hot, moderate, and cold. I chose the moderate one and really enjoyed it.

On Monday, December 13, I got up around 7:15 thinking that we would soon be on our way back to Barberton. However, Mike explained to me that Shaddy wanted me to go back into the hydro pool for another 30 minutes before leaving. Even though I had not expected to go back into the pool I must say that I am glad that I did and I thoroughly enjoyed it.

We left the resort area at or about 10:15 for the drive back to Barberton. The remainder of the day was spent relaxing and making last minutes plans for a trip to a game reserve. It was about two hours away from Barberton, and it was another first for me. I was excited about the idea.

I also traveled to a nearby town, Nelspruit, South Africa, with Mike, Enid, Dephnee, and Shaddy. It was a nice town about the size of Dothan, Alabama. I was impressed with it cleanliness and beauty.

Tuesday, December 14, after enjoying a very restful and peaceful night, I arose around 4:45 A.M., showered, shaved, dressed, and had my private devotional. It was a very beautiful morning with blue skies and sunshine in abundance. However, there was a 40% chance of rain in the forecast.

Our plans for the day included a two-hour drive to the Kruger National Park and Game Reserve. I was looking forward to this experience with eager and happy anticipation. Mike and Enid had a tent, and we pitched it and camped out. Dephnee, Enid's sister, made all of the arrangements, and she and her two children, Lyndyll and Josh, accompanied us.

We began the trip around 9:30 A.M. It was a very enjoyable and scenic route that included many beautiful farms, some of which produced sugar cane, bananas, grapes, mangoes, and oranges.

The travel guide that we received at Kruger National Park was very informative. Kruger National Park was one of the few places on Earth where mammals, plants, birds, and insects were in their natural environment. The more informed about the bushveld you are, the more pleasure Kruger will give you. Camouflage was of vital importance to many animals for survival. When standing still, their colors and shapes blend in perfectly with their surroundings. Even if you drove past slowly, you needed to look very carefully to find them. The roads in Kruger were not only for motorists. Animals and birds often used them to move around more easily so you needed to travel slowly to avoid scaring away any wildlife close to the road. Speeding could result in a collision with game which would be tragic for the animal and also damage your car.

The Lord blessed us with a safe arrival at the park and game reserve, and it was fantastic. It was interesting how it was designed to drive through and watch for the animals. When an animal was spotted, Mike stopped the vehicle to watch; and we would take pictures, if interested.

The first animals that we spotted were a deer and an impala, which seemed more abundant than any of the others. Next we saw several baboons and an equal number of giraffes, which were also very visible. On one occasion, as we drove along, Mike spotted another baboon sitting on the side of the road as if he/she was not the least bit frightened by us. The blue wildebeest was the next animal that we saw, followed by the sighting of several zebras.

By this time Dephnee suggested that we should locate the camping area, choose a site, pitch the tent, and eat lunch. After the tent had been pitched, the ladies prepared and served a delicious picnic lunch. After enjoying our lunch, we relaxed until about 5:30 P.M., after which we went on another drive through the park to see what other animals we might see. The gate to the camping area closed at 6:30; so, we were careful not to get locked out. On this trip we saw three or four hippopotamuses in a nearby river. The other animals that we saw on this drive were the same ones we had seen earlier in the day.

After the trip, the ladies prepared and served a very delicious supper. Once the remaining details were finished, we turned in for the night. Mike and I slept in the Venturebus, while the others slept in the tent. I enjoyed a good night's sleep interrupted periodically by the screaming or barking of the animals. I was the first to arise, which was around 4:45 A.M. It was interesting to note that it was already daylight. I enjoyed a good hot shower and was ready to begin another day of exploration in the park.

Enid had advised me that I should take malaria tablets; so, she gave me the first two the previous night with the understanding that I was to take two more each week on the same day. I was surprised that they were so bitter. Nevertheless, I intended to take them as prescribed. I was not aware of being bitten by a mosquito while in the park; so, I hoped that I was home free, so to speak.

Wednesday, December 15, before breaking camp, we went on an early morning drive through the park to see what animals we might see. As had been the case on Tuesday, the deer were the most visible. However, before the drive ended, we had seen a Kudu, two or three lions, several storks, a large number of monkeys, several baboons, and a jaguar. Our number-one priority was to spot an elephant; but it was not to be, at least not on that trip. Therefore, we decided to return to our campsite, eat breakfast, and take down our tent, fold it, and pack it for the road. By this time it was around 11:00 A.M., so we decided to go on another drive through a different part of the park with the hope that we would spot the elephants that had thus far eluded us. We could see their droppings on the road as evidence that they had recently been there, then it finally happened. I was not sure who spotted our first elephant. At first I thought that it was one of the children, but closer investigation confirmed that it was Mike. He was just driving along slowly when suddenly he saw him/her crossing the road, just ahead of us. This set off much excitement and glee. However, after we spotted our first elephant, they started coming out of the forest every few minutes. Usually, they would be in herds of six or more. In my opinion, when it was all over, we had seen thirty-five or forty before leaving the park.

We also saw an impala and several water buffaloes. Enid's sister promised a prize to the first one of the children to spot a lion. That prize was collected by Joel, Mike and Enid's son, in the amount of ten rand.

Before leaving the park area, the ladies served a very delicious picnic lunch.

We checked out of the park around 5:30 P.M.; and the drive home to Barberton took about four hours, but we were blessed with a safe arrival, just a little past 10:00 P.M.

Because of the lateness of the hour in returning from the National Park, we stopped at a Papa's Pizza place in Nelspruit, South Africa, before continuing on home to Barberton. This made the children very happy.

I think it worthy of note that it was extremely dry in some parts of the park; and, in my opinion, some of the animals were having a difficult time surviving.

Finally, I appreciated the cleanliness of the restroom facilities. They were fantastic, and the showers were spic and span.

I thank the Lord for blessing me to have had such a fulfilling and exciting experience.

Thursday, December 16, after enjoying a restful night's sleep, I arose around 6:00 A.M., enjoyed a good hot shower, and wrote some of my notes while they were still vivid in my memory. It was another beautiful day, and we were to leave for Capetown later on that morning; so at that point, it promised to be an excellent day for traveling.

I was told by Shaddy that this day was a national holiday in commemoration of a day of prayer for White South Africans.

Shaddy and Dephnee had been fantastic in showering me with their warm hospitality. I could not have hoped for more. They served us another delicious breakfast, after which we loaded our things into the Venturebus. With that task completed, we said our goodbyes around 11:00 A.M.

Mike filled the fuel tank on the Venturebus with petrol and checked to see whether or not anything had been overlooked. These details were completed in time for a 12:00 noon departure.

The route that we took was via Johannesburg not because it was the most direct route but Mike needed to check with Peter Drew, a ham radio operator and repairman, about a radio that he had repaired for him. Also, I wanted to see Raymond Smith, the husband of Mrs. Beauty Lewis Smith. She gave me his telephone number before I left the United States, both his residential and business phone. I was able to call him before leaving Barberton for the trip to Johannesburg, and he thought that it would not be a problem. When we arrived in Johannesburg, Mike called him again; and they went over the directions again, but something went wrong, and there was a mix up. When we tried to call him, we were only able to get his answering service; so, after the better part of two hours of trying, we reluctantly gave up. It was a real disappointment. I was really impressed by Mike's patience in trying to find Raymond, especially when we had so many more miles to travel before reaching Capetown. However, I prayed that there will be another time, if not for me, maybe the children, Mike and Enid, before their service in South Africa terminates.

I was happy that Mike's business and visit with Peter Drew went well and he was able to explain to Mike the repairs that he had made on his "rig" and what he should do to avoid a reoccurrence of the problem in the future. We were also able to meet Peter's son, Jeff, and his wife. Jeff is a practicing physician in the Los Angeles area. He and his wife were almost ready to leave for the airport to begin their flight back to the U. S.

The drive from Barberton to Johannesburg was quite enjoyable and scenic. In my opinion, many of the farms were just as modern as what we have in the United States. Their equipment included John Deere tractors and hay rollers for harvesting their hay.

Friday, December 17, unfortunately we were able to spend only a few hours in Johannesburg; however, I was really impressed with the beauty and cleanliness of the city. I would very much like to return when I have more time. We went within a few miles of Pretoria, the capital of South Africa, but did not stop, hopefully there will be another opportunity.

When we finally got on the road for Capetown it was after 8:00 P.M. Mike drove until about 1:00 A.M. before taking a break for some much-needed rest and sleep. There were many well-lighted rest areas along the way where you could park, rest, and sleep. The one that Mike chose was called Ultra City and was part of a chain operated by Shell Oil Company. Their facilities were first class and well maintained. We stopped at several of them before reaching Capetown and without exception, we were well pleased.

It was about 5 A.M. when we resumed our trip and arrived in Capetown around 6:15 P. M. It was a long trip but safe, and I thanked the Lord for His traveling mercies each moment and mile of the way.

For the most part, our travel on Friday was through the desert; and the only animals I saw were sheep. However, as we got nearer to Capetown, we saw grape vineyards and a variety of other fruit being grown.

Upon our arrival at Mrs. Pekeur, Enid's mother's home, she had food almost ready to be served. Therefore, it was not long before we enjoyed a very delicious meal.

After vespers, I enjoyed a good warm bath and a restful night's sleep.

Sabbath, December 18th, everyone was up by 8:00 A.M. and enjoyed a fruit and cereal breakfast, after which we attended service at the Riverside Seventh-day Adventist Church. It is interesting to note that it was Enid's family church and her mother still worshiped there. I found the members to be very cordial and hospitable. I really enjoyed the good Christian fellowship.

The church was celebrating the ordinance of humility by foot-washing and the communion service, which was partaking of the bread and the unfermented grape juice. I thank the Lord for blessing Mike and me with the rare opportunity of washing each other's feet and praying with and for one another. We had not expected that, so it was a pleasant surprise. The remainder of the service was just as spiritual and thought-provoking.

After the conclusion of our spiritual feast at the church, we drove to Enid's sister Naomi's home, where we were joined by several other family members, primarily brothers and sisters-in-law and their children for a delicious pot luck dinner. I enjoyed the food and the fellowship.

Enid was from a large family, and everyone that I met was friendly, cordial, and hospitable.

Mike was invited to bring the vespers thought; so, we returned to church around 6:00 P.M. for a very inspirational service featuring sharing the experiences different ones had had as they interacted with their prayer partners.

According to my plans, I only had one more Sabbath in South Africa; and that was December 25. I had thoroughly enjoyed myself and I was looking forward to worshiping at the Riverside Seventh-day Adventist Church for my final Sabbath celebration in that part of the Lord's vineyard.

Sunday, December 19, was a very beautiful day, with plenty of sunshine and mild temperature. We began the day with a good breakfast, after which we drove across town to Enid's sister Naomi and her husband Colin Trotter's home. We were met there by Enid's sister, Lettie, her husband Len, and their two children. They packed food to take along for a picnic lunch later in the day. We then traveled to Cape

Good Hope Nature Reserve. It was one of South Africa's most valuable nature reserves, in which there were over 1500 fynbos plant species. Many birds, reptiles, small mammals, and some large antelope could be seen; and magnificent scenes were being preserved for posterity.

The reserve also protected interesting cultural and historical sites as well as being a popular recreational facility.

Upon our arrival at the reserve, we were joined by Enid's sister Marie, her husband Percy, and their son Justin. The first order of business was to choose a picnic site and set up our nets and picnic umbrellas so that the food could be prepared and served for our lunch. Once this task was accomplished it wasn't long before the food was ready to be served, as always while I was there, it was delicious.

The beauty of the area was almost indescribable. We were right on the shores where the Atlantic Ocean and the Indian Ocean merge. The Atlantic is cold and the Indian Ocean is warm. There were hundreds, if not thousands, of people enjoying the beaches, swimming, and picnicking.

We left our picnic area around 5:00 P.M. at which time I thought we were going home. However, I discovered that we were going even further up into the mountain and the shoreline. When we reached the end of the road, there was a parking lot where we parked our vehicles. A bus was provided for transporting those who could not or did not want to walk up the steep incline to the Cape Point, the tip of Africa, where the lighthouse is located. Mike, Enid, the children, and Len walked to the top. However, Percy, his wife Marie, their son Justin and I rode the bus. I must say that the bus ride was an exciting experience. On the trip up the driver had to keep the bus in its lowest gear, and it seemed that it required all of its power to get to the top. Whereas, on the return trip back down to the parking lot, the reverse was true. The driver still had to keep the vehicle in its lowest gear, as well as use the brakes to a very large extent.

I must say that it was a fun-filled day, with many unique experiences for me.

It was interesting to note that there were several baboons in the parking lot and also on a cliff close to the parking lot.

The visit to the Cape Point and the lighthouse culminated our activities for the day, and we enjoyed the return trip along the shores of the Indian Ocean.

As I reflected over the mighty rocks, the rolling tides, the mighty waves, the animals, and the natural beauty of nature, I was able to appreciate the handiwork of God even more. In my opinion, even the most beautiful scenery that I had the privilege to see on this trip cannot even begin to compare with what it will be like when we all get to heaven. I am reminded of the text in 1 Corinthians 2:9 that states "Eye hath not seen, nor ear heard, neither have entered into the heart of man, the things which God hath prepared for them that love Him." I want to be there, don't you?

Monday, December 20th, after such a physically exhaustive day on Sunday, we decided that we should unwind a little bit before trying to do any more exploring.

It was interesting that it was in the Capetown area that Amy Biehl, the American student, was killed earlier this year. I am very impressed with the very Christian way her parents have been able to accept her death. They stated that "We have no regrets about her coming to South Africa. It is what she wanted, too," her father stated. He further stated that his daughter was well prepared when she came to South Africa. He also said, "It is not like she was ill prepared. She knew what the political situation in South Africa was." She had worked in Nombia before and after the election.

She was there to teach people and to help bring about democracy.

Miss Biehl was to have returned to the United States on August 27 but was murdered in Guguletu two days before. However, her intention was to return to South Africa for the elections.

It grieved me much to see one who was so concerned and willing to give her life to help bring about change. In my opinion, it was not appreciated, but even now I pray that her sacrifice was not in vain. I also grieved for her Christian parents, yet I appreciated the way that they handled such a traumatic experience. I have not detected any animosity or ill will in any response they have made thus far. I firmly believed that this is indicative of a true Christian. I prayed that the Lord will continue to sustain them.

The highlight of this day was a drive into Capetown to see the Christmas lights. They were very beautiful and comparable to what we have in the United States.

Tuesday, December 21, we kept somewhat of a low profile, but I did ride out with Mike, Enid, and the children, during which time I saw the Southern Publishing Association, The Adventist Book Center, and the office building for the Good Hope Conference of Seventh-day Adventists.

Enid also pointed out to me the school she attended before leaving home.

Mike and Enid attended a funeral in the afternoon at one of the nearby Seventh-day Adventist churches.

It was interesting to note that there was a large Moslem population in South Africa. In fact, there is a mosque located down the street from Enid's mother's house. The Moslem call to prayer is played over their public address system periodically throughout the day and night.

Wednesday, December 22, was very thrilling and rewarding. It started with a drive downtown to do a little shopping. However, we encountered a major traffic jam and decided to go to the harbor and an area called the Waterfront. It was here that Mike and Enid persuaded me to go on my first cruise. It lasted less than an hour, and I was glad that I went, even though it took a little arm-twisting on the part of Mike and Enid.

While at the Waterfront, I was able to see Robben Island in the distance. It was interesting to note that this was the prison in which Nelson Mandela was incarcerated for twenty-seven years. I was really glad for this unexpected event.

Another surprise that I experienced while in Capetown was the presence of the double-decked buses similar to the ones in England.

I was also surprised to see that there were so many big trucks over there, a few of which were American-made, with the controls on the left as in the United States.

Thursday, December 23, was one of the hottest days while I was there. It was difficult for me to realize that it was the day before Christmas Eve.

The first thing that Mike needed to do was to drive the Venturebus to a Toyota dealership. He was successful in getting the information he needed, including an owner's manual. He was also able to schedule an appointment for the next morning for routine maintenance.

Our next stop was in Claremont where Enid did some additional shopping.

Around 1:00 P.M., we enjoyed a very delicious meal with Brother and Sister Leslie Davis and their daughter Carol. I enjoyed the meal and the Christian fellowship.

While in Claremont, Mike and I confirmed my return flight with the travel agency.

Our final appointment for the day was Percy's birthday celebration.

Friday, December 24, was Christmas Eve. I was reminded that this was my first Christmas spent outside the United States.

Many people in Capetown were trying to get in some last minute shopping. Consequently, it was very congested in the downtown areas.

I did not have any specific plans for the day other than getting my things packed for my return trip the next night.

Enid's sister Dephnee, her husband Shaddy, and their two children, Lyndyll and Josh, arrived around 11:00 A.M. and spent their holidays with family and friends.

Our vespers included the singing of several Christmas carols, a review of Matt and Joel's Sabbath School lesson, and the prayer by me. I thanked the Lord that "while we were yet sinners, Christ died for us."

Saturday, December 25th was a beautiful Christmas in Capetown. Many of the churches had special services in the celebration of Christ's birth.

I was celebrating my final Sabbath in South Africa and was to depart from the Capetown International Airport at 9:50 that night.

We worshiped at the Riverside Seventh-day Adventist Church, and there was a full house. Mike preached about the birth of Christ as recorded in Luke Chapters one and two. He used a rather creative technique to introduce his sermon; namely, a photo album of Enid's family, featuring her sister Dephnee's wedding pictures, among others. He contrasted those pictures with the photos that might have been in Mary and Joseph's photo album. He emphasized how Mary and Joseph went a day's journey before they realized that they had left Jesus behind. Even now it is so easy for us to let go of Jesus. The congregation seemed very much in tune with the challenging message.

Following the service, we returned to Enid's mother's house for a very special Sabbath/Christmas dinner. Those participating were Mike, Enid, their two boys, Enid's sister Marie, her husband, their two children, and myself. There was an abundance of the most delicious food imaginable and, as always, a variety was very much evident.

The remainder of the afternoon was spent enjoying each other's company. The children really enjoyed themselves.

Capetown International Airport, Capetown, South Africa
(The author was about to get his passport checked
for the return trip to the U.S.A.

Enid's mother had not felt well during my visit, but she felt well enough to attend church each Sabbath.

Before sunset, we had a very happy and inspiring vespers with the children singing a number of their favorite choruses.

Immediately after sunset, we headed for the airport so that I could check in for my return flight. I was informed that it was an hour late, which would be around 11:00 P.M. Capetown time. Everyone decided to remain at the airport, rather than return to Enid's mother's house and come back to the airport later. While we were waiting, four other friends of Mike and Enid joined us. I almost became emotional as I saw the delegation of friends and loved ones who took the time to drive to the airport to see me off and wish me a safe flight.

We said our final goodbyes around 10:15 P. M. and the flight took off around 11:15 P.M.

Sunday, December 26, the Lord blessed the flight from Capetown to Miami, and it arrived around 7:00 A.M. I was indeed thankful to be back on American soil. I was somewhat apprehensive about getting through Customs, but the Lord blessed me; and the process went as smoothly as possible.

My flight to Atlanta was not due to depart until 1:02 P.M. The layover time gave me an opportunity to make some calls on my calling card and also write down some of the details while they were still fresh in my mind. I was surprised to find it so cold when I arrived in Miami;

287

in fact, it was 30 degrees Fahrenheit. That was quite a contrast to the summer-like weather that I had enjoyed in Capetown.

I was saddened to learn that Sister Bradley's daughter had passed away and had been buried while I was away. Sister Bradley is a member of our church family in Blakely.

My flight to Atlanta on TWA was about forty-five minutes late; but, thanks be to God, it was safe. Wayne, Marilyn, and the children met me as previously planned.

We drove directly from the airport to the home of Pastor Efrain Poloche, Wayne and Marilyn's pastor, for dinner with his family and friends. It was a very delightful meal, including homemade wheat bread and rolls. After the meal the others played dominoes until almost 11:00 P.M., during which time I lay down for some much needed rest.

We arrived at Wayne and Marilyn's house in Stone Mountain around 11:30 P.M. I made phone calls to Cheryl, Annette, my sister, and Mike and Enid in Capetown, South Africa, to let them know that I had a safe arrival and to convey once again my thanks for what they had done, individually and collectively to make my stay there fulfilling and rewarding, after which I enjoyed a restful night's sleep.

Monday, December 27, my first full day back in the United States began with bright sunshine and blue skies, with the temperature around 40 degrees Fahrenheit. I spent the day with Wayne, Marilyn and the children before driving home to Blakely on Tuesday.

I talked with Brother and Sister Rugless, Mike's former members from Modesto, who presently live in Decatur. They appreciated the update on Mike and Enid's ministry in South Africa.

My drive home on Tuesday was safe and enjoyable, and I was happy to find everyone in my extended family doing fine.

Eric, my nephew, did an excellent job of seeing about the cows during my absence; and I was happy to find them in good shape.

This closes the book on my visit to South Africa, and I hereby officially thank my children and Enid's family for their efforts in making my visit one that I will cherish for the rest of my life.

"It is better to light one small candle than to curse the darkness."

—Confucius

APPENDIX A BIOGRAPHICAL SKETCH

(John R. Harris)

A native of Early County (having been born near Cedar Springs, Georgia), his family moved to the Allen Chapel Community shortly after his birth where he grew up as a farm boy. (He is second in a family of twelve children of the late Mr. and Mrs. Rufus Harris.)

Educational opportunities were quite different from what they are today. In fact, it may sound unreal but there were more than thirty Black schools in Early County at that time, primarily of the "one or two-teacher" type, many of which were housed in churches. It was in this type of school setting that his elementary grade training was received.

In 1941, he entered the eighth grade of Washington High School, Blakely, Georgia. This posed a serious problem in that there was no public transportation provided at that time. Also, being the oldest son, his assistance was needed with farm chores. So, an old bicycle was acquired to be used in commuting to and from school. This was done for two years and proved to be a real challenge due to the distance (11 miles one way) and adverse weather conditions, at times. During his junior and senior high school years, this situation improved somewhat as his parents purchased an old pickup truck which he and his sister used for getting to and from school.

After high school graduation, with encouragement and sacrifice from his mother, he entered Albany State College, Albany, Georgia. Requirements for the B.S. degree were completed in March of 1949. Immediately, he returned to Early County and started his teaching career by completing the school year for a teacher who had recently taken a maternity leave. The school consisted of one room (church) and forty students in grades one through eight.

When his colleagues learned that he was seriously considering remaining as a teacher in his home area, many of them counseled against it. Jesus even stated that "A prophet is not without honour, save in his own country, and his own house." Nevertheless, he decided to "buck the odds" and try it. (He has not regretted this decision.)

At this time transportation was just beginning for black students, and buses were privately owned. Six hundred dollars, annually, was appropriated for bus driver salaries, and the difference was made up by the parents whose children rode the bus.

His day began when he drove his father's school bus to the Washington High School campus, dropped off the high school students, and continued to Zion Hope, the one-room school.

This first job was a real learning situation in that his professional training had not equipped him to effectively deal with such a program. Nevertheless, the school year was brought to a successful completion and thus marked the beginning of what he considers a very challenging and rewarding experience in the Early County School System.

He continued to upgrade his professional skills by doing graduate work at Atlanta University, Atlanta, Georgia, where he received the M.A. degree in School Administration.

Additional course work was completed at Florida A. & M. University, Tallahassee, Florida; University of Chicago, Chicago, Illinois; and the University of Kentucky, Lexington, Kentucky.

He has served continually in the Early County School System since beginning in March of 1949 with the exception of a brief tour of duty in the U.S. Army during the Korean Conflict.

His professional experience follows:

Teacher-Principal	Two yrs.	Washington High School	1949–1951
Principal	Five yrs.	Carver Elem. & High Jakin, Georgia	1951–1956
Principal	Four yrs.	Kestler Elem. & High Damascus, Georgia	1956–1960
Principal	Ten yrs.	Washington Elem. & High Blakely, Georgia	1960–1970
Principal	Nineteen yrs.	Early County Middle Blakely, Georgia	1970–1989

Whatever success he has realized, he feels, can be attributed to:
1. having tried to make the Lord first, last and always in his life;
2. his mother's encouragement and sacrifice;
3. the cooperation and support of a lot of people, including the late Superintendent, Early County School System, Mr. Lonnie B. Chester.

His most coveted honor was bestowed upon him on March 15, 1981, when the Early County Board of Education named and dedicated the Middle School Media Center for him. It was a most humbling experience due in large measure to the fact that it occurred in his lifetime.

He holds membership in the Calvary Seventh-day Adventist Church, Cedar Springs Road, Blakely, Georgia, where he serves as a lay elder and Sabbath School teacher.

Presently, he holds life membership in Georgia Retired Teachers Association; member, Blakely-Early County Chamber of Commerce; Member of Advisory Board of Washington High School Alumni Association; Member of Literacy Task Force for Early County; Member of the RESA Advisory Board, Leary, Georgia; and was appointed to Georgia Agrirama Development Authority, Tifton, Georgia, in 1985 by Gov. Joe Frank Harris. Gov. Harris appointed him to a second four-year term in January 1989.

He was married to the late Herdisene Robinson Harris, and they are the parents of three children—Jon Michael, Cheryl Lynnette, Wayne Bernard—two daughters-in-law, Enid Christina and Marilyn Margaret and one son-in-law, Phil WaNdambi. To date they have been blessed with five precious grandchildren.

APPENDIX B CHRONOLOGY
OF SIGNIFICANT EVENTS

1925—Rufus Harris and Charlie Mae Webb (parents) were married.

1926—Dorothy Mae Franklin Harris, my parent's first child, was born.

1927—John Rufus Harris' birthday.

1929—Nellie Bessie Deloris Harris, my parents' third child, was born.

1930—Dorothy Franklin Harris, my parents' first born, was fatally burned.

1931—Charles Reefus Harris, my parents' fourth child, was born.

1933—Mary Ellen Harris, fifth child, was born.

1935—Charity Etta Annette Harris, the sixth child, was born.

1936—Vunice Juanita Harris, my parents' seventh child was born.

1938—James Woodrow Harris, eighth child, was born.

1939—Vunice Juanita Harris died as a result of burns.

1939—Benny Roney Sanford Harris, ninth child, was born.

1941—Eugene Collins Harris, tenth child, was born.

1943—Ruth Sirphronia Harris, eleventh child was born.

1945—My graduation from High School.

1945—William Arnold Harris, twelfth child was born.

1947—Grandma Mary, my paternal grandmother, died.

1949—My first teaching job.

1949—My graduation from Albany State College with a B.S. in Elementary Education.

1949–51—My teaching and principal's job at Washington High School.

1950—Drafted into the United States Army.

1951—Discharged from the United States Army.

1951—United in holy matrimony to Herdisene Theresa Robinson.

1951–56—Teaching/principal at Carver School.

1953—Graduated from Atlanta University.

1954—Birth of Jon Michael Harris, our first born.

1956—Birth of Cheryl Lynette Harris, our second child.

1956–60—Principal of Kestler Elementary and High School.

1957—Birth of Wayne Bernard Harris, our youngest child.

1960–70—Principal of Washington High School.

1964—My maternal grandmother passed away.

1965—Herk, my wife, graduated from University of Kentucky, Lexington, Kentucky with a Master's Degree in Guidance and Counseling.

1968—Charles, my brother's, death.

1968—CRH Enterprises was formed.

1969—Elected to South Atlantic Conference of Seventh-day Adventist Executive Committee. Served under three presidents; namely, Banfield, Woodfork and Hairston, for a total of ten years.

1970–89—Principal of Early County Middle School.

1974—My brother, William's, death.

1978—My father's death.

1979—My mother's death.

1979—Mike received his M.A. Degree in Religion from Atlanta University.

1980—Cheryl graduated from Rush University's Nurse Practitioner program.

1980—Mike, our first born's, marriage.

1981—Mike called to pastor in the Central California Conference of Seventh-day Adventists.

1981—My appointment to a five-year term on the Executive Committee of the Southern Union Conference of Seventh-day Adventists.

1981—Middle School Media Center named and dedicated to my honor.

1981—Wayne, our youngest, was married.

1983—Birth of Matthew Ariel Harris, Mike and Enid's first born.

1983—Mike awarded Master of Divinity from Atlanta University.

1983—Herk, my wife, died.

1983—Cheryl's marriage.

1984—Delivered high school graduation address.

1985—My appointment to the Executive Board of Georgia Agrirama, Tifton, Georgia.

1985—Joel, the second son of Mike and Enid, was born.

1986—Mike's ordination into the gospel ministry.

1986—Marilyn completed requirements for her Ph. D in Clinical Psychology from California School of Professional Psychology, Los Angeles, California.

1987—Ruben, Wayne and Marilyn's son, was born.

1987—Jessica, Cheryl and Phill's daughter, was born.

1987—Mike, Enid, Matt, and Joel left for the foreign mission service at Bethel College, South Africa.

1988—Wayne graduated from Loma Linda University Medical School and was admitted to the Residency Program at Emory University School of Medicine in Atlanta, Georgia.

1989—Special retirement and appreciation program given for me.

1989—Herk's father, Granddaddy, died.

1990—Rebekah's birth, Wayne and Marilyn's second child.

1990—Mike, Enid and the boys came back on their first furlough.

1990—Invited to be guest speaker at the 25th class reunion for the class of 1965.

1990—Family reunion.

1990—My appointment to the Southwest Georgia RESA.

1991—Wayne completed Residency in Internal Medicine at Emory University School of Medicine.

1992—Inducted into Blakely Rotary Club.

1992—Dedication of Herdisene Robinson Harris Memorial Campsite and Family Reunion.

1993—Completion of three-year term on Southwest RESA Board.

1993—Wayne completed two years of service with the Public Health Department in Chattanooga, Tennessee.

1993—David Gabriel, Wayne and Marilyn's, third child was born.

1993—Trip to South Africa to visit Mike, Enid, Matt, and Joel. (November 28-December 26)

1994—Harris Family Reunion.

1994—Death of Marie Lois Kibble Robinson.

1994—Birth of Conrad Steffahn to Cheryl and Phill.

1995—Wayne began Oncology Fellowship.

1995—Death of Kirk Robinson, Herk's youngest brother.